Harcourt Language

SENIOR AUTHORS
Roger C. Farr ◆ Dorothy S. Strickland

AUTHORS
Helen Brown ◆ Karen S. Kutiper ◆ Hallie Kay Yopp

SENIOR CONSULTANT
Asa G. Hilliard III

CONSULTANT
Diane L. Lowe

Harcourt

Orlando   Boston   Dallas   Chicago   San Diego

Visit *The Learning Site!*
www.harcourtschool.com

Contents

Social Studies

2

Unit 2

Science

Grammar: More About Nouns and Verbs
Writing: Informative/Expository Writing (Explanation) 90

Writer's Craft:
CHAPTER 9 ## Organizing Information

Unit 3

Art/Creativity

Grammar: More About Verbs
Writing: Persuasive Writing 162

Unit 4

Science

Grammar: Pronouns, Adjectives, and Adverbs
Writing: Informative/Expository Writing (Classification) 232

Unit 5

Social Studies

Grammar: Phrases and Clauses
Writing: Informative/Expository
Writing (Research Report) . 306

10

Unit 6

Health/Recreation

Handbook

At a Glance

Listening and Speaking

Grammar: How Language Works

We all learn to speak without thinking about how words work. For example, children who grow up speaking English learn to say *the green leaf* instead of *the leaf green* before they learn about adjectives and nouns. Later, we study grammar, the rules our language follows. Learning about grammar helps us talk about language and become better writers.

The Building Blocks of Language

Words in English can be grouped into different parts of speech. These are the building blocks of language.

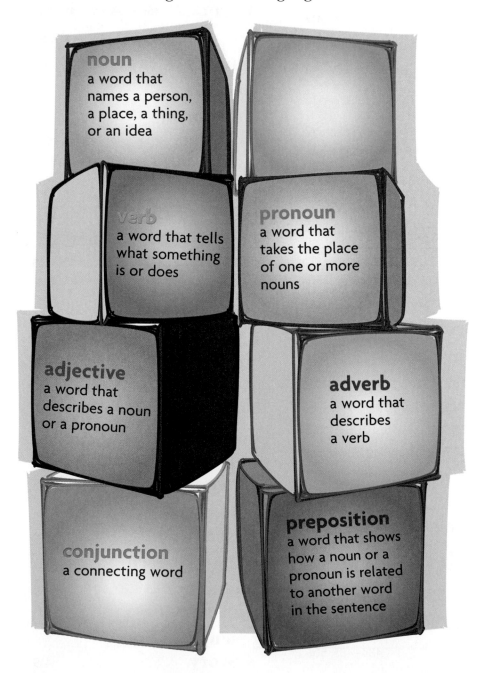

noun
a word that names a person, a place, a thing, or an idea

verb
a word that tells what something is or does

pronoun
a word that takes the place of one or more nouns

adjective
a word that describes a noun or a pronoun

adverb
a word that describes a verb

conjunction
a connecting word

preposition
a word that shows how a noun or a pronoun is related to another word in the sentence

Writing: Understanding the Writing Process

When you look at a book, you do not see the process the writer used to make it. What you see in print might not be much like the first plan for the book. The author might have rewritten many times.

The writing process is often divided into five stages. Most writers go back and forth through these stages. There is no one correct way to write.

Prewriting

In this stage, you plan what you are going to write. You choose a topic, identify your audience and purpose, brainstorm ideas, and organize information.

Drafting

In this stage, you write your ideas in sentences and paragraphs. Follow your prewriting plan to write a first draft of your composition.

Revising

This stage is the first part of editing your writing. You may work by yourself or with a partner or a group. Make changes that will improve your writing.

Proofreading

In this stage, you finish your editing by polishing your work. Check for errors in grammar, spelling, capitalization, and punctuation. Make a final copy of your composition.

Publishing

Finally, you choose a way to present your work to an audience. You may want to add pictures, make a class book, or read your work aloud.

Using Writing Strategies

A **strategy** is a plan for doing something well. Using strategies can help you become a better writer. Read the list of strategies below. You will learn about these and other strategies in this book. As you write, look back at this list to remind yourself of the **strategies good writers use**.

Strategies Good Writers Use

- Set a purpose for your writing.
- Focus on your audience.
- List or draw your main ideas.
- Use an organization that makes sense.
- Use your own personal voice.
- Choose exact, vivid words.
- Use a variety of effective sentences.
- Elaborate with facts and details.
- Group your ideas in paragraphs.
- Proofread to check for errors.

Keeping a Writer's Journal

Many writers keep journals. In your journal, you can list your ideas for writing. You can also reflect and write freely, keep notes, and experiment with words.

To start your own writer's journal, choose a notebook. Decorate the cover if you wish. Then start filling the pages with your notes and ideas.

Vocabulary Power

In addition to writing in your journal, you may also want to keep a "word bank" of different kinds of words to use in your writing. Look for the Vocabulary Power word in each chapter. You can also add other new words, such as interesting adjectives and strong verbs.

Keeping a Portfolio

A portfolio is a collection of work, such as writings and pictures. It is sometimes used to show a person's work to others.

Student writers often keep two types of portfolios. **Working portfolios** include pieces on which you are working. **Show portfolios** have pieces that you are finished with and want to show to others. You choose the pieces you want to move from your working portfolio into your show portfolio.

You can use either kind of portfolio in writing conferences with your teacher. In a conference, talk about your work. Tell what you are doing and what you like doing. Talk about the progress you have made. Set new goals for yourself as a writer.

Unit 1

Grammar **Sentences**

Writing **Expressive Writing**

AS IN TH
FOR WHOM
THE MEMORY OF
IS ENSHRINED F

My Journal

September 28

Today I visited the
Lincoln Memorial with
Aunt Abbie. The statue
of Abraham Lincoln
was so impressive

Declarative and Interrogative Sentences

A **sentence** is a group of words that tells a complete thought.

A **declarative sentence** makes a statement. Use a period (.) at the end of a declarative sentence. An **interrogative sentence** asks a question. Use a question mark (?) at the end of an interrogative sentence.

Examples:
Declarative Sentence
Some mail carriers work on foot.

Interrogative Sentence
What skills do mail carriers need?

Vocabulary Power

oc·cu·pa·tion
[ok′yə·pā′shən] *n.*
The work by which a person earns a living.

Guided Practice

A. **Tell whether each sentence is declarative or interrogative. Tell how you know.**

Example: Do you like outdoor occupations?
interrogative, because it asks a question

1. My neighbor is a mail carrier.
2. Mail carriers work for the United States Postal Service.
3. They deliver and collect mail.
4. Can I become a mail carrier at age eighteen?
5. People take a written test to apply for the job.
6. Do you have to read a map?
7. What other tests do you take?
8. You take a driving test.
9. Do you need a good driving record?
10. Yes, you must have a good driving record.

Independent Practice

B. **Write whether each sentence is declarative or interrogative.**

    Example: A career is a person's lifework.
                    declarative

    11. There are many ways to choose a career.

    12. One way is to think about what you like to do.

    13. Do you like to work with people?

    14. Do you prefer working indoors or outdoors?

    15. Would you like to travel?

C. **Write each declarative or interrogative sentence. Capitalize the first word of the sentence. End each sentence with the correct end mark.**

    Example: you might like to be a computer programmer
                    You might like to be a computer programmer.

    16. do you like to read and write stories

    17. you might become a writer

    18. did you know that there are many kinds of writers

    19. reporters write for newspapers, radio, and television

    20. they explain information clearly

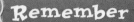

Remember

that a **declarative sentence** makes a statement. An **interrogative sentence** asks a question.

Writing Connection

Writer's Journal: Writing Idea Think about one or two jobs or careers that interest you. Describe what you would do in that work. Read your description, and write down questions you may have about that type of work. Be sure to use correct capitalization and punctuation in your sentences.

Imperative and Exclamatory Sentences

Imperative sentences give commands. **Exclamatory sentences** show strong feelings.

Most imperative sentences begin with an action word, such as *call*, *tell*, or *go*. The naming word *you* is understood. Use a period (.) at the end of an imperative sentence. Use an exclamation point (!) at the end of an exclamatory sentence.

Examples:

Imperative Sentences	Exclamatory Sentences
(You) Call a veterinarian.	Oh no, Bosco hurt his paw!
(You) Tell him something is wrong with Bosco's paw.	He's limping so much!

Guided Practice

A. Tell whether each sentence is imperative or exclamatory.

Example: Lift Bosco into the car. *imperative*

1. Put Bosco on my examination table.
2. Give me your sore paw, Bosco.
3. Oh no, here's a thorn in his paw!
4. Hold Bosco still while I remove it.
5. It's out!
6. Give Bosco two of these pills every day.
7. Put this medicine on his paw once a day.
8. Bring him back in a week.
9. What a brave boy you are, Bosco!
10. Wow, you're a great dog!

Independent Practice

B. Tell whether each sentence is imperative or exclamatory.

> **Example:** I would love to be a veterinarian!
> *exclamatory*

11. Get good grades in school.

12. Take science courses about animals.

13. Wow, there are so many science courses!

14. Find out how much education you will need.

15. Seven years of college is such a long time!

C. Write each imperative and exclamatory sentence. Capitalize the first word of the sentence. End each sentence with the correct end mark.

> **Example:** watch the zoo doctor as she checks an orangutan
> *Watch the zoo doctor as she checks an orangutan.*

16. give the orangutan the sleeping drug

17. wow, that formula really works

18. what a large animal it is

19. check his heart and breathing rates

20. listen to his heart and lungs

Writing Connection

Writer's Craft: Kinds of Sentences Imagine that you are a dog trainer. How do you talk to the dog? Write five imperative sentences and five exclamatory sentences that you might use when training a dog.

USAGE AND MECHANICS
Punctuating Four Kinds of Sentences

Punctuation is one way to express the meaning of a sentence.

You know that every sentence begins with a capital letter and ends with an end mark. The end mark you use depends on the type of sentence. Declarative and imperative sentences end with a period (.). Interrogative sentences end with a question mark (?). Exclamatory sentences end with an exclamation point (!).

Examples:

Declarative: Ben is excited about a computer career.

Interrogative: What kind of career is it?

Imperative: Ask him to tell you about it.

Exclamatory: It sounds like such a great job!

Guided Practice

A. **Tell whether each sentence is declarative, interrogative, imperative, or exclamatory. Then tell the end punctuation for the sentence. Tell how you know what kind of sentence it is.**

Example: Ben wants to be a computer animator
declarative, period, because it makes a statement

1. What does a computer animator do
2. A computer animator makes moving pictures on computers
3. Tell me how I can be a computer animator
4. You can study at an art school or in college
5. Oh, I want to be an animator for a video game

Independent Practice

B. **Tell whether each sentence is declarative, interrogative, imperative, or exclamatory. Then write the end punctuation for the sentence.**

    Example: Carmen wants to work on the Internet
                declarative, period

    6. What kind of Internet job does Carmen want
    7. She wants to be a Web master
    8. Web masters manage sites on the World Wide Web
    9. What a great job that is
  10. Tell me more about Web masters

C. **Write whether each sentence is declarative, interrogative, imperative, or exclamatory. Then write the sentence, using the correct end punctuation mark.**

    Example: Where do Web masters work.
                interrogative, Where do Web masters work?

  11. Do you know how many companies hire Web masters.
  12. Think about the kinds of companies that have websites?
  13. Any company that has a website has a Web master!
  14. Web masters work for companies in the computer and entertainment businesses?
  15. Wow, there must be lots of jobs.

Writing Connection

Social Studies Choose a career about which you want to learn more. Write five questions to ask someone who works in this career. Check to make sure that you have punctuated each sentence correctly.

Extra Practice

A. The word in parentheses ( ) following each sentence tells what kind of sentence it is. Write each sentence correctly. *pages 24–29*

Example: my father works as a firefighter (declarative)
My father works as a firefighter.

1. describe what firefighters do on the job (imperative)
2. firefighters put out fires (declarative)
3. they rescue people from burning buildings (declarative)
4. it is such a dangerous occupation (exclamatory)
5. firefighters also clean up the fire scene (declarative)
6. cleaning up a whole burned building is such a difficult job (exclamatory)
7. did you know that firefighters do safety inspections (interrogative)
8. now tell us something else (imperative)
9. what do firefighters do between fire alarms (interrogative)
10. they dry their hoses and stretch them into shape (declarative)

B. Add words to each word group to make the type of sentence indicated in parentheses ( ). *pages 24–29*

Example: other firefighting jobs (imperative)
Tell us about other firefighting jobs.

11. Fire inspectors (declarative)
12. How do (interrogative)
13. inspect buildings for fire hazards. (declarative)
14. what inspectors could find (imperative)
15. a really interesting occupation (exclamatory)

Remember

that a **sentence** expresses a complete thought. A **declarative sentence** makes a statement. An **interrogative sentence** asks a question. An **imperative sentence** gives a command. An **exclamatory sentence** expresses strong feelings. A sentence begins with a capital letter and ends with an end mark.

For more activities with different kinds of sentences, visit *The Learning Site:*

www.harcourtschool.com

C. Write the following sentences. Add the correct capitalization and end mark to each one.

pages 28–29

Example: what tests must you pass to become a firefighter

What tests must you pass to become a firefighter?

16. most firefighters must have a high school education
17. what are some of the other requirements
18. they must meet certain physical standards
19. tell us what they are
20. those physical standards are so tough

D. Write each sentence, correcting the errors.

pages 28–29

21. Do you know why firefighters must be in good shape.
22. It's because they must carry 80 to 100 pounds of equipment?
23. Imagine carrying that weight up so many stairs
24. firefighters must also chop through doors with heavy axes.
25. No wonder firefighters must be strong?

Writing Connection

Real-Life Writing: Interview Work with a partner. Your partner will ask you the questions you wrote for the previous lesson. Listen carefully. Answer the questions as though you were the person in the career you described. Give clear and complete answers. Then trade places and interview your partner.

DID YOU KNOW?
Benjamin Franklin, a leader during the Revolutionary War, started the nation's first fire department. He founded it in the city of Philadelphia in 1736.

Chapter Review

Read the passage. Some sentences are underlined. Choose the best way to write each underlined sentence, and mark the letter for your answer. If the underlined sentence needs no change, choose _No mistake_.

STANDARDIZED
TEST PREP

> Mark is a geologist. He studies rocks. (1) <u>How does he do that?</u> First, Mark makes a map of an area. (2) <u>He might spend days making the map?</u> Next, he does field work. (3) <u>picture Mark in a distant place.</u> Mark drills into the earth. (4) <u>Why does he do this!</u> He wants to get rocks from deep in the earth. (5) <u>Mark writes a report about rocks.</u> (6) <u>He shares the report with others?</u>

TIP Make sure that you understand the directions before you begin answering the questions.

1 A how does he do that.

  B How does he do that!

  C How does he do that

  D No mistake

2 F He might spend days making the map.

  G He might spend days making the map

  H he might spend days making the map!

  J No mistake

3 A picture Mark in a distant place!

  B Picture Mark in a distant place?

  C Picture Mark in a distant place.

  D No mistake

4 F Why does he do this.

  G Why does he do this?

  H why does he do this.

  J No mistake

5 A Mark writes a report about rocks!

  B Mark writes a report about rocks?

  C Mark writes a report about rocks

  D No mistake

6 F he shares the report with others?

  G he shares the report with others.

  H He shares the report with others.

  J No mistake

For additional test preparation, visit _The Learning Site:_
www.harcourtschool.com

Being a Good Listener and Speaker

Listening is one of the best ways to learn things. Speaking is a way of sharing ideas and feelings with others. Here are some tips to help you become a better listener and speaker.

If you are listening:

- Give the speaker your full attention.
- Look at the speaker.
- Don't disturb other listeners.
- Ask questions when the speaker is finished.
- Take notes to help you remember what the speaker said.

If you are speaking:

- Speak clearly and correctly.
- Take your time and don't talk too fast.
- Look at your audience.
- Use hand and body movements to illustrate your point.
- Show that you are interested in what you are saying.
- Ask your audience for questions.

YOUR TURN

WHO AM I? Form small groups and play a game of "Guess the Mystery Career." Dress as though you were going to a particular job. Then introduce yourself to the group. Don't tell your career. The group should ask you questions to guess your occupation. Practice the speaking and listening skills you have learned as you play the game.

Vocabulary Power

vol•un•teer
[vol•ən•tir′]: *n.* A person who offers to help or to work without pay.

Complete and Simple Subjects

The **subject** of a sentence names the person or thing spoken about in the rest of the sentence.

The complete subject includes all the words that tell who or what is doing the action in the sentence. The **simple subject** is the main word or words in the complete subject.

In the following examples, the complete subject is underlined once. The simple subject is underlined twice.

Examples:

Justin Smith is a firefighter.

Many firefighters are volunteers.

The volunteers' equipment is always ready.

Guided Practice

A. Identify the complete subject in each sentence.

Example: Many volunteers help at the fire station.
Many volunteers

  1. Some volunteers wash the fire trucks.
  2. Other people test the hoses.
  3. The station needs to be cleaned.
  4. The chief's name is Garrison.
  5. Garrison tells people how to help.

B. Identify the simple subject in each sentence.

Example: Ron works at the fire station. *Ron*

  6. He teaches volunteers how to fight fires.
  7. Ron's friends work there, too.
  8. This town is very small.
  9. Many people work for the fire department.
  10. Some volunteers work hard.

Independent Practice

C. Write each sentence. Underline the complete subject once. Underline the simple subject twice.

Example: Many places need volunteers like Maggie.
Many places need volunteers like Maggie.

11. Hospital patients like Maggie very much.
12. The local hospital always needs volunteers.
13. Roger volunteers on the second floor.
14. Roger's patients like the magazines he brings.
15. Roger likes to bring funny ones.
16. Funny stories can help people feel better.
17. Some volunteers read stories aloud.
18. A local artist paints pictures for some patients.
19. This artist cheers people up with her pictures.
20. The nurses like the pictures, too.
21. Many gentle animals are volunteers in hospitals.
22. Therapy animals help people get better.
23. Gentle animals help people relax.
24. Animal volunteers must be well behaved.
25. Hospital patients enjoy having animals visit them.

Writing Connection

Writer's Journal: Writing Idea Writers often let their personality show in their writing. Choose a subject that you know well. Write a poem, letter, song, story, or review. Show your personality by using words and phrases that seem lively and natural to you. Underline your complete subjects once, and your simple subjects twice.

Nouns in Subjects

The simple subject of a sentence is often a noun.

You know that the subject of a sentence names the person or thing spoken about in the sentence. A noun is a word that names a person, place, thing, or animal.

Examples:

The Little League **coaches** are Larry and Ann.
The simple subject is coaches.

Twelve **children** play on their team.
The simple subject is children.

Guided Practice

A. **Identify the simple subject in each sentence. Notice that each simple subject is also a noun.**

Example: My favorite sport is baseball.
sport

1. The baseball field is cared for well.
2. The coach stands near the dugout.
3. The home plate umpire keeps the baseballs.
4. The snack bar is close to the bleachers.
5. Buttered popcorn is sold at the snack bar.
6. Hard helmets protect the players' heads.
7. The baseball bats are kept in the dugout.
8. The tall bleachers are made of concrete.
9. The umpires have not arrived yet.
10. The team's coaches are volunteers.

Independent Practice

Remember that simple subjects are often nouns.

B. Write each sentence. Underline the complete subject once. Underline the noun that is the simple subject twice.

Example: _Some people volunteer to help animals._

11. Sid was walking on a beach.
12. White seagulls gather on the beach.
13. The waves are very big.
14. A large sea lion walks toward the ocean.
15. This animal walks slowly because it is hurt.
16. A tall woman phones Animal Rescue to help.
17. Three workers arrive to help the sea lion.
18. Many children watch the scene.
19. One person works on the sea lion's flipper.
20. The sea lion will be able to swim again.
21. A small crab crawls out of a hole in the sand.
22. A little boy runs after the crab.
23. The crab's claws could pinch him.
24. His mother warns him not to touch the crab.
25. A wave takes the crab into the ocean.

Writing Connection

Real-Life Writing: Newspaper Article Imagine that you are a reporter for your community newspaper. Think of an enjoyable event in your community, such as a fair, a parade, or a concert. Work with a partner, and write a news article about the event. Write about volunteers who help. Include the names of all volunteers, and tell what each does to help. Underline your complete subjects once, and then circle the noun that is the simple subject.

USAGE AND MECHANICS

Combining Sentences: Compound Subjects

A **compound subject** is made up of two or more subjects joined by *and* or *or.* Compound subjects have the same predicate.

Simple sentences that have the same predicate can be combined to make one sentence with a compound subject. If a compound subject has three or more subjects, use commas to separate them. Join the last two subjects with *and* or *or.*

Examples:

Gloria will paint the mural.

Roger will paint the mural.

> **Gloria and Roger** will paint the mural.

The mayor will be in the mural.

The governor will be in the mural.

The President will be in the mural.

> **The mayor, the governor, and the President** will be in the mural.

Guided Practice

A. Identify the compound subject in each sentence.

Example: Wood and plaster can be painted.
Wood and plaster

1. Boys and girls have been asked to help.
2. Thomas or Elizabeth is going to paint.
3. A child, a librarian, and a carpenter stop to look.
4. The older man, the younger man, and the young woman ask what the mural will be.
5. Children, deer, and rivers will be painted.

Independent Practice

B. Write each sentence. Underline the compound subject.

    Example: Beaches and parks need cleaning.
          <u>Beaches and parks</u> need cleaning.

  6. Students and teachers are going to help.
  7. Plastic bottles and cans litter the ground.
  8. May and October are cleanup months.
  9. Tom, Jeff, or Luke will pull weeds.
10. Tina, Leah, or Mark will pick up trash.

C. Combine each pair of sentences to form one sentence with a compound subject. Use *and* or *or* to join the subjects.

    Example: Emily decided to volunteer.
             Mia decided to volunteer.
             Emily and Mia decided to volunteer.

11. Good food made everyone happy. Cool drinks made everyone happy.
12. More cleanup will come after lunch! More work will come after lunch!
13. Emily may walk on the beach. Linda may walk on the beach.
14. Cans go into the trash. Bottles go into the trash.
15. The beaches are clean. The paths are clean.

Writing Connection

Social Studies Imagine that you have been asked to get other people to help in your community. Design a poster that will persuade people to volunteer. Using some compound subjects, write several reasons explaining why people should volunteer.

Remember

that a **compound subject** is made up of two or more simple subjects that are joined by *and* or *or*.

Extra Practice

A. **Write each sentence. Underline the complete subject once. Underline the simple subject twice.** *pages 34–35*

Example: The neighbors let Tom play in their yard.
The neighbors let Tom play in their yard.

1. Tom heard tires screeching.
2. His friend heard it, too.
3. A large truck ran a stop sign.
4. The stop sign is hidden by a tree.
5. The driver stopped just in time.
6. A small car was passing the corner.
7. The truck barely missed the car.
8. The driver's quick actions kept them from wrecking.
9. The air smelled like rubber.
10. Bigger stop signs should be put in at the corner.

B. **Use at least two words to write a complete subject for each sentence. Then write the sentence, and underline the simple subject.** *pages 34–35*

Example: _____ is the mayor's son.
That boy is the mayor's son.

11. _____ heard about the accident from his son.
12. _____ read some newspaper articles.
13. _____ was called to a meeting.
14. _____ liked his new ideas.
15. _____ asked them to vote to add new stop signs.
16. _____ would make the town safer.
17. _____ would have to stop at the corners in town.
18. _____ could cross the streets safely.
19. _____ are now happy about the signs.
20. _____ have made the neighborhood a safer place.

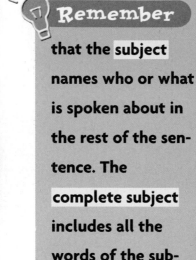

Remember

that the **subject** names who or what is spoken about in the rest of the sentence. The **complete subject** includes all the words of the subject. The **simple subject** is the main word in the complete subject. A **compound subject** is two or more subjects joined by *and* or *or*.

For more activities using complete and simple subjects, visit *The Learning Site:*

www.harcourtschool.com

C. **Write the sentence. Underline the compound subject. Circle the connecting word.** *pages 38–39*

Example: Girls, boys, men, and women are working all over the country to help each other.
<u>Girls, boys, men,</u> (and) <u>women</u> *are working all over the country to help each other.*

21. Cities and regions have programs you can join.
22. Volunteers, workers, and others work hard.
23. Children and adult volunteers are helpful.
24. Indoor jobs and outdoor jobs need to be done.
25. Volunteers, people in need, and the whole community benefit.

D. **Combine each pair of sentences to form one sentence with a compound subject. Use *and* or *or* to join the subjects.** *pages 38–39*

Example: Frank tried to climb the mountain.
Liz tried to climb the mountain.
Frank and Liz tried to climb the mountain.

26. Frank needs help climbing a mountain. Liz needs help climbing a mountain.
27. Emergency rescue teams race to the scene. Volunteers race to the scene.
28. Men and women help out. Teenagers help out.
29. Heavy snow and sleet make the work hard. Darkness makes the work hard.
30. Frank yells for help. Liz yells for help.

Writing Connection

Writer's Journal: Recording Ideas Think of a friend, a classmate, or an animal you have helped. Using compound subjects, write a paragraph that describes what you did and how it was helpful. Tell how you can do more to help others.

Chapter Review

Read the two sentences in the box. Then choose the answer that shows how the two sentences can *best* be combined.

STANDARDIZED
TEST PREP

TIP Two short sentences can often be combined into one sentence with a compound subject. Review the rules for punctuating compound subjects before you begin.

1 Lois Jones volunteers at a daycare center. Judy Engels volunteers at a daycare center.

   A Lois Jones and Judy Engels they volunteer at a daycare center.

   B Lois Jones and Judy Engels volunteer at a daycare center.

   C Lois Jones volunteers at a daycare center, Judy Engels volunteers at a daycare center.

   D At a daycare center, Lois Jones and Judy Engels volunteer.

2 Judy and Lois will make bowls next week. The younger children will make bowls next week.

   F Judy Lois and the younger children will make bowls next week.

   G Judy, Lois and, the younger children will make bowls next week.

   H Judy and Lois next week, the younger children will make bowls.

   J Judy, Lois, and the younger children will make bowls next week.

3 The teachers appreciate the girls' help. The children appreciate the girls' help, too.

   A The teachers and the children appreciate the girls' help.

   B The teachers, and the children appreciate the girls' help.

   C The teachers and the children, they appreciate the girls' help.

   D The teachers appreciate the girls' help, and the children appreciate the girls' help.

4 Judy and Lois enjoy arts and crafts. I enjoy arts and crafts, too.

   F Judy, Lois and I, we enjoy arts and crafts.

   G Judy and Lois and I, enjoy arts and crafts.

   H Judy, Lois, and I enjoy arts and crafts.

   J Judy and Lois enjoy arts and crafts, I enjoy them, too.

For additional test preparation, visit *The Learning Site:*
www.harcourtschool.com

Test-Taking Strategies

After you have studied, there are skills that will make it easier for you to do well on a test. The next time you are taking a test, try these strategies:

1. Listen closely while the teacher gives directions. If the directions are written, read them carefully before you begin. If the directions are asking you to do more than one thing, make sure that you understand all of the different steps.

2. Read all of the answer choices before you choose the one you believe is correct. Possible answers can be very similar, and if you work too quickly, it is easy to pick the wrong one.

3. Eliminate answers which you know are incorrect. This will help you find the right choice.

4. Answer the easier questions first. If you are not sure of an answer, leave a space and go to the next item. Then go back and answer the harder questions. This way, you won't run out of time before you have answered all of the questions whose answers you know.

5. Mark your answers and check your work. Be sure you understand how to mark the answer. You may be asked to underline it, circle it, or write its letter or number. If you have time, review your answers and check to be sure that you marked each one correctly.

YOUR TURN

TAKING A TEST Work with a partner to make up a multiple-choice test. First, write a paragraph containing five sentences. Each sentence must have one error. Underline the error. Then, write questions that give four ways to correct the error. Only one choice should be correct. Go back and write directions explaining how to take the test. Exchange tests with another pair. Using the tips on this page, work with your partner to take the test.

Writer's Craft

Personal Voice

DESCRIPTION You probably express yourself by **describing** things every day. When you give a **description**, you tell what something looks like. You might also tell how it sounds, how it feels, how it smells, how it tastes, or what it does.

Read the following passage. Notice how the writer describes this special day.

LITERATURE MODEL

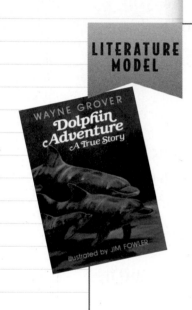

> That morning the sea was as smooth as glass with no waves and no wind blowing at all. With the mist rising up and the sun beating down to warm our bodies, it was a very special morning.
>
> As I looked down into the water, I could see the bottom approximately eighty feet under the boat. It was perfectly clear; the sky was a deep blue, and the air was cool and comfortable. There had been other perfect days, but for some reason, that day was like no other.
>
> —from *Dolphin Adventure: A True Story* by Wayne Grover

Analyze THE Model

1. What was special about this day in particular?

2. What words and phrases does the writer use to describe the day?

3. How did the writer help you understand what that morning was like?

Vocabulary Power

ap•prox•i•mate•ly
[ə•prok′sə•mit•lē]
adv. About; around; almost exact.

Using Personal Voice

When you describe something, you use your **personal voice** or your own special way of expressing yourself. Every writer has a unique personal voice. Study the chart on the next page.

How to Develop Your Personal Voice

You can develop your personal voice by using **figurative language** and **imagery** and by expressing your **viewpoint**.

Figurative language compares two different things. Types of comparisons include **similes**, which use *like* or *as*, and **metaphors**, which say one thing is the other.

Simile: Sam's bike was like a runaway horse charging down the road. (compares bike to horse, using *like*)

Metaphor: Sam's bike was a runaway horse charging down the road. (compares bike to horse)

Imagery is using vivid language to help readers form a mental picture.

Example: Large drops of juice dripped from the slice of melon.

Express your own **viewpoint** to let your reader know how you feel about the subject. For example, depending on your viewpoint, you might describe a spider as *scary* or as *magnificent*.

YOUR TURN

ANALYZE DESCRIPTIVE WRITING Work with several classmates to find examples of descriptive writing in stories, articles, or poems. Talk about how the authors used their personal voices.

Answer these questions:

1. What does the writer describe? Can you picture it in your mind?
2. Does the writer use figurative language? If so, point out and discuss examples.
3. Does the writer use imagery? Point out and discuss examples.
4. What is the writer's viewpoint? How do you know?

Figurative Language and Imagery

A. Choose a word from the box to complete each simile or metaphor. Write the completed sentence on your paper.

bell	blanket	basketball
stars	snowflakes	soldier

Similes

1. Bits of white paper fell like _____.
2. The puppy is as round as a _____.
3. A tall tower stands like a _____ near the castle.

Metaphors

4. The little girl's eyes were sparkling _____.
5. His voice was a _____ ringing across the yard.
6. The snow is a _____ of white on the ground.

B. Revise each sentence. Use imagery to help your reader create a vivid mental picture. Write the revised sentence on your paper.

1. The wind blows through the trees.
2. The ball went over the fence.
3. He ate the grapes.
4. Her house is on a hill.
5. I love the smell of roses.

Writer's Viewpoint

C. Read each description. On your paper, identify the writer's viewpoint and explain how the writer expresses that viewpoint.

   1. We walked through the dim shadows of the forest, tripping over tangled roots. Once we heard a strange cry of a bird or animal in the distance. Then all was silent again, except for the loud beating of our hearts.

   2. The small amount of sunlight that reached the forest floor made patterns like sparkling diamonds. The peaceful silence was broken now and then by the quiet rustle of leaves or the song of an unseen bird.

D. Read each of the following descriptions. On your paper, write a sentence that adds to the description and expresses the same viewpoint.

   1. The tomato looked delicious.
   2. The bird made a terrible squawking noise.
   3. Tonight it is rainy and unpleasant.
   4. That pig is a handsome animal.
   5. What a funny little bird!

Writing and Thinking

Writer's Journal

Write to Record Reflections Do you think your personal voice comes through in your writing? Why or why not? What can you do to help readers hear your personal voice more clearly? Write your reflections in your Writer's Journal.

Descriptive Paragraph

The author of *Dolphin Adventure: A True Story* described a beautiful morning on a boat in the ocean. When Jenny read that description, she thought about the many fine days she had spent on the lake with her grandfather. Read this descriptive paragraph that Jenny wrote about her grandfather's boat.

MODEL

author's viewpoint

imagery
metaphor

simile

imagery

simile

imagery

author's viewpoint

My grandfather's boat isn't big and fancy. It is very small, just the right size for Grandpa and me. It is painted the blue of the sky on a sunny summer day. Grandpa says that the motor is a cranky old mule when he tries to get it started. Once he gets it running, though, it purrs like a content cat. I sit on the middle seat and watch the ripples the boat makes as it moves across the lake. I listen for the quick splash of a fish leaping like an acrobat. Sometimes I see a turtle sunbathing on a log or a heron stepping along on its long legs near the shore. Grandpa's little blue boat is the perfect place to spend a happy afternoon.

Analyze THE Model

1. What is Jenny's purpose for writing this paragraph?
2. How does Jenny use figurative language and imagery?
3. What viewpoint does Jenny express?
4. Does Jenny's paragraph give you a clear picture of the boat and the lake? Explain your answer.

YOUR TURN

WRITING PROMPT **Write a paragraph to describe an object. Choose something that you have strong feelings about or that has special meaning to you. Use figurative language and imagery to make your description come alive. Express your viewpoint in your writing.**

STUDY THE PROMPT **Ask yourself these questions:**

1. What is your purpose for writing?
2. Who is your audience?
3. What object will you describe?

USING YOUR
Handbook

Use the Writer's Thesaurus to find vivid words that will help you describe the object.

Prewriting and Drafting

Plan Your Paragraph Make a web like this one to plan your paragraph.

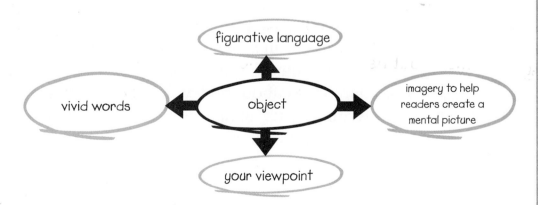

49

Editor's Marks

℘	delete text
∧	insert text
↻	move text
¶	new paragraph
≡	capitalize
/	lowercase
○	correct spelling

Editing

Read over the draft of your descriptive paragraph. Can you change or add anything to create a more vivid picture in your reader's mind? Use this checklist to help you revise your paragraph:

☑ Will your readers be able to picture the object in their minds?

☑ Do you think your readers will recognize your personal voice?

☑ Can you add figurative language or imagery to your description?

☑ Have you expressed your viewpoint clearly?

Use this checklist as you proofread your paragraph.

☑ I have begun sentences with capital letters.

☑ I have used the correct end punctuation for each sentence.

☑ I have used compound subjects to combine sentences where possible.

☑ I have used a dictionary to check my spelling.

Sharing and Reflecting

 Writer's Journal Make a final copy of your paragraph and share it with classmates in a small group. Tell what you like best about your classmates' descriptions. Share ideas about how you can improve your descriptive writing by using figurative language and imagery and by expressing your viewpoint.

Looking at Fine Art

Each writer has a unique personal voice. Artists have their own personal style as well. Each artist who looks at an object or a scene sees details in different ways. The work of an artist reflects his or her own way of seeing the world.

Look at this print made from a woodblock. The artist's name is Hiroshige Ando. The print is called *In the Eyes of the Cat.*

YOUR TURN

Discuss *In the Eyes of the Cat* in a group with two or three classmates. Talk about these questions:

STEP 1 **Why did the artist call this print *In the Eyes of the Cat*?**

STEP 2 **What does the cat see?**

STEP 3 **How would you describe the scene in words? What examples of figurative language and imagery would you use?**

Now look out the window of your classroom. Imagine that you are a cat on the windowsill. Take turns with the members of your group describing what you see from the viewpoint of the cat. Use figurative language and imagery in your description.

Complete and Simple Predicates

The **complete predicate** includes all the words that tell what the subject of the sentence is or does. The **simple predicate** is the main word or words in the complete predicate of a sentence.

You know that the subject names the person or thing spoken about in the rest of the sentence. A subject cannot tell enough to form a complete thought. A sentence needs a predicate, too.

Examples:	The predicate tells
Jeremy **saved** his allowance every week.	*what* Jeremy saved and *when*
Jeremy **shopped** at the mall for a present.	*where* Jeremy shopped and *why*
Kate **is** a salesperson during the week.	*what* Kate is and *when*

Guided Practice

A. Identify the complete predicate of the sentence. Then identify the simple predicate. Be ready to explain your answers.

Example: Jeremy studied books about oceans.
studied books about oceans: complete predicate; studied: simple predicate

1. Europeans came to New England by boat.
2. Towns moved goods by sea.
3. Cities grew because of trade.
4. Many communities depended on the ocean.
5. Fishing boats hunted whales for many years.

Independent Practice

B. Write the sentence. Underline the complete predicate. Then circle the simple predicate.

Example: *New Englanders* (use) *the resources around them*.

6. People in New England harvest the area's trees.
7. Farmers plant crops.
8. New England communities trade food and lumber.
9. Most people use money or credit for trade.
10. Trade builds a strong economy.
11. The fishing industry creates many jobs.
12. Manufacturers sell nets and fishing gear.
13. Skillful workers build boats.
14. Other jobs are necessary.
15. Every town needs workers.
16. Families need schools and stores.
17. Much of New England's economy comes from fishing.
18. The sea played a part in the area's growth.
19. Fishing boats dock in Massachusetts's harbors.
20. The fishing season lasts for months.
21. Fishers catch lobsters in wire pots.
22. Then fishers sell the lobsters.
23. Many sailors learn skills from their parents.
24. Some teach their children.
25. People in Massachusetts share resources.

Writing Connection

Social Studies Think about people's jobs in your community. Write five sentences about how their work helps other people. Include interesting information in your complete predicates. Be sure to capitalize and punctuate your sentences correctly.

Verbs in Predicates

Every predicate has a verb that tells what the subject is or does.

The simple predicate is always a verb. It is the main part of the predicate.

Examples:

Mrs. Lee **works** in town.

She **is** a teacher.

She **shops** after work at the town market.

The market **closed** at 2:00 P.M. yesterday.

Mrs. Lee **went** to another store.

DID YOU KNOW?
People have used many forms of money to trade for goods. The people of Tibet once used dried tea. Native Americans once used shell beads and sometimes wove them into belts.

Guided Practice

A. **Identify the verb in the complete predicate.**

Example: Each region has a local economy.
has

1. Natural resources create jobs and communities.
2. Farmers in Massachusetts grow cranberries.
3. Foresters in Maine cut timber.
4. Vermont dairies make cheddar cheese.
5. Many Pennsylvania farmers are dairy farmers.
6. Some New Jersey businesses manufacture chemicals.
7. These Maryland fishing crews trapped crabs.
8. The oranges in many markets grew on trees in Florida.
9. Some California farmers planted olive trees.
10. These growers made their olives into olive oil.

Independent Practice

B. Write the sentence, and underline the verb.

> **Example:** California's economy grows steadily.
> *California's economy <u>grows</u> steadily.*

11. California has many resources and industries.
12. Californians make many products.
13. Businesses once communicated by mail.
14. People in Japan buy food from California.
15. Californians purchase cameras from Japan.
16. Many people in California work in factories.
17. Some factories build airplanes.
18. High-tech workers design computers.
19. Some of these workers are experts.
20. They studied computer science in school.

C. Add a complete predicate to each subject to make a complete sentence. Write the sentence, and underline the verb.

> **Example:** Visitors to Virginia
> *Visitors to Virginia <u>enjoy</u> Williamsburg.*

21. Visitors to my state
22. Tourists in my town
23. Workers in my community
24. People in my family
25. People in my neighborhood

Remember that the simple predicate is always a **verb.**

Writing Connection

Writer's Craft: Strong Verbs Which products make your state famous? Which holidays have special celebrations? With a small group of students, make a list of these products or events. Each student should write three complete sentences about one topic. Use strong verbs in each sentence. Combine the group's sentences, and present them orally to the class.

GRAMMAR–WRITING CONNECTION

Combining Sentences: Compound Predicates

A compound predicate is two or more simple or complete predicates that have the same subject.

Simple sentences that have the same subject can be combined to make one sentence with a compound predicate. Use commas to separate three or more predicates. Join the last two predicates with a conjunction such as *and, but,* or *or.*

Examples:

We **read** about the land.
We **learned** about crops.

} We **read** about the land **and learned** about crops.

Crops **did** well last year.
Crops **failed** this year.

} Crops **did** well last year **but failed** this year.

Guided Practice

A. Identify the compound predicates and the conjunctions that join them.

Example: Some farmers grow vegetables or raise dairy cattle.
grow vegetables or raise dairy cattle

1. Some farmers have plum orchards and make prunes from the plums.
2. Some farms grow crops but also raise cattle.
3. Farmers hire different kinds of workers and help other businesses.
4. Trucks carry heavy loads and transport goods.
5. Truckers drive late at night or start out early in the morning.

Independent Practice

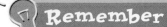
Remember

that a **compound predicate** is made up of two or more predicates that are joined by a **conjunction.**

B. **Write the sentence. Underline the compound predicate.**

> **Example:** *Companies create plans and buy materials.*

  6. Some families start businesses or run them.
  7. Companies help people and make money.
  8. Communities grow quickly and improve.
  9. Consumers buy products and use services.
  10. People buy things and help the economy grow.

C. **Write the sentence. Underline the simple predicates (verbs) and the conjunction that connects them.**

> **Example:** *Companies pay taxes and add money to the economy.*

  11. The government collects taxes and provides services.
  12. Some taxes pay for schools or build roads.
  13. Tax money buys library books and pays a firefighter's salary.
  14. Workers earn a salary, spend some money, and save a little every week.
  15. The store did poorly at first but made a profit after a few months.

Writing Connection

Real-Life Writing: Writing a Note Suppose that a new neighbor has asked you about your neighborhood. Write a short note that explains to your new neighbor why you like a particular store near where you live. Include at least one sentence with a compound predicate.

Extra Practice

A. Read each sentence. Write the complete predicate. Then underline the simple predicate. *pages 52–55*

Example: Many businesses operate in Pennsylvania.
operate in Pennsylvania

1. The economy of Pennsylvania is strong.
2. Coal and steel companies provide many jobs.
3. Many people work in manufacturing plants.
4. Some companies improve high-tech computers.
5. Scientists from Philadelphia design robots.
6. Robots are machines.
7. These machines help in factories.
8. Men and women share the work at factories.
9. People work on assembly lines.
10. Each person has a special job.

B. Write the sentence. Underline the complete predicates in each compound predicate. Circle the word that connects them. *pages 56–57*

Example: *People work at home or have outside jobs.*

11. People in the service industry work hard and help others.
12. Restaurant workers cook meals or serve them.
13. Salespeople advertise products and sell goods.
14. Doctors care for teeth, treat injuries, or cure illnesses.
15. Teachers study hard and share their knowledge.
16. Police arrest lawbreakers but help other people.
17. Postal workers sort letters, sell stamps, or deliver mail.
18. Firefighters risk their lives and face danger.
19. People live in cities and need these services.
20. A community values its workers and pays them for their services.

Remember

that a **complete predicate** includes all the words that tell what the subject of the sentence is or does. The **simple predicate** is the verb in the complete predicate. A **compound predicate** is two or more predicates that have the same subject.

C. Combine each group of sentences into one sentence with a compound predicate. Write the sentence. Use commas where needed. *pages 56–57*

Example: Gardeners plant seeds. Gardeners pick flowers.
Gardeners plant seeds and pick flowers.

21. Carpenters build homes. Carpenters repair them.
22. Some workers collect trash. Some workers clean streets.
23. Plumbers install water pipes. Plumbers fix leaks.
24. Librarians order books. Librarians also spend time with younger readers.
25. Hotel workers greet guests. Hotel workers sort guests' mail.
26. Tourists see new sights. Tourists buy souvenirs. Tourists eat new foods.
27. Washington, D.C. guides provide tours of government offices. Washington, D.C. guides offer museum tours.
28. Some visitors explore museums. Some visitors travel to historic sites.
29. California's tourists visit redwood forests. California's tourists travel to Yosemite National Park.
30. Visitors to Maine can climb a mountain. Visitors to Maine can watch boats on Penobscot Bay.

Writing Connection

Writer's Journal: Interesting Facts Write some interesting facts about the economy in your area. Does your area have a rural economy built around farming or an urban economy built around manufacturing and industry? What businesses contribute to that economy? Use simple and compound predicates in your writing.

For more activities with simple, complete, and compound predicates, visit *The Learning Site:*

www.harcourtschool.com

STANDARDIZED
TEST PREP

Chapter Review

Choose the best way to write each underlined section, and mark the letter for your answer.

> (1) <u>Inventions change the economy and.</u> (2) <u>Farmers planted seeds harvested crops by hand.</u> (3) <u>Then farm machines were invented. Machines saved labor.</u> (4) <u>They planted the seeds harvested the crops, or packed the food.</u>

1 A Inventions and change the economy.

B Inventions or change the economy.

C Inventions change the economy.

2 F Farmers planted seeds and harvested crops by hand.

G Farmers planted seeds harvested crops and by hand.

H Farmers planted seeds, and harvested crops by hand.

3 A Then farm machines were invented, and saved labor.

B Then farm machines were invented and, machines saved labor.

C Then farm machines were invented and saved labor.

4 F They planted the seeds harvested the crops or packed the food.

G They planted the seeds, harvested the crops, or packed the food.

H They planted the seeds, or harvested the crops or packed the food.

For additional test preparation, visit *The Learning Site:*

www.harcourtschool.com

Understanding Time Lines

A **time line** is a diagram that shows important events in the order in which they happened. This time line shows important events in the life of Carmen, a fourth grader. Can you see how Carmen changed as she grew?

Every event points to the year in which it happened.

The date on the left tells when the time line begins.

The date on the right tells when the events on the time line stop.

I learned to walk.

I started preschool and met Alice.

We went to the Grand Canyon.

I learned how to swim.

1993 1994 1995 1996 1997 1998 1999 2000 2001 2002

I was born in Austin, Texas, on June 10. My parents named me Carmen.

My brother Luis was born in March.

I started kindergarten with Mrs. Holcomb.

My family moved to Tucson, Arizona.

I am in the fourth grade.

Spaces on the line show how much time has passed. Usually, equal spaces show equal lengths of time.

YOUR TURN

Make a time line of your life by following these steps:

- Choose paper with no lines. Turn the paper sideways, so that you will have more room to write.

- Use a ruler to draw a long, straight line. Then at equal spaces (one-inch spaces, for example) make a small mark for each year of your life.

- Above the first mark, write the year you were born. Write a year for each of the next marks. Finish by writing the current year above the last mark.

- Beneath each mark, write a short sentence or two telling what happened that year.

Sentences

A **sentence** is a group of words that tells a complete thought.

A **complete sentence** must have a subject and a predicate. The subject names the person or thing the sentence is about. The predicate tells what the person or thing is or does.

Examples:

Incomplete Sentences	Complete Sentences
are not all the same **(missing subject)**	People are not all the same.
People in the United States **(missing predicate)**	People in the United States come from many places.

Vocabulary Power

cul·ture [kul′chər] *n.* The ideas and way of life of a group of people. Culture includes language, customs, music, art, food, and games.

Guided Practice

A. Tell if the word group is a sentence or not a sentence. Tell how you know.

Example: Is a way of doing things.
              not a sentence; no subject

1. I was a bridesmaid at my cousin's wedding.
2. Holiday cards are mailed to friends and family.
3. Is a way to celebrate a birthday.
4. The children in my class.
5. Many people in the United States.
6. Are types of Mexican food.
7. My family ate turkey on Thanksgiving Day.
8. Mieko's family comes from Japan.
9. My favorite type of music.
10. Often use chopsticks.

B. Read each word group. If the words make a sentence, write *sentence*. If the words do not make a sentence, write *not a sentence*. Then write whether the word group is missing a subject or a predicate.

> **Example:** Foods like stew and pasta.
> *not a sentence; no predicate*

11. Many Americans eat carrots and potatoes.
12. However, foods from other cultures.
13. Are very popular, too.
14. Bagels and pasta are served almost everywhere.
15. Some treats from around the world.

C. Add the subject or predicate that is needed to make a complete thought. Underline the word or words you add.

> **Example:** (Add a subject) have different customs.
> <u>People</u> have different customs.

16. (Add a subject) celebrate holidays in many ways.
17. Mother's Day (add a predicate)
18. Some mothers (add a predicate)
19. Some greeting cards (add a predicate)
20. (Add a subject) is the first day of the new year.

Writing Connection

Technology Suppose you lived when there were no televisions or computers. With a partner, write four questions to ask older adults about inventions that have been made during their lifetimes. For example, how did the invention change people's lives? Then interview an older adult and take notes. Using complete sentences, write a paragraph telling what you learned.

> **Remember**
> that a **complete sentence** tells a complete thought. A complete sentence has a subject and a predicate.

Simple and Compound Sentences

A **simple sentence** expresses one complete thought. A **compound sentence** is made up of two or more simple sentences, usually joined by a comma and the conjunction *and, or,* or *but.*

Simple sentences may have a compound subject or a compound predicate or both. However, each part of a compound sentence has its own subject and its own predicate.

Examples:

Simple Sentences

Some Americans live on farms.

Others live in cities.

Some boys and girls live on farms in the Midwest.

Compound Sentences

Some Americans live on farms, **but** others live in cities.

Farmers can buy land, **or** they can rent it.

Guided Practice

A. Tell whether each sentence is simple or compound. Tell how you know.

Example: Some farms grow corn, but others grow rice.
compound; two simple sentences joined by a comma and but

1. A combine and a tractor are farm machines.
2. Combines cut wheat, and tractors pull plows.
3. Healthy seeds and rich soil produce big crops.
4. Farmwork may be hard, but machines help.
5. One family and a helper can farm many acres.

Independent Practice

B. Write the sentence. Underline each simple subject once and each simple predicate twice. Then write *simple* or *compound* to describe the sentence.

> **Examples:** Some <u>people</u> <u>live</u> outside the city, and <u>they</u>
> <u>commute</u> to work.
> *compound*

6. City people often live and work in tall buildings.
7. Many buildings have twenty to fifty floors, and some are even taller.
8. Thousands of people work in these buildings and ride to their offices in high-speed elevators.
9. Many workers in cities travel to their jobs by train, but rural workers use cars more often.
10. Many city people live in apartments, but some have private houses.
11. Many city and country dwellers keep pets.
12. Wild animals live in the country, but many species are found in cities, too.
13. Birds, squirrels, and raccoons live in city parks.
14. You might spot a coyote late at night, but you probably would not see bears.
15. Falcons live on tall buildings or build nests on bridges.

Remember that a **compound** **sentence is made** up of two or more **simple sentences.** They are joined by a comma and a conjunction.

Writing Connection

Science Think about new inventions that will change the future. What new kinds of phones, video equipment, or computers do you think will be invented during your lifetime? Using simple and compound sentences, write a paragraph about some of these inventions and how they may change your life.

USAGE AND MECHANICS
Combining Sentences

You can combine two simple sentences to make one compound sentence.

Join the simple sentences with *and*, *but*, or *or*. Place a comma before the conjunction in the new compound sentence.

Examples:

Simple Sentences	Compound Sentences
Maria is in fourth grade. Her brothers are in high school.	Maria is in fourth grade, **and** her brothers are in high school.
Maria was born in Mexico. Now she lives in Texas.	Maria was born in Mexico, **but** she lives now in Texas.

Guided Practice

A. Use a conjunction to combine each group of sentences into a compound sentence.

Example: Maria's brothers speak English and Spanish.
Maria speaks only English.
Maria's brothers speak English and Spanish,
***but** Maria speaks only English.*

1. The newcomers adopt United States customs. Many of the newcomers keep their own customs.
2. Children speak English in school. Family and friends speak another language at home.
3. Can you speak two languages? Do you speak only one?
4. We enjoy the dances and songs of many cultures. We enjoy local dances and songs, too.
5. Would you like to learn to play a Spanish guitar? Would you rather try an African thumb piano?

Independent Practice

B. Use a conjunction to rewrite each group of sentences as one compound sentence. Add the comma in the correct place.

Example: Have you seen pictures of the Amish people? Have you ever visited an Amish community?
Have you seen pictures of the Amish people, or have you ever visited an Amish community?

6. The Amish are friendly to visitors. They live apart in their own communities.
7. They do not have cars, televisions, radios, telephones, or computers. They do not want them.
8. They live by farming. They raise large crops.
9. They sell their extra food. They give it to needy neighbors.
10. Boys dress like their fathers. Girls dress like their mothers.
11. Married men have beards. Single men do not.
12. Gas or kerosene lamps light Amish homes. Wood is used for heat.
13. Amish children enjoy having fun. They play baseball, basketball, and other games.
14. Building a barn is a group project. Everyone helps.
15. The men and boys build the barn. The women and girls cook meals for the workers.

Writing Connection

Writer's Craft: Point of View Ask someone to tell a story of how he or she came to this country or lived through an important time. Think of another character who could tell the story. Then write the story from that character's **point of view**. How might the story be different if the speaker's friend were telling it? Use at least two compound sentences in your writing.

> **Remember**
> that two simple sentences can be joined to make a compound sentence. They are joined by a comma and a conjunction.

DID YOU KNOW?
Many Amish use horses and buggies (old-fashioned carriages) to get from place to place. They also use horses for plowing. An Amish family might have as many as fifteen horses.

Remember

that a simple
sentence expresses
one idea. A
compound sen-
tence is made up
of two or more
simple sentences,
joined by a comma
and the conjunc-
tion *and, but,* or *or.*

Extra Practice

A. **Read each word group. If the words make a complete sentence, write *complete*. If the words do not make a complete sentence, write *not complete*. Then write whether a subject or a predicate is missing.** *pages 62–63*

Example: Drinks hot tea from a glass.
not complete, no subject

1. Is the language and customs of a group.
2. Customs are traditional ways of doing things.
3. The Amish live an old-fashioned life.
4. Modern inventions, such as computers and telephones.
5. Modern farmers in the Midwest.
6. Harvest grain with a combine.
7. Are used by most United States residents.
8. The customs of many cultures.
9. Have moved to all parts of the country.
10. People in many countries.

B. **Write each sentence. Underline each simple subject once and each simple predicate twice. Then write *simple* or *compound* to describe the sentence.** *pages 64–65*

Example: <u>People</u> <u>come</u> to the United States from all over the world.
simple

11. People from many other countries settle in the United States.
12. Each new group brings its way of life, and different customs make our culture richer.
13. United States residents come from many backgrounds, but we have much in common.
14. Citizens elect local representatives, and they vote for national officials.
15. Many groups hold festivals or celebrations.

For more activities
with simple
and compound
sentences, visit
The Learning Site:

www.harcourtschool.com

C. Use the conjunction—*and, but,* or *or*—that fits best to combine the sentences into one compound sentence. Write the new sentence, and put the comma in its proper place. *pages 66–67*

Example: Most cultures celebrate birthdays. Some birthdays are especially important.
Most cultures celebrate birthdays, but some birthdays are especially important.

16. A Mexican American birthday celebration is like most birthday parties. There might be a piñata.

17. Parents fill the piñata with toys and treats. Children break it open with a stick.

18. Birthday candles are a popular custom. They are used in Europe, too.

19. Can you blow out the candles with one breath? Does it take two?

20. We often sing "Happy Birthday" at birthday celebrations. People in France and in Italy sing it, too.

Writing Connection

Writer's Journal: Writing Idea Write a paragraph about someone who has been important in your life. This person could be a family member, a teacher, or another adult whom you admire. In your paragraph, use both simple and compound sentences to tell why the person has been important to you.

STANDARDIZED
TEST PREP

Chapter Review

The underlined words in each sentence contain a mistake. Choose the answer that is the best way to write the underlined section of the sentence.

1 You may think the yo-yo came from the United
States, it came from the Philippines.

A States it came

B States, but it came

C States but it came

2 The yo-yo was used for hunting it was deadly.

F hunting, and it was

G hunting and it was

H hunting, it was

3 It was a weapon or it was not a toy.

A weapon but it

B weapon it was

C weapon, and it

4 It flew at an animal and the string caught its legs.

F animal, and the string

G animal, or the string

H animal, the string

5 The animal fell, or hunters caught it.

A fell, and hunters

B fell and hunters

C fell, but hunters

TIP Answers to
questions are often
very similar. Be sure to
read each answer
carefully. Pay attention
to differences in punc-
tuation, as well as to
word choices.

**For additional test
preparation, visit
The Learning Site:**

www.harcourtschool.com

Using a Library's Electronic Card Catalog

Libraries have card catalogs to help you find books. A card catalog has a card for every book or resource in that library. These cards are filed alphabetically in drawers. An electronic card catalog contains the same information, but it is stored on a computer. An electronic card catalog may also contain listings of resources that can be found in other libraries.

If you know the name of the author or the book title, you can use the **author search** or **title search** in the library's electronic card catalog to find the book in the stacks.

If you need to find library resources on a particular topic, you can do a **subject search**. Use one or more keywords to find exactly what you need. For example, the keyword *Korea* will give you a list of resources on everything about that country. If you want to know about *Korean American children*, use **all three keywords**. Then the listings will refer only to this particular topic.

YOUR TURN

USING CARD CATALOGS Go to the library. Use the computer catalog and the card catalog to look up the topic "Mexican Americans." Which catalog helped you find resources more quickly? Which was easier to use? Which catalog contained more information? Write down your answers to these questions. Be ready to share your answers with the class.

Authors

Call Number

Illustrator

Title

author search

J 973.04M MacMillan, Dianne, and Dorothy Freeman

My Best Friend Mee-Yung Kim:

Meeting a Korean-American Family

Pictures by Bob Marstall

Eloise Greenfield and Lessie Jones Little

Childtimes

A THREE-GENERATION MEMOIR

LITERATURE MODEL

ALA Notable
Boston Globe–
Horn Book
Honor

Many writers keep diaries to record and to reflect on ideas and feelings. In these passages from *Childtimes*, by Eloise Greenfield and her mother, Lessie Jones Little, Eloise describes some of her childhood memories. As you read, think about how the author writes from her own point of view.

Childtimes

by Eloise Greenfield and Lessie Jones Little

Childtimes is written like a diary. Each of these entries tells about an important memory from Eloise Greenfield's childhood. In the following selections, she remembers that she was a quiet and shy little girl. Eloise Greenfield grew up to become a famous children's author and poet.

First Days

It's the first day of my life—my remembered life. I'm three years old, sitting on the floor with Mama. I'm cutting out a picture for my scrapbook, a picture of a loaf of bread. I'm cutting it out and pasting it in my book with the flour-and-water paste I had helped to make.

As far as I know, that was the day my life began.

My school life began two years later. Mama walked my cousin
Vilma and me down P Street, through the open doors of John F.
Cook School, and into Mrs. Staley's kindergarten class. Vilma and
I were both scared. I was scared quiet. She was scared loud. I sat
squeezed up in my chair, and Vilma screamed.

A Play

When I was in the fifth grade, I was famous for a whole day,
and all because of a play. The teacher had given me a big part,
and I didn't want it. I liked to be in plays where I could be part
of a group, like being one of the talking trees, or dancing, or
singing in the glee club.

I used to slide down in my chair and stare at my desk while
the teacher was giving out the parts, so she wouldn't pay any
attention to me, but this time it didn't work. She called on me
anyway. I told her I didn't want to do it, but she said I had to. I
guess she thought it would be good for me.

On the day of the play, I didn't make any mistakes. I remembered all of my lines. Nobody in the audience heard me, though. I couldn't make my voice come out loud.

For the rest of the day, I was famous. Children passing by my classroom door, children on the playground at lunchtime, kept pointing at me saying, "That's that girl! That's the one who didn't talk loud enough!"

Analyze THE Model

1. From what point of view is the author telling the story?
2. How do you think the author felt about her day of being famous?
3. Why do you think Eloise Greenfield chose to tell about these two events in *Childtimes*?

READING — WRITING CONNECTION

Parts of a Personal Narrative

Eloise Greenfield recalled important days in her childhood. Read this personal narrative by a student named Erica. Note the parts of a personal narrative.

MODEL

writer's viewpoint

beginning

using *my*

middle

> *A Winter Discovery*
>
> Last winter, my family and I visited my Uncle Garth at his farm in Minnesota. When we got there, my brother Luke and I played outside in the snow until dinnertime.
>
> After dinner, it was too dark to go back outside and play. Luke and I tried to turn the television on, but Aunt Ruth said the television was broken. We were disappointed that we were going to miss our favorite shows. What would we do?
>
> Then my uncle's friend Stefan came over. He brought his violin. Uncle Garth sat down at the piano, and Aunt Ruth got out her guitar. They all played together in the living room, and my family and I sat down and listened. Aunt Ruth showed my brother how to play music with spoons. I got to play the tambourine. My aunt and uncle sang songs like "Turkey in the Straw" and "Clementine." Stefan taught us all a song from Germany, his homeland. He sang the words in German and then in English. Luke and I

learned some German words, like <u>Ach</u>, <u>ja</u>, <u>Herz</u>, and <u>Liebe</u>.

After we played, I was very tired, but I didn't want to go to bed. I wanted to hear more music. Mom said, "I bet you didn't even miss your television show."

using I

She was right! I had completely forgotten about the show! I was so glad Aunt Ruth hadn't gotten the television fixed.

end/writer's viewpoint

Analyze THE Model

1. Why did Erica write about her first visit to Uncle Garth's farm?
2. Who do you think is the audience for Erica's sketch?
3. Why does Erica tell about Stefan's visit?

Summarize THE Model

Use a chart like this one to help you identify the elements of Erica's story. Then use your chart to write a summary of her personal narrative.

Who?
Where?
When?
What happened?
1.
2.
3.

Writer's Craft

Personal Voice Erica wrote her personal narrative from her own point of view. What sentences in her story show how Erica thinks and feels? How would the sentences be different if Stefan or her aunt were telling the story?

Prewriting

Purpose and Audience

You probably have good memories about some events that took place when you were younger. In this chapter, you will share your memories with your classmates by writing a personal narrative.

WRITING PROMPT Think of an event in your childhood that made you think about something in a different way. Write a personal narrative about that experience to share with your classmates. Use your personal voice to express your thoughts and feelings.

Before you begin, think about your audience and purpose. Who will your readers be? What event changed your thinking and how should you tell about it?

MODEL

Erica decided to write about her visit to her uncle's farm. She thought about her memories of that visit and how it made her think differently about something. Then she used a chart to decide what she would say.

Strategies Good Writers Use

- Remember your purpose for writing.
- Include details that will help your audience share your experience.

YOUR TURN

Decide what experience you are going to write about. Jot down your memories, including details about the people, the place, and the event.

Who? mother, brother, aunt, uncle, Stefan
Where? farm in Minnesota
When? last winter

What do I remember?
1. Luke and I could not watch television.
2. Uncle Garth, Aunt Ruth, and Stefan all played music.
3. Luke and I got to play music, too.
4. I forgot about watching television.

Organization and Elaboration

Follow these steps to help you organize your personal narrative:

STEP 1 **Identify the Place and Time**
Establish the setting: who was there, where you were, how old you were, and what you were doing.

STEP 2 **Write in Your Own Voice**
Use comparisons and language that help your readers share your memory.

STEP 3 **Tell Why the Experience Was Important**
Tell what you learned. Your personal narrative should be more than just a list of things you did.

MODEL

How does Erica begin her personal narrative? What gives us the sense that Erica is telling the story in her own voice?

> Last winter, my family and I visited my Uncle Garth at his farm in Minnesota. When we got there, my brother Luke and I played outside in the snow until dinnertime.

YOUR TURN

Use the chart you created in prewriting to guide you as you draft your personal narrative. Remember to tell your memory in your own natural voice.

Strategies Good Writers Use

- Identify the place and time.
- Tell your story in chronological order.
- Write in your own voice.

Use a computer to write your draft. With a computer you can easily delete and rewrite passages to get the voice and the descriptions the way you want them.

Revising

Organization and Elaboration

Reread your draft, and ask yourself these questions:

- Have I written my narrative in my own voice?
- Have I told the reader where and when this event happened?
- Have I told the story in chronological order?
- Have I told the reader why this experience is important to me?

MODEL

When Erica reread her draft, she decided that her description of Stefan's visit needed some revision.

> Then my uncle's friend Stefan came
> over. He brought his violin. Uncle Garth
> sat down at the piano, and Aunt Ruth got
> out her guitar. They all played together in
> the living room, and my family and I ~~and~~ ^sat down/
> listened. Aunt Ruth showed my brother
> ~~and me how to play music.~~ My aunt
> and uncle sang songs. ~~Stefan~~ taught us /Stefan
> all a song from Germany, where he is
> from. ~~We all played along and clapped~~

how to play music with spoons. I got to play the tambourine.

like "Turkey in the Straw" and "Clementine."

Luke and I learned some German words, like <u>Ach</u>, <u>ja</u>, <u>Herz</u>, and <u>Liebe</u>.

He sang the words in German and then in English.

YOUR TURN

Revise your personal narrative. Ask yourself if the voice telling the story sounds like you telling a story. Be sure that you include details that help your reader share your memory.

<u>S</u>trategies
<u>G</u>ood <u>W</u>riters <u>U</u>se

- Read your writing aloud to yourself.
- Think about the descriptive language.
- Ask if the ideas you want to focus on are the ones that get the most attention.

 Use your word processing program's Cut and Paste feature to move words around without having to retype them.

Proofreading

Checking Your Language

Make sure that your writing contains no mistakes in spelling. Misspelled words are confusing and make your work hard to read.

MODEL

When Erica proofread her work, she discovered that she had some punctuation and spelling errors.

> After dinner, it was too dark to go back outside and play. Luke and I tried to turn the television on, but Aunt Ruth said the television was broken. We Were disappointed Because we were going to miss our favorite shows What would we do?

that

YOUR TURN

Proofread your revised work. You may want to proofread several times to:
- check sentence punctuation.
- check capitalization.
- check spelling.

Strategies Good Writers Use

- Make sure sentences are complete.
- Check sentence punctuation.
- Look in a dictionary to find the spelling of words that may be misspelled.

Editor's Marks

❞	delete text
∧	insert text
ᵟ	move text
¶	new paragraph
≡	capitalize
/	lowercase
◯	correct spelling

Publishing

Sharing Your Work

Now you are ready to publish your personal narrative. Answer these questions to help you decide how to share your writing with your audience.

1. Who is your audience? Where could you publish your personal narrative so that your audience would see it and read it?

2. Would it be better to print your work or write it in cursive? To decide, think about your audience.

3. Does your personal narrative need illustrations? Can you draw them, or should you look for photographs?

4. Should you read your personal narrative aloud? Use the information on page 83 to help you prepare.

USING YOUR
Handbook

- Use the rubric on page 506 to evaluate your personal narrative.

Reflecting on Your Writing

 Using Your Portfolio What did you learn about your writing in this chapter? Write your answer to each question below.

1. How well did your writing reflect your voice?

2. How did you make the description of your experience real for your readers?

3. How does your personal narrative show your feelings about the experience?

Add your personal narrative to your portfolio, along with your written answers. Review the work in your portfolio. Write a sentence about one way you have improved as a writer. Then write another sentence about one thing you would like to do better.

Being an Effective Speaker

Erica chose to publish her personal narrative by presenting it aloud to small groups of her classmates. Plan to publish your personal narrative in the same way. Here are the steps you can follow as you get ready for your presentation:

STEP 1 Practice reading your work aloud. Read it often enough so that you can read easily and comfortably.

STEP 2 If possible, record yourself reading your personal narrative. Listen to the recording and decide if you are speaking too loudly or too softly. Decide if you are speaking too fast or too slow.

STEP 3 Practice reading your work. You tried to use natural language when you wrote the story so it would sound as if you were telling the story. Now you should try to read the story in a natural way, as if you were telling it and not reading it.

Strategies for Listeners

As your classmates present *their* personal narratives, use these strategies to appreciate and share their memories:

- Focus on the speaker.
- Try to visualize what the speaker is describing.
- Ask yourself if you have ever had a similar experience.

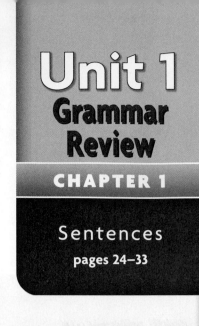

Unit 1
Grammar Review

CHAPTER 1

Sentences
pages 24–33

Declarative and Interrogative Sentences *pages 24–25*

Write whether each sentence is declarative or interrogative.

1. My aunt is an artist in New York City.
2. She works in an art gallery.
3. Her friend makes picture frames next door.
4. Have you ever visited an art gallery?
5. Do you know how many paintings are shown?

Imperative and Exclamatory Sentences *pages 26–27*

Write whether each sentence is imperative or exclamatory.

6. Follow these directions to my aunt's art gallery.
7. How far it seems!
8. Turn left when you walk out the front door.
9. Walk three blocks to Madison Avenue.
10. How long those three blocks seem!
11. Walk two blocks down Madison Avenue.
12. Then go one more store to the Midway Gallery.
13. So many people with different jobs work here!
14. What a large gallery this is!
15. How exciting it is to see the work of young artists!

Punctuating Four Kinds of Sentences *pages 28–29*

Write the sentence. Write whether it is declarative, interrogative, imperative, or exclamatory. Add the correct end punctuation.

16. Have you ever thought about working in a museum
17. My uncle works at the Museum of Natural History
18. He sets up displays about Native American life
19. What a great place it is
20. Make sure you take some photos

Complete and Simple Subjects

pages 34–35

Write the sentence. Underline the complete subject once, and underline the simple subject twice.

1. Students from our school helped out at Austin Creek.
2. The eager helpers repaired the homes of wild salmon.
3. The wild salmon need deep, cool pools.
4. Many excited volunteers showed up on Saturday.
5. Members of the Helpers Club worked hard all week.

Nouns in Subjects *pages 36–37*

Write the sentence. Underline the complete subject once. Underline the noun that is the simple subject twice.

6. Fallen trees in the woods must be cleared.
7. Students with their own equipment shoveled sand.
8. This fourth grade class wanted to help the fish.
9. Rural and city communities depend on volunteers.
10. The student volunteers planted willow trees.

Combining Sentences: Compound Subjects *pages 38–39*

Combine each pair of sentences to form one sentence with a compound subject. Underline the compound subject, and place commas where they are needed.

11. Willows and rocks were placed next to the creek. Branches were placed next to the creek.
12. Creeks are homes for many fish. Streams and rivers are homes for many fish.
13. Students volunteered their time. Parents volunteered their time.
14. Fishers were happy with the results. Hikers were happy with the results.
15. Jenny and Yusaku were proud of their week's work. Michael and Jake were proud of their week's work.

Unit 1
Grammar Review

CHAPTER 4

Predicates/
Verbs

pages 52–61

Complete and Simple Predicates *pages 52–53*

Write the complete predicate of each sentence. Underline the simple predicate.

1. French people spend francs.
2. Italians earn lire.
3. Russians buy things with rubles.
4. People in Japan use yen.
5. In the United States, money is counted in dollars.

Verbs in Predicates *pages 54–55*

Write the sentence. Underline the verb.

6. People sell their products.
7. The ancient Chinese used coins.
8. They also created paper money.
9. In 800 A.D., people first bought things with money.
10. Ancient peoples traded goods, too.
11. Some groups exchanged shells or food.
12. Some people made tools.
13. Other people raised animals.
14. Today governments make coins and paper money.
15. Shoppers pay with cash or credit cards.

Combining Sentences: Compound Predicates *pages 56–57*

Combine each group of sentences into one sentence with a compound predicate. Underline the compound predicate. Use commas where needed.

16. People keep money in banks. People write checks. People use credit cards.
17. A check states an amount. A check names a bank.
18. Countries around the world use money. Countries around the world exchange goods.
19. A person can borrow money. A person can buy a home.
20. A bank may lend money. A bank may refuse a loan.

Sentences *pages 62–63*

Read the word group. If it is not a sentence, write *not complete*, and write whether it is missing a subject or a predicate.

1. Mario and his family.
2. Makes a big family dinner.
3. They will celebrate his tenth birthday tomorrow.
4. A piñata in the shape of a camel.
5. Contains gifts from his family.

Simple and Compound Sentences *pages 64–65*

Write the sentence. Underline each simple subject once and each simple predicate twice. Then write *simple* or *compound* to describe the sentence.

6. Our school is in Texas and is close to Mexico.
7. Mexico has a rich culture, and many Mexicans are proud of it.
8. Many students come from Mexico and speak Spanish.
9. We sing Spanish songs, and everyone learns them.
10. We ate at a celebration, and I tried new foods.

Combining Sentences *pages 66–67*

Rewrite the sentences in each group as a compound sentence using *and* or *but*. Add commas where needed.

11. Serena's grandparents have been in America for twenty years. They still speak Vietnamese at home.
12. They miss their Vietnamese relatives back home. They are happy in their new home.
13. Meiko is from Japan. Her mother always speaks Japanese.
14. Rinaldo was born in Mexico. Now he lives in the United States.
15. Customs are different all over the world. We enjoy learning about different cultures.

Unit 2

Grammar   More About Nouns and Verbs

Writing   Informative Writing: Explanation

How to Start a Seashell Collection

1. Look for shells on the sand or in the water.

2. Collect shells that are not chipped or broken.

3. Don't take shells that still have animals living in them.

4. Sort the shells by size, shape and col...

Common and Proper Nouns

A noun is a word that names a person, a place, a thing, or an idea. A noun can tell who or what.

A common noun names any person, place, thing, or idea. A common noun begins with a lowercase letter.

A proper noun names a particular person, place, or thing. Words that name people's titles, holidays, days of the week, and months are also proper nouns. Each main word in a proper noun begins with a capital letter.

	People	Places	Things
Common Noun	girl	city	month
Proper Noun	Erica Davis	Austin, Texas	November

Examples:

Common Nouns: The **basketball player** helped his **team** win the **game**.

Proper Nouns: Michael Jordan helped the **U.S. Olympic team** win the gold medal for basketball.

Vocabulary Power

a•nat•o•my
[ə•nat′ə•mē] *n.* The study of the different parts and organs of people and animals.

Guided Practice

A. **Read the sentences. Tell whether the under-lined words are common or proper nouns.**

Example: Tabitha, the baby, fell, but she was not hurt.
proper, common

1. She did not break a bone.
2. It happened on Valentine's Day.
3. A baby's skeleton is soft.
4. A skeleton is like a frame for the body.
5. Mrs. Garcia, our science teacher, teaches us about anatomy.

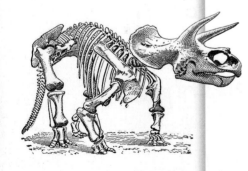

Independent Practice

B. Read the sentences. Write whether the underlined words are common nouns or proper nouns.

Example: Muscles help you move.
common

6. Your body is filled with muscles.
7. Each muscle has a different job.
8. Annie studies anatomy at Rice University.
9. She also plays tennis.
10. How does Annie hit the ball?
11. Her brain sends a message to her arm.
12. The message travels along a nerve.
13. A muscle in her arm becomes shorter.
14. That muscle pulls on the bone.
15. It lifts her arm and hand.

C. Read the sentences. Write the noun or nouns in each sentence. Write whether each noun is a common noun or a proper noun.

Example: A worm wriggles.
worm, common

16. Animals sometimes move strangely.
17. They use muscles to move.
18. The elephant walks slowly.
19. The snake slithers quietly.
20. The Springtown Zoo is nearby.

> **Remember**
> that a **noun names** a person, place, thing, or idea. A **common noun** names any person, place, thing, or idea and begins with a lowercase letter. A **proper noun** names a particular person, a place, or a thing and begins with a capital letter.

Writing Connection

Writer's Journal: Taking Notes Ask your partner about his or her favorite television shows, books, movie stars, and music groups. Take notes so that you remember your partner's responses. Then write three sentences about your partner's favorite things.

Singular and Plural Nouns

A **singular noun** names one person, place, thing, or idea. A **plural noun** names more than one person, place, thing, or idea.

Most nouns become plural when you add *s* or *es*. Add *s* to nouns that end in a vowel or most consonants. Add *es* to nouns that end in *s*, *x*, *ch*, or *sh*. To form the plural of a noun that ends in a consonant and *y*, change the *y* to *i* and add *es*.

Regular Nouns			
Singular	bone	day	country
Plural	bones	days	countries

Some nouns are **irregular** and have special spellings in the plural form. Other irregular nouns have the same spelling for both the singular and the plural forms.

Irregular Nouns			
Singular	foot	child	deer
Plural	feet	children	deer

Guided Practice

A. **Tell whether the underlined noun or nouns are singular or plural.**

Example: Exercises may build your <u>strength</u>. *singular*

1. Strength training involves lifting <u>weights</u>.
2. Running is good for your <u>heart</u>.
3. <u>Runners</u> need comfortable <u>shoes</u>.
4. Can you run as fast as a <u>deer</u> can?
5. <u>Deer</u> are especially fast runners.

Independent Practice

B. **Read the sentences. Write the noun or nouns in each sentence. Then tell whether each noun is singular or plural.**

Example: Our hands are amazing.
hands, plural

6. A hand is very useful.
7. It can do many tasks.
8. Have you noticed that hands and feet are alike?
9. Toes are similar to fingers.
10. A wrist moves the same way that an ankle does.

C. **Read the sentences. Write the plural form of the noun in parentheses.**

Example: Muscles have different (section).
sections

11. Muscles are often connected to (bone).
12. The connecting (part) are tendons.
13. Tendons are thin, like (rope).
14. When you move, you can feel some (tendon) pulled tight under your skin.
15. Anatomy is the study of parts of (person) and animals.

Remember

that a **singular** **noun** names one person, place, or thing. A **plural** **noun** names more than one person, place, or thing.

There are 27 bones in the hand.

Writing Connection

Real-Life Writing: Introduce a Classmate Read your notes from the interview with your partner. Then write an introduction of your partner. An introduction lets others know what your partner is like. Include sentences about your partner's favorite sports, hobbies, and other interests. Then read what you have written to the class.

Common Abbreviations

Ave.	Avenue
Blvd.	Boulevard
Dr.	Drive
Rd.	Road
St.	Street
E.	East
N.	North
S.	South
W.	West

Abbreviations in Titles

Mr.	title for all men
Ms.	title for all women
Dr.	Doctor
Capt.	Captain
Gov.	Governor
Prof.	Professor

Time Words

| A.M. | before noon |
| P.M. | after noon |

USAGE AND MECHANICS

Abbreviations and Titles

An abbreviation is a shortened form of a word.

Many abbreviations begin with a capital letter and end with a period. Titles before names, such as *Mrs.*, *Ms.*, *Mr.*, *Dr.* (Doctor), *Gov.* (Governor), and *Sen.* (Senator) begin with a capital letter. *Miss* is also a title. *Miss* begins with a capital letter but is not abbreviated.

Examples:

The twins were born at 1:00 P.M. at Jackson Hospital on **N.** Whitson **Blvd.**

Their father is **Capt.** Harris.

Ms. Hart lives near **Dr.** Brown and **Prof.** Murphy.

Use abbreviations when you take notes, make lists, write in a journal, or address an envelope. In other kinds of writing, use the complete word (except for *Mr.*, *Mrs.*, and *Ms.*, which are always abbreviated).

Guided Practice

A. Find the abbreviation or abbreviations in each sentence. Tell what they mean.

Example: Brad Carlin had a bad cough and went to see Dr. Patel.
Dr., Doctor

1. The doctor's office is on Lincoln Ave.
2. It is near E. Market St.
3. First the nurse, Ms. Sims, measured Brad's height and weight.
4. Then the doctor listened to Brad breathe while Mr. Carlin watched.
5. The doctor told Brad to come back the next day at 4:00 P.M.

Independent Practice

B. **Write the sentences. Correct any mistakes in abbreviations.**

> **Example:** In 1628, dr William Harvey explained how blood moves through the body. *Dr.*

6. Ms Teresa Robles teaches anatomy.
7. She teaches at j. f. Kennedy High School.
8. She spoke to students at the Elm st School.
9. The students also heard from dr. Poston that day.
10. He works at the hospital on n. Wolcott ave.
11. The school nurse, ms Ortiz, showed us how to listen to our own hearts beat.
12. Our gym teacher, mr. Armbruster, reminded us that exercise helps keep hearts healthy.
13. I like to jog near my house on E Carolina rd.
14. I have time on Friday after 4:00 pm.
15. Today gov Sampson declared this month to be Healthy Heart Month.

Writing Connection

Health Exercise can keep your heart in good shape. Make a list of ways you like to exercise. Do you walk, run, skate, jump rope, ride a bicycle, dance, or play different sports? Make a chart listing the days of the week. Write down the different kinds of exercise you do each day. If you think you need more exercise, plan some activities to add to your chart where you can fit them in.

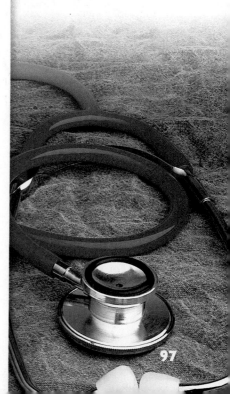

Extra Practice

For more help
with nouns, visit
The Learning Site:

www.harcourtschool.com

98

A. **Read each sentence. Write whether the underlined noun is a common noun or a proper noun.**
pages 92–93

Example: Mrs. Ortiz is the <u>nurse</u> at our school.
common

  1. How can <u>children</u> stay healthy?
  2. You must do two important <u>things</u>.
  3. Exercise and eat healthful <u>foods</u>.
  4. <u>Mrs. Ortiz</u> teaches us which foods to eat.
  5. <u>Mr. Handel</u> cooks healthful school lunches.

B. **Read each sentence. Write whether the underlined noun is singular or plural.** *pages 94–95*

Example: Coach Vega encourages everyone to play
active <u>games</u>.
plural

  6. Volleyball is good for your <u>heart</u>.
  7. Soccer helps build up the <u>muscles</u> in your legs.
  8. Jumping rope is great <u>exercise</u>.
  9. <u>Children</u> need to exercise every day.
10. Exercise builds strong <u>bodies</u>.

C. **Write each sentence. Use the correct plural
form of the noun in parentheses.** *pages 94–95*

Example: Growing (child) choose exercises that are fun.
children

11. Riding (bicycle) is enjoyable.
12. We can feel the muscles of our (leg) become
stronger as we pedal.
13. Be careful not to fall off the bike and break your
(bone).
14. Swimming can make your (arm) strong.
15. Kicking your (foot) as you swim builds muscles.

D. Each of the following sentences contains an incorrect plural noun or an incorrect abbreviation. Rewrite each sentence correctly.

pages 94–97

> **Example**: Nerveses have a very important job.
> *Nerves*

16. Nerves send signales to the muscles.

17. Every part of the human body has branchs of nerves.

18. Nerves link the brain and spine to other parts of our bodys.

19. Our braines can send messages through nerves to facial muscles.

20. The resultes of these messages can be smiles or laughs.

21. Other brain messages can result in frownes.

22. Our teacher told us to tickle our feets with grass.

23. Then mr. Lee, our teacher, asked what we felt.

24. Most of the childs felt gentle, ticklish feelings.

25. The nerves in the foots felt the grass and sent messages to our brains.

DID YOU KNOW?
The heart is a very busy organ. The average heart pushes more than three million quarts of blood through the body every year.

Writing Connection

Writer's Craft: Write a Title The title of a passage usually tells its main idea. Work with a partner to take turns reading a paragraph aloud. As you listen, write down the most important ideas you hear. Then write a title that fits the main idea of the paragraph.

Chapter Review

Read the passage and decide which type of mistake, if any, appears in each underlined section. Mark the letter for your answer.

> On <u>Jan 16,</u> a cold, dry morning, the fourth grade
> (1)
> at <u>Highland avenue school</u> went outdoors
> (2)
> for a <u>Science lesson.</u> Some of <u>the childern were</u>
> (3)   (4)
> <u>not very happy</u> about this activity. They were afraid
> that <u>their hands or feet or whole bodys</u> would
> (5)
> freeze. <u>The teacher, Mr Liu,</u> asked them to breathe
> (6)
> in and out very slowly. They laughed when they saw
> that their breath looked like steam from a kettle. Mr.
> Liu explained, "The air <u>inside your mouthes</u> is warm
> (7)
> and <u>has Water in it."</u>
> (8)

TIP Remember that abbreviations usually end with a period. Abbreviations of proper nouns begin with a capital.

1 A Spelling
  B Capitalization
  C Punctuation
  D No mistake

2 F Spelling
  G Capitalization
  H Punctuation
  J No mistake

3 A Spelling
  B Capitalization
  C Punctuation
  D No mistake

4 F Spelling
  G Capitalization
  H Punctuation
  J No mistake

5 A Spelling
  B Capitalization
  C Punctuation
  D No mistake

6 F Spelling
  G Capitalization
  H Punctuation
  J No mistake

7 A Spelling
  B Capitalization
  C Punctuation
  D No mistake

8 F Spelling
  G Capitalization
  H Punctuation
  J No mistake

For additional test preparation, visit *The Learning Site:*
www.harcourtschool.com

Listening for Purpose and Main Idea

Reading is not the only way to learn new information. You can learn a lot by listening, too. Sometimes you can get information from a speaker. Listen for the speaker's purpose and main idea. Follow these tips when listening to new information:

- Pay close attention to what the speaker is saying. Do not let your mind wander.

- Picture in your mind what the speaker is saying.

- Determine the speaker's purpose. Does the speaker want to give you information? Does the speaker want to entertain you with interesting stories? Does the speaker want to persuade you to agree with his or her opinion?

- Ask questions if you did not understand what the speaker said. Write down questions as you listen.

- Take notes about interesting and important points. These notes can help you ask questions later and remember what you heard.

- Try to summarize what the speaker said. A *summary* is a short review of the most important information.

YOUR TURN

LISTEN TO YOUR PARTNER Think of a sport or an activity you enjoy. Tell a partner about it. Your partner should listen and take notes. Then have your partner ask you three questions about the activity. Switch roles and listen to your partner. Do not forget to take notes and ask three good questions. Finally, use your notes to write a short paragraph about your partner's activity. Make sure that your paragraph includes the most important information.

Singular Possessive Nouns

Possessive nouns show ownership. A **singular possessive noun** shows ownership by one person or thing.

To form the possessive of most singular nouns, add an apostrophe (') and an *s*. The apostrophe takes the place of the words *of*, *of the*, *of a*, and *of an*.

Examples:

the mother of the baby seal ⟶ the baby **seal's** mother

the weight of an infant seal ⟶ an infant **seal's** weight

the seals of Russia ⟶ **Russia's** seals

Vocabulary Power

hab·i·tat [hab'ə·tat] *n.* The place where an animal or plant naturally lives or grows.

Guided Practice

A. Identify the possessive noun in each sentence.

Example: The photographer's picture shows a seal pup.
photographer's

1. Eric's trip to find seals took him and his son Ted north.
2. His many questions about seals showed Ted's excitement.
3. This flight was the boy's first trip to visit seals.
4. Eric showed his son the pilot's map.
5. He answered his son's questions.

Independent Practice

B. Write the possessive noun in each sentence.

Example: There is a meadow behind my family's house.
family's

6. We often see a robin's nest in the nearest tree.
7. My sister's name is Kate.
8. Kate's dog lies under that tree on hot days.
9. Our neighbor's cow grazes in the meadow.
10. The cow's calf is fun to watch.
11. The warbler, a small songbird, is Dad's favorite.
12. This bird's nest is found in the grass.
13. My mom's favorite animal is the deer.
14. A ladybug's food is insects that kill plants.
15. This beetle's help can save a tree.

C. Write each sentence. Replace the underlined words with the possessive noun.

Example: Imagine <u>the surprise of the boy</u>.
Imagine the boy's surprise.

16. <u>The fawn of the deer</u> stands at the edge of the meadow.
17. <u>The spots of the fawn</u> make it difficult to be seen.
18. <u>The ears of the mother</u> turn toward a sound.
19. <u>The ears of the doe</u> alert it to a nearby snake.
20. <u>The habitat of the doe</u> is full of danger.

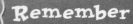

Writing Connection

Real-Life Writing: Write an Advertisement Think of a real or imaginary product that you want to sell. Name the product after yourself—for example, Sara's Special Soap. Write a short advertisement for it. Explain what it can do.

that **possessive nouns** show ownership. A **singular possessive noun** shows ownership by one person or thing. Add an apostrophe (') and *s* to most singular nouns to form a possessive noun.

Plural Possessive Nouns

Plural possessive nouns show ownership by more than one person or thing.

Plural possessive nouns are formed in two ways. To form the possessive of a plural noun that ends in *s*, add only an apostrophe ('). To form the possessive of a plural noun that does not end in *s*, add an apostrophe and *s*.

Examples:

the cameras of the tourists ⟶ the **tourists'** cameras

the work of the men ⟶ the **men's** work

the size of the bears ⟶ the **bears'** size

the drawings of the women ⟶ the **women's** drawings

Guided Practice

A. Identify the plural possessive nouns.

Examples: The visitors' goal on this tour is to see wild animals.
visitors'

These tours are often too dangerous to be children's trips.
children's

1. The guides take care of travelers' food and shelter.
2. One of the tour leaders' jobs is to find animals, such as elephants.
3. What are elephants' habitats like?
4. These huge animals' home is in Africa.
5. The guides' jeeps take tourists to flat grasslands there.

Independent Practice

B. Write the plural possessive noun in each sentence.

Examples: The zebras' homes are here.
zebras'
They are the people's favorite.
people's

6. The children's park has many animals.
7. The wildebeests' hooves stir up dust.
8. The elephants' food is waist-high grass.
9. The lionesses' hunting skills are excellent.
10. The giraffes' diet includes leaves.

C. Write each sentence. Change the underlined words to a plural possessive form.

Examples: The vacation was the idea of my parents.
The vacation was my parents' idea.

The shouts of the children rang out.
The children's shouts rang out.

11. The campfires of the families lit the night.
12. The hooting of the owls came from the trees.
13. The fishing gear of the men lay on the dock.
14. We heard the honking of the geese in the morning.
15. The hive of the bees was hidden.

Writing Connection

Science Imagine that you are a guide at a zoo or animal farm. Take a group of visitors on a tour of the main areas of the zoo. Write a paragraph describing some of the animals' habitats. Use possessive nouns in your paragraph.

Remember that a plural **possessive noun** shows ownership by more than one person or thing.

DID YOU KNOW? About 1,500,000 wildebeests and 750,000 zebras take part in the yearly migration, a move to find food and water.

USAGE AND MECHANICS

Possessive Noun or Plural Noun?

Do not confuse plural nouns with possessive nouns.

You know that a plural noun names more than one person, place, thing, or idea. A possessive noun shows ownership.

Examples:

We watched the whale **calf's** birth.
singular possessive

The **babies'** bodies were quite big.
plural possessive

The **sailors** are ready to ship out.
plural not possessive

Guided Practice

A. **Tell whether the underlined noun in each sentence is a singular possessive noun, a plural possessive noun, or a plural noun that is not possessive.**

Examples: Sue's wish is to go on a whale watch.
singular possessive

The children's tickets are free.
plural possessive

My parents show their excitement.
plural not possessive

 1. The passengers' backpacks contain food.
 2. A few passengers are watching for whales.
 3. At times they can see only the whales' tails.
 4. The travelers got pictures of whales.
 5. I bet that some of the photos are great.

Independent Practice

Remember

that a possessive noun shows ownership. Do not confuse possessive nouns with plural nouns that do not show ownership.

B. Read each sentence. Write whether each under-lined noun is singular possessive, plural possessive, or plural not possessive.

Examples: A <u>calf's</u> protection comes from its mother.
singular possessive

Baby <u>whales</u> are called calves.
plural not possessive

Different <u>people's</u> work tells us about whales.
plural possessive

6. Where does <u>scientists'</u> knowledge about whales come from?
7. <u>Scientists</u> watch whales' activities.
8. Sea <u>captains'</u> diaries tell where sailors have seen whales.
9. A <u>researcher's</u> tag identifies a particular whale.
10. A <u>whale's</u> body may have <u>markings</u>.
11. A whale <u>calf's</u> body has almost no fat.
12. A <u>mother's</u> rich milk quickly fattens a calf.
13. Fat protects the <u>calves'</u> bodies from icy waters.
14. <u>Whales'</u> diets include krill and plankton.
15. <u>Whales</u> can scoop up 3 tons of food at one feeding.

Writing Connection

Writer's Craft: Giving Reasons Imagine that you are an animal keeper in a zoo. Write down some ideas for animal care. Support your choices with reasons. (For example, "I would make their home look like their habitat in the wild.") Explain your ideas to a partner. Each of you should record the other's key ideas and reasons and should present the other's ideas to the class. Use possessive nouns and plural nouns correctly.

Extra Practice

A. Write the possessive noun in each sentence. Write whether the possessive is singular or plural. *pages 102–105*

Examples: My aunt's cabin is near the Sonoran Desert. *aunt's, singular*

Relatives' visits are common in autumn. *Relatives', plural*

1. My sister's binoculars help us see many things.
2. There are woodpeckers' nests in a cactus.
3. The same hole can be many creatures' home.
4. A woodpecker's babies are safe inside the cactus.
5. A cave may be a bobcat's shelter.

B. Write each sentence. Replace the underlined words with the possessive form. *pages 102–105*

Examples: The long, curved beak of the hummingbird lets it reach inside flowers.
The hummingbird's long, curved beak lets it reach inside flowers.

The strong legs of the kangaroos help these animals jump.
The kangaroos' strong legs help these animals jump.

6. The habitat of an animal is where it lives.
7. The homes of many animals are in the same place.
8. The pointed bill of the greenfinch helps the bird crack seeds.
9. The short beak of the bullfinch helps the bird eat buds.
10. Garbage of people can be food for some animals.

Remember

to add **'s** to form the possessive of a singular noun or plural noun that does not end in *s.* Add only an apostrophe to form the possessive of a plural noun that ends in *s.*

For more activities with possessive nouns, visit *The Learning Site:*

www.harcourtschool.com

C. Write each sentence, using the correct noun in parentheses. *pages 106–107*

Example: That Emperor penguin's egg rests on its (father's, fathers') feet.

That Emperor penguin's egg rests on its father's feet.

11. Is it far to the (penguins, penguins') nesting areas?
12. The (birds, birds') travel in darkness.
13. The (mothers, mother's) lay eggs in early May.
14. Sometimes it is the (father's, fathers) job to keep the eggs warm.
15. The (father's, fathers') bodies lose about half their weight while keeping eggs warm.

D. Write each incorrect sentence, using the correct possessive or plural noun. If the sentence is correct, write _correct_. *pages 106–107*

Example: We used Ellens flashlight to follow the path.

We used Ellen's flashlight to follow the path.

16. We were hoping to see these birds' tonight.
17. We saw two owl's nests.
18. The twins flashlights were broken.
19. Ellen has loved owl's for a long time.
20. Ellen said that she heard an owl's hoot last night.

> **Remember**
> that a **possessive**
> **noun** shows own-
> ership. A **plural**
> **noun** does not
> show ownership.

Writing Connection

Writer's Journal: Recording Ideas Choose a habitat that you know, such as a nearby park. What kinds of animals live in this habitat? Is this habitat worth keeping as it is? Why? Write your ideas in your journal. Check your use of possessive and plural nouns.

Chapter Review

Read the passage and choose the word that belongs in each space. Mark the letter for your answer.

STANDARDIZED
TEST PREP

One __(1)__ work has changed __(2)__ ideas about __(3)__ . Jane Goodall lived in a forest in Tanzania for __(4)__ to learn about them. __(5)__ notes tell about the __(6)__ forest habitat and the animals themselves. She watched a chimp named David use a piece of grass to get __(7)__ from their mound. Goodall's research proved that chimps use __(8)__ to get food.

TIP Sometimes test questions are part of a paragraph. Read the whole paragraph first to get a general idea of the subject. Use this information to help you answer each question.

1 A womans
   B woman's
   C womans'
   D women's

2 F peoples'
   G people
   H peoples
   J people's

3 A chimpanzees
   B chimpanzee's
   C chimpanzees'
   D chimpanzee

4 F years'
   G years
   H year
   J year's

5 A Goodall'
   B Goodalls
   C Goodalls'
   D Goodall's

6 F chimp's
   G chimps
   H chimps'
   J Chimps'

7 A termites
   B termite's
   C Termites
   D termites'

8 F tools'
   G tools
   H tool's
   J toolses'

For additional test preparation, visit *The Learning Site:*
www.harcourtschool.com

Using Reference Materials

When you have a research project to do, it is important to know how to use reference materials.

Encyclopedias

An encyclopedia is a book or set of books that gives information about a wide variety of subjects. The subjects are arranged in alphabetical order. An encyclopedia can also be on a CD-ROM.

There are twelve volumes in this set. This is volume one.

If you are looking for facts about ponds, you would look here.

This volume covers subjects that begin with the letters *T* and *U*.

Periodicals

Periodicals, such as magazines and newspapers, have recent facts about a topic. Periodicals are published every day, week, or month. Look in a periodical index, or guide to articles, to find facts on a topic.

YOUR TURN

WORDS ABOUT ANIMALS Work with a partner to choose an animal habitat such as polar ice, forests, or deserts. Use an encyclopedia and periodicals to find and record facts about this habitat and the animals that live there. Make a list with the heading *What This Habitat Is Like*. Make another list with the heading *Animals That Live Here*.

Writer's Craft

Organizing Information

How often do you explain how to do something or share a fact that you know? Every time you do this, you are giving **information**. If you write down the information, you are doing **informative writing**.

Read the following passage from *Hold the Anchovies! A Book About Pizza*. Notice how the writer explains the steps in time order.

LITERATURE MODEL

Vocabulary Power

se•quence
[sē′kwəns] *n.* The order or arrangement in which one thing comes after another.

Pizza is made from many things. The first is dough. The dough is made by adding warm water and yeast to the flour. When the dough rises and stretches just the right amount, it is ready to be tossed into the shape of a pizza pie.

The next thing we need is sauce made from sweet, ripe tomatoes. The sauce is spread evenly on the dough. Now the cheese is grated and sprinkled onto the pizza. Now everything is ready to go into the oven.

—from *Hold the Anchovies! A Book About Pizza*
by Shelley Rotner and Julia Pemberton Hellums

Analyze THE Model

1. What is the writer explaining?

2. Why does the writer put the steps in time order?

3. How does the writer help you understand which step comes first, next, and so on?

When you write to explain something, you want the information to make sense to your reader. You need to **organize** your information or put it in good order. Look at the chart on the next page.

Strategies for Organizing Information

Applying the Strategies

Order ideas.

- Put ideas in an order that makes sense, such as time order or order of importance.

Use sequence words.

- Use words such as **first, next, now,** and **after** to help readers understand sequence, or time order.

YOUR TURN

ANALYZE TEXT ORGANIZATION **Work with a partner. Look in your science text for an explanation of an experiment or other information that is presented in time order. Talk about how the information is organized.**

Answer these questions:

1. What is the writer explaining?

2. Why is it important for this information to be explained in time order?

3. How does the writer indicate the sequence of steps or ideas?

Ordering Ideas

A. Put each set of sentences in time order. Then write the sentences on your paper in paragraph form.

1. Soon the seed begins to sprout.
   A seed is carried on the wind.
   The stem grows larger, and leaves appear.
   The seed falls to the ground.
   A tiny stem pushes up through the soil.

2. It sent back amazing pictures of Uranus and its moons.
   After passing Saturn, the spacecraft headed for Uranus.
   It flew past Mars, Jupiter, and Saturn.
   Voyager 2 then flew past Neptune and out of our solar system.
   Voyager 2 was launched from Earth.

3. Add one egg to the cake mix.
   First, preheat the oven to 325°.
   Pour the cake mix into a bowl.
   After the cake has cooled, frost it.
   Then add the third ingredient, one cup of water.
   Bake for 25 minutes.
   Mix all the ingredients well.
   Pour the batter into a greased cake pan.

Using Sequence Words

B. Write the paragraph below on your paper. Add sequence words from the box to show the order of ideas. Remember to capitalize the first word of each sentence.

during	after	finally	first	next

The cooling stage begins _____ a volcano has finished erupting. At _____, gases and vapor continue to escape from the volcano. _____ the _____ step in the cooling stage, the volcano may form hot springs. _____, the volcano loses the last of its heat, and springs of cold water may form in and around it.

Writing and Thinking

Writer's Journal

Write to Record Reflections You might follow directions for many reasons, such as to bake a cake, to learn a new game, or to take a test. What might happen if you can't understand the directions or the order in which to do the steps? From your own experiences, what can you learn about how directions should be organized? Write your reflections in your Writer's Journal.

Writing Directions

The authors of *Hold the Anchovies! A Book About Pizza* explained the steps you would follow to make a pizza. Hector knows how to make a tornado in a jar! His teacher wanted to know how he did it, so Hector wrote the directions for her. Read the directions that Hector wrote.

MODEL

order—list
materials first

sequence
words

steps in time
order

sequence
words

time order

> It's easy to make a miniature tornado. The materials you will need are a glass jar with a lid, water, food coloring, and some dishwashing detergent.
>
> First, fill the jar about 3/4 of the way with water. Add a teaspoon of dishwashing detergent and as much food coloring as you need to get the color you want. Next, put the lid tightly on the jar. Shake the jar hard for about twenty seconds.
>
> After shaking the jar, give it a quick twist. Then watch as a tiny tornado forms in the water inside the jar.

Analyze THE Model

1. Will Hector's teacher have difficulty following his directions? Why or why not?

2. Do the steps seem to be in correct order?

3. What might happen if Hector did not put the steps in the right order?

4. How does Hector's use of sequence words help you understand his directions?

YOUR TURN

WRITING PROMPT **Think of something you know how to do that requires several steps. Maybe you know how to do a science demonstration, play a simple game, or make a milk shake. Write a set of directions that your classmates can follow.**

STUDY THE PROMPT **Ask yourself these questions:**

1. What is your purpose for writing?

2. Who is your audience?

3. What writing form will you use?

Prewriting and Drafting

Organize Your Ideas Plan the order of steps for your directions. Use a chart like this one to organize your thoughts.

Tell what you are explaining. List any materials or ingredients that might be needed.

Explain the first step.

Explain each of the other steps in the correct order. Use sequence words to make the order clear.

USING YOUR
Handbook

Use the Writer's Thesaurus to find sequence words to explain the order of the steps in your directions.

Editing

Read over the draft of your directions. Can you improve the directions to make them easier to understand? Use this checklist to help you revise and proofread your directions:

☑ Will your classmates be able to follow these directions?

☑ Have you explained the steps in an order that makes sense?

☑ Are there steps you should add or leave out to make the directions easier to follow?

☑ Did you use sequence words to help your reader?

Use this checklist as you proofread your paragraph:

☑ I have used capitalization and punctuation correctly.

☑ I have used singular and plural nouns correctly.

☑ I have distinguished between possessive nouns and plural nouns.

☑ I have used a dictionary to check my spelling.

Editor's Marks

ℐ delete text

∧ insert text

ᓂ move text

ᑫ new paragraph

≡ capitalize

/ lowercase

◯ correct spelling

Sharing and Reflecting

Writer's
Journal

After making a final copy of your directions, share them with a partner. Read your partner's directions and then role-play following the steps. Discuss what you like about your partner's directions, and talk about strategies for writing clear directions in the future. Write your reflections in your Writer's Journal.

Giving Spoken Directions

When you give directions, you don't always write them down. Often the directions you give are oral, or spoken. In some situations, you might draw a simple map or diagram to illustrate your spoken directions.

How are spoken directions different from written ones? How are they the same? Study the Venn diagram.

Written Directions
If necessary, reader can go back and reread.

Both
Should be clear and organized.
Should be given in order.
Should include sequence words to make them easier to understand.

Spoken Directions
Listener needs to remember directions or ask speaker to repeat them.

YOUR TURN

Work in a small group to practice giving spoken directions. Follow these steps.

STEP 1 Decide on a task you do well. For example, you might give directions for playing a game.

STEP 2 Have members of your group take turns giving spoken directions. If you wish, draw diagrams and maps to illustrate your directions.

STEP 3 As each person is speaking, the rest of the group should listen carefully and try to visualize following the directions.

STEP 4 Talk about what you learned from listening to each other's directions. Point out strategies that were used for giving directions.

Strategies for Listening and Speaking

Use these strategies to help you give, as well as understand and follow, spoken directions:

• Speakers should remember to adjust rate, volume, pitch, and tone to fit their audience and purpose.

• Listeners should listen carefully to identify and remember the sequence of steps.

119

Action Verbs

An **action verb** is a word that tells what the subject of a sentence does, did, or will do.

You know that the predicate of a sentence tells what the subject of the sentence is or does. The main word in the predicate is a verb. Every sentence has a verb. Most verbs are action verbs.

Examples:

A volcano **explodes**.

Hot, melted rock **shoots** out of the volcano.

The melted rock **covers** the land around the volcano.

Vocabulary Power

ge•ol•o•gist
[jē•ol′ə•jist] *n.* A scientist who studies the history and structure of the earth.

Guided Practice

A. Read the sentence. Identify the action verb.

Example: Many people live near active volcanoes.
live

1. Some volcanoes damage nearby areas.
2. Lava, or hot, melted rock, covers the land.
3. The air fills with ashes.
4. Some geologists study volcanoes.
5. These scientists tell about volcanic activity.
6. Not all volcanoes explode.
7. Lava flows slowly and quietly.
8. Smoke sometimes rises from these volcanoes.
9. People often see small streams of lava and clouds of ash.
10. People sweep the ash from the roads.

Independent Practice

B. Write the sentence. Underline the action verb.

Example: *Scientists <u>collect</u> information about volcanoes.*

11. Scientists wonder about the future of volcanoes.
12. They watch volcanoes all over the world.
13. Some geologists study only volcanoes.
14. These people travel to dangerous places.
15. Some geologists even go inside volcanoes.
16. The scientists carry special tools with them.
17. These tools record information about volcanoes.
18. One tool measures gases in the air.
19. Another tool shows movements under the ground.
20. Geologists teach other people about volcanoes.
21. Washington's Mount St. Helens volcano exploded in 1980.
22. Volcanic ash filled the air.
23. The ash fell like snow onto the streets.
24. Experts told everyone to leave the area.
25. Most people survived the disaster.

Remember

that an **action verb** tells what the subject of a sentence does, did, or will do.

Writing Connection

Writer's Journal: Using a Thesaurus Use a thesaurus to find verbs with meanings similar to the verbs in the Guided Practice and Independent Practice exercises. Substitute the verb in the sentence with the verb you find in the thesaurus. What difference does the new verb make? Write the new words in your word bank.

Common Linking Verbs	
be	seem
look	feel
become	appear
smell	taste
sound	grow

Linking Verbs

A linking verb connects, or links, the subject of a sentence to a word or words in the predicate.

You know that an action verb tells what the subject of a sentence does, did, or will do. Some verbs are linking verbs. A linking verb is followed by a word or words in the predicate that rename or describe the subject.

Examples:
Mount St. Helens **is** a volcano.
(*Volcano* is another name for *Mount St. Helens.*)

Some volcanoes **become** inactive.
(*Inactive* describes *volcanoes.*)

Some verbs can be either action verbs or linking verbs, depending on how they are used.

Examples:
Mount St. Helens **looks** calm. (linking verb)

Jack **looks** at Mount St. Helens. (action verb)

Guided Practice

A. Read the sentence. Identify the linking verb. Tell which word or words are connected to the subject by the linking verb.

Example: Volcanoes seem safe most of the time.
linking verb seem *connects subject to* safe

1. Volcanoes become dangerous during eruptions.
2. Mount St. Helens was the source of volcanic ash.
3. Volcanic ash looks different from ash in a fireplace.
4. Volcanic ash is pieces of rock.
5. Eruptions are very powerful.

Independent Practice

Remember that a **linking verb** connects the subject to a word or words in the predicate.

B. The simple subject in the sentence is underlined. Write the linking verb and the word in the predicate that is connected to the subject by the linking verb.

> **Example:** Some <u>volcanoes</u> are old.
> *are, old*

6. <u>Volcanoes</u> are common on other planets.
7. Mars's tallest <u>volcano</u> seems huge to us.
8. Its <u>name</u> is Olympus Mons.
9. <u>It</u> was active a long time ago.
10. The <u>surface</u> of Venus appears volcanic.

C. Write the verb in each sentence. Tell whether it is an action verb or a linking verb.

> **Example:** Volcanoes create new land. *create*, action verb

11. Wind and water change volcanic rock into soil.
12. They also move volcanic soil into the ocean.
13. Most volcanic rock erodes over time.
14. Volcanoes are the source of much of the Earth's new land.
15. Lava and ash become new rock and soil.

Writing Connection

Writer's Craft: Strong Verbs Write three sentences about volcanoes using action verbs and three sentences using linking verbs. Exchange papers with a partner. Replace your partner's linking verbs with action verbs and some of his or her action verbs with stronger verbs. How does the meaning of the sentence change? Keep a list of strong action verbs to use in your writing.

USAGE AND MECHANICS

Using Forms of *Be*

The most common linking verbs are forms of *be*.

You know that a linking verb connects the subject to a word or words in the predicate. Always use the form of *be* that agrees with, or matches, the subject.

Rules for Using *Be*:	Examples:
Use **am**, **is**, or **was** with a singular subject.	A mild earthquake **is** not serious. A big earthquake in Turkey during 1999 **was** destructive. I **am** happy that the Turkish people got help.
Use **are** or **were** with *you* and with a plural subject.	Many people **were** homeless. Strong earthquakes **are** problems in many countries.
Use **be** in an imperative sentence.	**Be** sure to follow safety rules.

Guided Practice

A. Identify the form of *be* in parentheses that completes each sentence correctly.

Example: An earthquake (is, are) sometimes scary.
is

1. Imagine that you (is, are) asleep in your bed.
2. Suddenly you (is, are) aware of shaking.
3. The lamp near your bed (is, are) not steady.
4. Your pets (is, are) nervous.
5. Why do you think the animals (are, is) scared?

Independent Practice

B. Write the form of *be* in parentheses that completes the sentence correctly.

Example: Only a few earthquakes (is, are) major disasters.
are

6. There (is, are) 40,000 to 50,000 earthquakes each year.
7. Most of them (is, are) harmless.
8. In the past, earthquakes (was, were) big problems in some places.
9. These places (is, are) in earthquake zones.
10. An earthquake zone (is, are) a risky place to build a city.

C. Write the sentence. Use the correct form of *be* in the blank.

Example: I _____ glad that scientists can predict earthquakes. *am*

11. There _____ over twenty earthquake zones.
12. Much of California _____ in an earthquake zone.
13. I _____ curious about animal behavior before an earthquake.
14. Before an earthquake, some animals _____ very restless.
15. They seem to know that something _____ wrong.

Writing Connection

Real-Life Writing: Write a Letter Discuss how people might feel after an earthquake. List things earthquake victims might need. Work with a partner to write a letter to your school or local newspaper. Use forms of *be* to describe conditions and to tell how people can help.

Remember

to use *am, is,* and *was* with singular subjects. Use *are* and *were* with *you* and with plural subjects. Use *be* with commands.

DID YOU KNOW?
This seismograph has a pen that moves from side to side. It records the movements of an earthquake.

Extra Practice

Remember

that **action verbs** tell what the subject of a sentence does, did, or will do. **Linking verbs** connect the subject of a sentence to a word or words in the predicate. The verb changes to match its subject.

A. **Write each sentence, and underline the verb. Write *action* or *linking* to tell what kind of verb it is.** *pages 120–123*

Example: People in other communities and countries <u>help</u> victims of earthquakes. action

1. In 1999 a terrible earthquake hit Turkey.
2. Many people were hurt.
3. The earthquake caused a great deal of damage.
4. Many people needed food and clothing.
5. People were trapped under buildings.
6. Greece and Israel are countries near Turkey.
7. They gave generously to the Turkish people.
8. The United States sent rescue teams.
9. Other countries rushed volunteers to Turkey.
10. The Turkish people were grateful.

B. **Write each sentence, using the verb form in parentheses that completes the sentence correctly.** *pages 122–125*

Example: The Red Cross (is, are) a helpful organization.
    is

11. One problem (is, are) damage to buildings.
12. Other problems (is, are) a lack of electricity and gas.
13. Sometimes it (seem, seems) impossible to rebuild a town.
14. (Is, Are) people ready to give up?
15. People (appears, appear) eager to rebuild their homes.

For more activities with action and linking verbs, visit *The Learning Site:*

www.harcourtschool.com

C. Write each sentence. Use the correct form of _be_ in the blank. *pages 124–125*

Example: What _____ the best houses to build in an earthquake zone?

are

16. The best house _____ one that will not fall when shaken.
17. Wood buildings _____ safer than brick ones.
18. A light roof _____ better than a heavy one.
19. An earthquake-proof building _____ one that stands on solid rock.
20. _____ you surprised by this information?

D. Read each sentence. If it has an error, write the sentence correctly and underline the correction. If the sentence is correct, write _No mistake_.
pages 124–125

Example: There is many ways to stay safe.
There <u>are</u> many ways to stay safe.

21. If you is inside, do not run outside.
22. Taking an elevator is not a good idea.
23. The beach are another dangerous place.
24. There are no shelter.
25. Giant waves is likely to flood the area.

DID YOU KNOW?
The strength of an earthquake is measured by a number on the Richter scale. The number tells how much the ground moved.

Writing Connection

Art Design a poster or a group of pictures with captions about everyday safety. Your topic could be about riding a bike safely or preventing accidents at home. Use at least three action verbs and three linking verbs in your writing.

Chapter Review

Read the passage. Choose the word that belongs in each blank. Mark the letter for your answer.

STANDARDIZED
TEST PREP

> Did you know that a volcano __(1)__ not always harmful? Volcanoes __(2)__ helpful to many people. Bathing in hot springs heated by volcanoes helps some people __(3)__ better. Soil __(4)__ rich for farming when it gets minerals from volcanic rock and ash. Pumice __(5)__ hardened lava. Pumice __(6)__ useful for many things. Pumice pieces __(7)__ useful in grinding and polishing and for scrubbing objects. Pumice can even smooth the rough skin on the soles of your feet. These benefits show that volcanoes do not always __(8)__ disasters.

TIP If you finish before the test time is up, read over your answers. You may want to change some of them.

1 A are
  B is
  C seem
  D am

2 F are
  G is
  H seems
  J was

3 A appears
  B feels
  C are
  D feel

4 F becomes
  G become
  H are
  J were

5 A is
  B be
  C were
  D become

6 F are
  G seem
  H is
  J am

7 A be
  B was
  C are
  D is

8 F be
  G are
  H become
  J seems

For additional test preparation, visit *The Learning Site:*
www.harcourtschool.com

Comparing Visual Images

Advertisements use pictures and words to persuade people to buy things. Read the advertisement below. How do the pictures and words work together to persuade readers to buy the product?

The product's box is shown so that you can find it in the store.

The happy smile makes you believe that the cereal tastes good.

HAPPY BEAR CEREAL

This picture appeals to children, who will think that bears love the cereal. The children will want the cereal, too.

The bowl of breakfast cereal shows you what the product looks like.

"Put a smile on your face! Eat Happy Bear Cereal!"

The caption gives the main message of the advertisement.

In a small group, discuss the message the advertiser is trying to communicate. How do the pictures get the message across? Do the pictures alone persuade you to buy the product? Why or why not? How do the words get the message across? Do the words alone persuade you to buy the product? Why or why not?

YOUR TURN

DESIGN AN AD Design a magazine advertisement for a product you like. Tell your readers why this product is good and why they should buy it. Then draw a picture and write words to communicate the message. Look at magazine ads to get ideas.

Common Helping Verbs

am	should
is	has, have
are	had
was	do, does
were	did
will	can
would	could

Vocabulary Power

ma•rine [mə•rēn′] *adj.* Having to do with, formed by, or found in the sea.

Main Verbs and Helping Verbs

Sometimes a predicate is made up of two or more verbs that work together. The **main verb** tells what the action is.

A **helping verb** works with the main verb to tell more about an action. The helping verb always comes before the main verb. When *be* is used as a helping verb, it is not a linking verb.

Examples:

All the waters of the five oceans **are connected**.

Some scientists **did note** two minor oceans.

Guided Practice

A. **Identify the two verbs in each sentence. Tell whether each verb is a main verb or a helping verb.**

Example: I am reading about the Pacific Ocean.
   am, helping verb; *reading,* main verb

1. The largest ocean is named the Pacific Ocean.
2. The Pacific does cover about 70 million square miles.
3. The Pacific Ocean could hold all the continents.
4. The average depth was measured at about 13,000 feet.
5. Mountains are found on the ocean floor.

Independent Practice

B. **Write the sentence. Underline each helping verb once and each main verb twice.**

Example: People <u>should</u> <u><u>keep</u></u> the ocean clean.

6. The ocean has provided food, energy, and minerals.
7. People have used ocean plants for food.
8. Seaweed has served as a source of food.
9. People can eat fish and shellfish also.
10. Vitamins are found in some seaweed.
11. Energy from the ocean does have several forms.
12. Oil has become an important energy source.
13. Oil is located beneath the ocean floor.
14. The changes in the depths of ocean waters are caused by tides.
15. Ocean tides can produce energy.
16. Many minerals were discovered at the bottom of the ocean.
17. The ocean does contain copper, iron, and zinc.
18. People may find pearls inside oyster shells.
19. Scientists can make medicines from ocean plants.
20. Everyone will need products from the ocean.

Remember

that the helping verb comes before the main verb in a sentence.

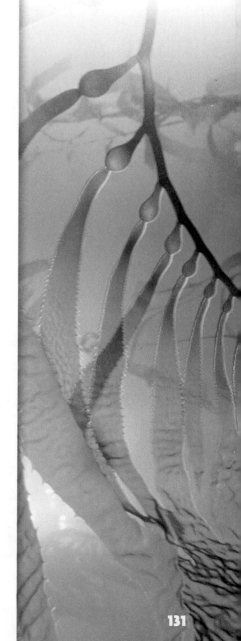

Writing Connection

Writer's Journal: Writing Idea Imagine that you are a fisher, a sailor, a lifeguard, or a marine scientist. Write a journal entry about what it is like to work in the ocean. Exchange journal entries with a partner. Underline the helping verbs once and the main verbs twice on your partner's paper.

More About Main Verbs and Helping Verbs

Sometimes a word such as *not* or *often* comes between the main verb and the helping verb.

You know that the helping verb always comes before the main verb. Words that come between the two verbs also tell about the action. These words may change the meaning of the sentence or make it more exact. In the following examples, the helping verb is underlined once, the main verb is underlined twice, and the word between the two parts of the verb is circled.

Examples:
Some types of fish could (not) survive in the ocean.

Ocean sand is (often) included in a cement mixture.

Guided Practice

A. Tell which word comes between the main verb and the helping verb in each sentence.

Example: The Arctic Ocean is often covered with ice.
often

1. This ice is mostly formed by frozen seawater.
2. Chunks of glacier ice will often float in the Arctic Ocean.
3. Glacier ice does not contain salt water.
4. The North Pole is also located in the Arctic Ocean.
5. Most plants will not survive in such cold temperatures.

Independent Practice

B. Write each sentence. Underline the helping verb once and the main verb twice. Circle the word that comes between the main verb and the helping verb.

Example: *Shrimp* <u>are</u> (also) <u>called</u> *shellfish.*

6. Shrimp are usually considered a valuable catch.
7. They will often hide in sand during the day.
8. Shrimp can then eat at night.
9. Some types of shrimp do not live in salt water.
10. Some shrimp can even change color.
11. Like shrimp, lobsters are also called shellfish.
12. People will sometimes catch too many lobsters.
13. Fishing laws should now protect the lobsters.
14. People have also eaten crabs.
15. Small crabs are often seen on the beach.
16. The oyster is usually protected by its shell.
17. Oysters would normally prefer calm waters.
18. An oyster will sometimes produce a pearl.
19. Some oysters do not make pearls.
20. Pearls are frequently used in jewelry.

Remember that a word may come between a main verb and a helping verb.

Writing Connection

Writer's Craft: Using Supporting Details Write a paragraph about an activity that all fish have in common. Then explain in three more sentences why that activity is important. Reread your paragraph to look for sentences in which words come between the helping verb and the main verb. Tell a partner how these words add to the meaning of each sentence.

**Common
Contractions**

isn't	couldn't
aren't	wouldn't
wasn't	shouldn't
weren't	don't
haven't	doesn't
hasn't	didn't
hadn't	

USAGE AND MECHANICS

Contractions with *Not*

A **contraction** is a shortened form of two words. It
is written as one word.

Often the word *not* is added to a helping verb to
form a contraction. The apostrophe (') takes the place
of the letter *o* in *not*. The main verb always follows the
contraction.

Examples:

I **have not** seen a whale. I **haven't** seen a whale.

Ocean waters **do not** stand still. Ocean waters **don't**
stand still.

Can't and *won't* have irregular forms.

can + not = can't   will + not = won't

Guided Practice

A. **Identify the contraction in each sentence. Then
tell the two words that form the contraction.**

Example: People <u>can't</u> prevent hurricanes. *can not*

1. Some hurricanes don't stay out over the ocean.
2. Some large storms aren't called hurricanes.
3. Tropical storm winds don't blow as hard as
   hurricane winds.
4. Hurricanes won't remain in the same place.
5. Scientists haven't learned everything about
   hurricanes.
6. Waves don't usually cause damage to docks.
7. An ocean wave doesn't move from side to side.
8. People shouldn't go outside during a hurricane.
9. Midwestern states don't get severe hurricanes.
10. Scientists couldn't always predict hurricanes.

Independent Practice

B. Write the contraction in each sentence. Then write the two words that form the contraction.

Example: Dolphins aren't considered fish.
aren't, are not

11. River dolphins don't live in salt water.
12. Dolphins can't smell.
13. Most dolphins won't live alone.
14. A dolphin doesn't usually dive deeply.
15. Dolphins wouldn't harm humans.

C. Write each sentence. Write a contraction for the underlined word or words in each sentence.

Example: Most sharks <u>would</u> <u>not</u> prefer cold water.
Most sharks wouldn't prefer cold water.

16. Sharks <u>do</u> <u>not</u> have bones.
17. Most sharks <u>can</u> <u>not</u> live without salt water.
18. Sharks <u>will</u> <u>not</u> take care of their young.
19. The nurse shark <u>does</u> <u>not</u> swim constantly.
20. Scientists <u>have</u> <u>not</u> identified all types of sharks.

Remember

that a **contraction** is two words written as one word with an apostrophe.

DID YOU KNOW?
The process of measuring the depth of the oceans is slow. Scientists estimate it would take about 125 years to complete this job!

Writing Connection

Writer's Craft: Organizing Ideas Imagine that you are a whale. Write a paragraph about your daily activities. What can you do that humans cannot do? Use contractions in at least three of your sentences. After you draft your paragraph, think about how your sentences are organized. Is there a clear topic sentence? Do the other sentences add important details about the topic? Revise your paragraph as needed to create a final draft.

Extra Practice

A. Write the two verbs in each sentence. Then write *helping verb* or *main verb* next to each verb. *pages 130–133*

Example: Penguins have lived for centuries on the shores of the South Atlantic Ocean.
have, helping verb; *lived,* main verb

1. Unlike most birds, penguins do not fly.
2. They have waddled along the icy shores.
3. Penguins can walk almost as fast as humans.
4. Penguins will spend time in the ocean.
5. They have become excellent swimmers.
6. Penguins will use their flippers like wings.
7. They are almost flying underwater.
8. Penguins can steer in the water with their feet.
9. Short, thick feathers should keep their bodies dry.
10. Penguins can dive deeper than any other bird.

B. Write each sentence. Underline the helping verb and the main verb. Circle the word that comes between these verbs. *pages 132–133*

Example: Scientists have often made new discoveries.
Scientists have (often) made new discoveries.

11. Researchers had never used computers in the past.
12. Marine scientists are also using new tools now.
13. Scientists could sometimes predict weather patterns.
14. Weather conditions do not remain the same.
15. Weather information would really help fishers.

Remember

that **helping verbs** and **main verbs** work together to express action. A **contraction** can be formed from a helping verb and the word *not*. An **apostrophe** takes the place of the letter *o* in *not*.

For more activities with main verbs and helping verbs, visit The Learning Site:

www.harcourtschool.com

C. Rewrite each sentence. Use a contraction for the helping verb and the word *not*. *pages 134–135*

Example: You should not drink ocean water.
You shouldn't drink ocean water.

16. Do not think that the ocean floor is flat.
17. You do not find warm water in the deepest parts.
18. Sunlight can not reach the bottom of the ocean.
19. The coldest waters do not freeze.
20. The water has not frozen because it is too salty.

D. Write the sentence, and correct each error. If the sentence has no errors, write *No error* after it. *pages 134–135*

Example: He has'nt studied marine life.
He hasn't studied marine life.

21. Scientists have'nt studied ocean floors for very long.
22. Marine scientists dont always work in the ocean.
23. Some wouldn't pass up the chance to teach.
24. Without the oceans, our planet would'nt have life.
25. The oceans arent' losing their mystery.

Writing Connection

Real-Life Writing: Giving Directions Imagine that you are teaching a friend to do something at the beach, such as build a sand castle, swim safely, or avoid sunburn. Draw pictures that explain at least four steps for doing the task. Write captions for the drawings. Warn your friend what could happen if he or she doesn't follow these steps.

STANDARDIZED
TEST PREP

TIP Answer the items
you are sure about first.
Then go back and try to
answer the others.

Chapter Review

Read each sentence. Look at the underlined words
in each one. There may be a mistake in punctuation or word usage. If you find a mistake, choose
the answer that is the best way to write the underlined section. If there is no mistake, choose
Correct as is.

1 <u>Most people dont
think</u> of the ocean
when they think of
farming.

   A Most people do'nt
   think

   B Most people not
   thinking

   C Most people don't
   think

   D Correct as is

2 People in Asia <u>have
farm the ocean</u> for
thousands of years.

   F have farmed the
   ocean

   G farming the ocean

   H are farming the ocean

   J Correct as is

3 Fish farming, however,
<u>has'nt always existed.</u>

   A hasn't always exist.

   B hasn't always existed.

   C hasnt existed always.

   D Correct as is

4 <u>Fish farming didn't
become popular</u> in
this country until the
1960s.

   F Fish farming did'not
   become popular

   G Fish farming not
   becoming popular

   H Fish farming did'nt
   become popular

   J Correct as is

5 <u>This pond will soon
become</u> a fish farm.

   A This pond soon
   becoming

   B This pond will soon
   becoming

   C This pond become
   soon

   D Correct as is

6 These fish farmers
<u>are raised catfish.</u>

   F are raise catfish.

   G has raised catfish.

   H are raising catfish.

   J Correct as is

For additional test
preparation, visit
The Learning Site:

www.harcourtschool.com

Group Discussions

Listening and speaking skills are important in presentations and in group discussions. A group discussion, however, is less formal than a presentation. In a group discussion, you make decisions about a topic. In a presentation, you present the decisions made in the group discussion.

Tips for a successful group discussion:

- Brainstorm ideas or solutions.
- Respect each other's ideas, even though you may not agree.
- Ask questions if something is unclear.
- Discuss the ideas. Give reasons why a solution will or will not work. Take a vote if necessary.
- Decide how to present your ideas to your audience.

Tips for speaking in a group discussion:

- Write a few notes to help you express what you want to say.
- Speak clearly.
- Summarize your main points.

YOUR TURN

Work with two or three classmates. As a group, collect research about an interesting fish, and discuss how you would present the information to a first-grade audience. In your discussion, take turns listening and speaking. Then, make a list of points you would teach and how you would teach them. Finally, write a paragraph about the things your group did well.

Writing Workshop

A how-to essay explains how to do a task. In this selection, you will learn how to grow a plant from a seed. As you read, think about what makes the explanation easy to understand.

FRUIT SEEDS

by Angela Wilkes
photographs by Dave King

Every time you eat fruit, you throw away the seeds or pit in the middle. Have you ever thought of planting them instead? If you give the seeds the right conditions and are patient, many seeds produce handsome plants. The best time of year to plant seeds is in the spring. Here you can find out how to plant an avocado pit and see how it grows.

You will need

• Potting soil or seed-and-cutting soil
• Different seeds and pits, such as grape seeds, a peach pit, orange or lemon seeds, apple seeds, or an avocado pit

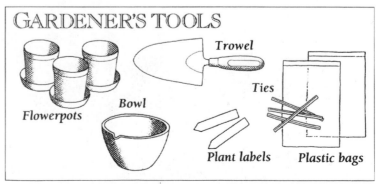

GARDENER'S TOOLS

Flowerpots   Trowel   Bowl   Plant labels   Ties   Plastic bags

141

What to do

1. Soak big pits in water for 24 hours. Put some soil in a bowl and water it. Stir it well, then fill small pots with the soil.
2. Plant avocado pits pointed end up, sticking out of the soil. Plant seeds about 1/2 inch down in pots of soil.
3. Label each pot to say what is in it. Put each pot in a plastic bag and tie the bag at the top, then put the pots in a warm, dark place.

The growing plant

Check the flowerpots every day. As soon as you see a shoot, move the pot to a light place and take off the plastic bag. Water the young plant regularly, just enough to keep the soil moist, and watch it grow. Here you can see the first stages in the development of an avocado plant.

From pit to plant

①

Avocado pits take six to seven weeks to sprout. The pit splits, a root grows down into the soil, and a shoot emerges at the top.

②

The stem grows quickly and the first leaves begin to open out. If the plant seems to be growing too tall, pinch off the growing shoot at the top. This encourages the plant to become bushier.

③

The first leaves soon grow quite large.

When the plant shows signs of growing too big for its pot, move it to a new, larger pot.

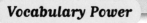

Vocabulary Power

thrive [thrīv] *v.* To grow vigorously.

Analyze THE Model

1. What is the author's purpose?
2. How does the writer clearly present the steps in this project?
3. Why must the steps be done in a particular order?

READING — WRITING CONNECTION

Parts of a How-to Essay

Angela Wilkes explained step-by-step how to grow a seed. Study this essay, written by a student named Peter. Look carefully at the parts of his how-to essay.

MODEL

Setting Up an Aquarium

topic sentence — *Have you ever wanted a pet fish, but didn't know where to put it? You can set up your own aquarium. Here's how!*

You will need the following items:

list of materials —
- *a glass tank*
- *a plastic tray for the bottom of the tank*
- *some gravel or very small stones*
- *an air pump with an air tube*
- *filters for the air tube*
- *1 or 2 goldfish*
- *fish food*

details — *You can find the gravel and small stones outside. You can buy the rest of the items at a pet store.*

Once you have all the materials, you should clean them well and let them dry on a flat surface. Then follow these steps:

steps in order — *1. First, put the plastic tray in the bottom of the tank. Put the plastic air tube holder into the hole in the tray.*

2. Now, put a filter on one end of the hose. Run the hose inside the plastic holder and attach the other end to the air pump.

    3. Then, spread the gravel evenly on the tray.

    4. Fill the tank with water.

    5. Finally, turn on the air pump.

    Let the water sit for an hour, and then put the fish in the tank. Feed them and see them swim around! You'll enjoy watching them.

steps in order

description of finished product

Analyze THE Model

1. What is Peter's purpose for writing?

2. Who do you think Peter's audience is?

3. How did Peter make the steps clear?

Summarize THE Model

Use a graphic organizer like this one to help you summarize Peter's essay. Include only the main points.

Writer's Craft

Organizing Information Peter's essay was organized. He put the steps in a logical order, he numbered the steps, and he used sequence words. What would happen if Peter changed the order of the steps? How would his essay be different if he took out the numbers or the sequence words?

Materials

Where to Get What You Need

What to Do
1.
2.
3.
4.

Prewriting

Purpose and Audience

In this chapter, you will write an essay that tells your classmates how to make something.

WRITING PROMPT Write a how-to essay which teaches your class-mates how to make something using items found in nature. For example, do you know how to use pine cones to make a wreath? Start with an interesting sentence. Be sure to put your steps in a logical order and use sequence words.

Before you begin, think about your purpose and audience. Who will your readers be? What would you like to teach them to make?

MODEL

Peter began by thinking of different projects he would like to teach others. He decided to explain how to set up an aquarium. He listed all the items that were needed. Then he wrote the steps. He knew that he might need to add more information later.

Purpose: to set up an aquarium
Audience: younger kids

Materials: glass tank, gravel, plastic tray for the tank, air pump with an air tube, air tube filters, goldfish, fish food

Steps: gather gravel, buy other items, clean materials, put tray in tank, attach air filter, fill tank, add fish

Strategies Good Writers Use

- Decide on your purpose and audience.
- Make a complete list of the project's materials and steps.
- Brainstorm ways to make your directions clear.

YOUR TURN

Choose a topic that includes objects from nature. Use a chart to organize your ideas.

Organization and Elaboration

Follow these steps to help you organize your essay:

STEP 1 **Introduce the Task**

Try to get your audience's attention by asking a question or making a surprising statement. Then explain your purpose for writing.

STEP 2 **List the Materials That Are Needed**

Make a clear list of all the materials. Include illustrations if possible.

STEP 3 **Explain Each Step in Order**

Write the steps. Number each one, or use sequence words that clearly show the order of the steps. Include tips to make the job easier. Use illustrations.

STEP 4 **Describe the Finished Project**

Tell about the values or benefits of the project and why it was worth doing.

MODEL

Here is the beginning of Peter's draft of his essay. How does he try to get his audience's attention? What is his topic?

> Have you ever wanted a pet fish, but didn't know where to put it? You can set up your own aquarium. Here's how!

YOUR TURN

Now draft your essay using the steps above. Review your prewriting notes and charts to help you get started.

Strategies Good Writers Use

- Begin by getting the reader's attention and telling what the reader will learn to do.
- List the materials that are needed.
- Organize your steps in the best order.
- Use sequence words.

Use a computer to draft your essay. When you've written the steps, you can move them around if you need to. Use the "click and drag" feature with your mouse.

Revising

Organization and Elaboration

Carefully reread your essay. Think about these questions:

- How well did I introduce my essay?
- Did I list all the materials that are needed?
- Have I used illustrations for the materials list?
- Are my steps easy to follow and in the most logical order?

MODEL

Here is part of Peter's essay. Notice that he added more details. He also explained where to find the items on the list.

You will need the following items:
- a plastic tray for the bottom of the tank
- a glass tank
- some gravel or very small stones
- filters for the air tube
- an air pump with an air tube
- 1 or 2 goldfish
- fish food

You can find the gravel and small stones outside, but you can will have to buy the rest of the items at a pet store.

YOUR TURN

Reread your essay to be sure you have included all the needed materials and have put your steps in the correct order. If you wish, trade your draft with a partner. Discuss each other's work.

- Take out words and phrases that may be confusing.
- Add steps to make your writing clearer.
- Rearrange steps to be more logical.
- Add photos or illustrations to make steps clearer.

If you have typed your essay on the computer, you can use the cut and paste features to organize your materials.

Proofreading

CHAPTER 12

How-to Essay

Checking Your Language

When you proofread, you should look for mistakes in grammar, spelling, punctuation, and capitalization. If you do not correct these mistakes, readers may have trouble following your directions.

MODEL

After Peter revised his essay, he proofread it. What mistakes did he fix?

> Once you have all the materials, you should (cleen) [clean] them well and let them dry on a flat surface. Then follow these steps:
> 1. First, put the plastic (trey) [tray] in the bottom of the tank. Put the plastic air tube holder into the whole in▲ [n] the tray.
> 2. now, Put a filter on (won) [one] end of the hose. Run the hose (innside) [inside] the plastic holder and Attach the other end to the air pump.
> 3. Then, spread the gravell evenly on the (trey) [tray].
> 4. Fill the tank with water.
> 5. (Finaly) [Finally] turn on the Air Pump.

YOUR TURN

Proofread your revised essay to:
- **check grammar and spelling.**
- **check punctuation and capitalization.**
- **make sure your list of materials and steps is complete.**

> S*trategies*
> G*ood* W*riters* U*se*

- Capitalize and punctuate correctly.
- Check for correct possessive nouns and contractions with <u>not</u>.
- Check for the correct forms of the verb <u>be</u>.

Editor's Marks

✗	delete text
∧	insert text
᧐	move text
¶	new paragraph
≡	capitalize
/	lowercase
◯	correct spelling

149

Publishing

Sharing Your Work

Now you can publish your how-to essay. Answer these questions to help you decide on the best way to share your work:

1. Who is your audience? What is the best way to publish your essay so that your audience will see it?

2. Think about your audience. Then decide whether you should print your essay or write it in cursive. Either way, be sure your handwriting is neat and easy to read.

3. What is the best way to make illustrations for your essay? Can you draw them? Can you include photographs? Can you do some of the work on a computer?

USING YOUR
Handbook

• Use the rubric on page 507 to evaluate your essay.

Reflecting on Your Writing

 Using Your Portfolio What did you learn about your writing in this chapter? Write your answer to each question below.

1. Do you think your essay was appropriate for your audience? Why or why not?

2. Using the rubric from your Handbook, how would you score your own writing? What things made it strong? What things made it weak?

Write your answers and add them and your essay to your portfolio. Then read through the work in your portfolio. Write a sentence that tells something that is strong about your writing. Then write a sentence that tells what you would like to improve.

Computer Graphics

After Peter finished his essay, he decided that he could make his essay clearer by adding **computer graphics**. You, too, can draw pictures or create charts to make your how-to essay easier to understand.

STEP 1 Pick one or two steps from your essay that you think could be explained more clearly with an illustration or diagram. You might want to make a chart for all the steps.

STEP 2 Decide what type of illustration you want to make. Pick a tool from the graphics toolbar. If you want to draw, select the drawing tool. If you want to make a chart, use boxes or straight lines.

STEP 3 Create a diagram, chart, or other image that works well with your essay. Check to see that the image is the right size.

STEP 4 Print your graphic. Cut out your graphic, and paste it near the text that it helps explain. If you are reading your essay aloud, you should hold your graphic up for your audience to see when you read that part of your essay.

TIP **Computer Strategies** Here are some tips for using a graphics program:

- Simple graphics programs provide squares, boxes, lines, and arrows. You can change or combine those designs to create an illustration for your essay.
- When drawing a line, hold the mouse until the line is finished.
- Click on the end or corner of a graphic to resize it. Click on the middle of a graphic to move it.

Common and Proper Nouns

pages 92–93

Read the sentence. Write whether the underlined words are common nouns or proper nouns.

1. The fitness center is near the jogging track in <u>Wiltshire Park</u>.
2. <u>Adam Chang</u> works there on <u>weekends</u>.
3. He helps <u>people</u> plan the perfect <u>workout</u>.
4. On <u>Tuesday</u> he showed <u>Allison</u> how to lift weights.
5. Everyone at the <u>gym</u> wants to have a healthier <u>body</u>.

Singular and Plural Nouns

pages 94–95

Read the sentence. Write whether the underlined nouns are singular or plural.

6. <u>Bones</u> join together to form the <u>skeleton</u>.
7. The skeleton protects the <u>heart</u>, lungs, and other <u>organs</u>.
8. A healthy <u>heart</u> pumps <u>blood</u> to the muscles.
9. The <u>muscles</u> contract and expand when we move.
10. Oxygen is carried in the <u>blood</u>.
11. When we exercise, our muscles need more <u>oxygen</u>.
12. Our <u>hearts</u> work harder to pump the blood.
13. Our <u>lungs</u> work harder to breathe in more oxygen.
14. Adam is helping <u>Bill</u> strengthen his heart.
15. A healthy heart can mean a long <u>life</u>.

Abbreviations and Titles   *pages 96–97*

Write the sentence. Correct each abbreviation.

16. Adam took a class with dr Hakura.
17. The class met at mt Shasta Hospital on n. Seller ave.
18. Classes were on weekdays from 9 AM to 2 PM.
19. Adam went to class on tues, jan 5, and wed, jan 6.
20. mrs Shields and mr Tillman were also in the class.

Singular Possessive Nouns

pages 102–103

Write the sentence. Replace the underlined words with the possessive form.

1. <u>The state bird of California</u> is the quail.
2. The <u>body of the quail chick</u> is tiny.
3. The <u>job of the male</u> is to guard the family.
4. He watches carefully for the <u>shadow of the cat</u>.
5. Andrew has seen quail on <u>the property of Maria</u>.

Plural Possessive Nouns   *pages 104–105*

Write the sentence, using the plural possessive form of the noun in parentheses.

6. We saw other _____ nests on our farm. (bird)
7. Andrew used his _____ cameras. (parent)
8. We were excited to see the _____ photographs. (children)
9. The children used the _____ zoom lenses. (camera)
10. The pictures looked like real _____ pictures. (photographer)

Possessive Noun or Plural Noun?   *pages 106–107*

Change the underlined noun to a singular possessive, a plural possessive, or a plural noun that is not possessive. Then write each sentence correctly.

11. We also saw some <u>hummingbird</u> nests.
12. A <u>hummingbird</u> wings beat very quickly.
13. Its long bill helps it sip a <u>flower</u> nectar.
14. Hummingbirds are the <u>world</u> smallest birds.
15. Their <u>wing</u> help them fly backward, too.
16. <u>Amy</u> favorite bird is the thrush.
17. This <u>bird</u> feathers have shades of brown.
18. These <u>singer</u> nests are found in many countries.
19. We see many <u>robin</u> searching for food in the spring.
20. A <u>robin</u> song reminds us that spring has arrived.

Action Verbs   *pages 120–121*

Write the sentence. Underline the action verb.

1. Rocks melt near the Earth's core.
2. Pressure and heat create diamonds and other gems.
3. Pressure also pushes up mountain ranges.
4. A thick layer of rock forms the surface of the Earth.
5. The Earth's crust shifts over thousands of years.
6. Ocean waves turn rocks into sand.
7. Rivers and streams carry pebbles, sand, and rocks downhill.
8. Scientists call this process *erosion*.
9. The top layers press on the bottom layers.
10. The pressure changes the sand into rock.

Linking Verbs   *pages 122–123*

Write the linking verb in each sentence. Write the word or words in the predicate that are connected to the subject by the linking verb.

11. Parts of the earth's crust are moveable.
12. Some scientists seem curious about earthquakes.
13. Many scientists become interested in learning more.
14. Scientists are aware of signs that show the beginning of an earthquake.
15. Still, it is difficult to know everything about an earthquake beforehand.

Using Forms of *Be*   *pages 124–125*

Write the form of *be* in parentheses that completes each sentence correctly.

16. The seismograph (is, are) an instrument that measures earthquakes.
17. Yesterday a seismograph (was, were) on display at the museum.
18. Three geologists (was, were) there, too.
19. They (is, are) all experts in their fields.
20. I (be, am) curious about their ideas.

Main Verbs and Helping Verbs

pages 130–131

Write the sentence. Underline each helping verb once and each main verb twice.

1. Special scientists are studying ocean life.
2. These scientists are called marine biologists.
3. They could examine the stomach of a fish.
4. Then scientists could know that fish's diet.
5. Marine biologists can tell the age of a fish.
6. They have studied the bones of the fish.
7. One scientist has figured the average size of a certain kind of fish.
8. Another marine biologist has weighed this fish.
9. Fishing boats are limited in certain areas.
10. Limited fishing does help certain fish.

More About Main Verbs and Helping Verbs pages 132–133

Write the sentence. Underline each helping verb once and each main verb twice. Then circle the word that comes between these verbs.

11. Coral reefs do not exist everywhere.
12. They are not located in cold, dark waters.
13. The reefs are only found in sunny, warm waters.
14. Coral reefs are often made of both living and dead coral animals.
15. The reefs have also provided homes for other sea life.

Contractions with *Not* pages 134–135

Write the sentence, making a contraction from the underlined words.

16. Deep-sea diving <u>is</u> <u>not</u> for everyone.
17. Some divers <u>will</u> <u>not</u> explore sunken ships.
18. They <u>do</u> <u>not</u> like the danger.
19. They <u>should</u> <u>not</u> take any chances.
20. A diver <u>cannot</u> see very much in the dark waters.

153

Unit 2 Wrap-Up

Writing Across the Curriculum: Science

One Square Foot of the World

An ecosystem is made up of a community of living things and the place, or environment, in which they live. How do the living things and the environment help each other survive? Find out, and share what you learn with your classmates. The steps below will help you.

Choose an Ecosystem to Study

- Take a ruler and string out into a field, your backyard, or a nearby park.

- Mark off a one-foot square space with the string.

Watch the Ecosystem Closely

- Visit your ecosystem several times every day for one week. Look closely at the insects, animals, and plants that live there or visit it.

- Record your observations on a chart. Write down the day and time. Tell what living things you saw and what they were doing.

Research and Write a Report

- Use an encyclopedia or the Internet to research the ways living things and their environment affect one another.

- Write a report to explain the relationship between living things and the environment.

Share Your Report

- Share your report with your classmates.

Danger on Crab Island
by Susan Saunders
REALISTIC FICTION
Dana and her family teach her cousin, Tyler, about the environment and share what they do to rescue injured sea animals.
Award-Winning Author

Dinosaur Tree
by Douglas Henderson
NONFICTION
The life cycle of a tree is followed from its beginning during the time of the dinosaurs, to its end over five hundred years later.
Award-Winning Author

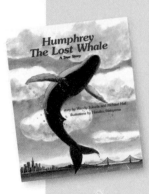

Humphrey the Lost Whale: A True Story
by Wendy Tokuda and Richard Hall
NONFICTION
When a humpback whale accidentally wanders into a shallow river, local townspeople work together to save him. In the process, they learn about the habits and habitats of whales.

Sentences *pages 24–29*

Write the sentence. Write whether it is *declarative*, *imperative*, *interrogative*, or *exclamatory*.

1. I want to be a wildlife biologist.
2. Do you know what a wildlife biologist does?
3. She often works to protect animals.
4. What a wonderful job that is!
5. Work hard in your science classes.

Subjects/Nouns *pages 34–39*

Write the sentence. Underline the complete subject.

6. Marni wants to be a writer.
7. She and her sister write for the school newspaper.
8. Marni's writing is very good.
9. Her stories appear in the town newspaper, too.
10. Marni's parents are very proud of her.

Predicates/Verbs *pages 52–57*

Write the sentence. Underline the complete predicate.

11. Liv's parents run a hardware store.
12. Her mother and father work very hard.
13. They sell paints and make keys.
14. People buy tools and rent supplies there.
15. Their store is important to the community.

Simple and Compound Sentences *pages 62–67*

Write the sentence. Write whether it is a *simple sentence* or a *compound sentence*.

16. Our community has farms, and it has a town.
17. I live in town, but Kim lives in the country.
18. The farmers raise livestock and crops.
19. They meet at the market or at the local diner.
20. Everyone knows each other here.

Nouns *pages 92–97*

Write each noun and whether it is *common* or *proper*.

1. There was an earthquake near San Diego.
2. The reporter said that the quake was not very strong.
3. The front window of Panini Restaurant broke.
4. Dogs and cats were terrified.
5. Big cracks ran across Pine Street.

Possessive Nouns *pages 102–107*

Write the sentence. Underline the possessive nouns, and write whether each is *singular* or *plural*.

6. The Arctic's tundra is home to many animals.
7. Polar bears' homes are in the frozen north.
8. A polar bear's dinner is often a seal.
9. Seals' homes are the cold arctic waters.
10. The waters' dwellers often include whales.

Action Verbs and Linking Verbs
pages 120–125

Write the sentence. Underline the verb, and label it as an *action verb* or a *linking verb*.

11. Mt. Vesuvius exploded many hundreds of years ago.
12. Nobody expected the explosion.
13. The explosion was sudden.
14. People fled in terror.
15. The volcano looks quiet now.

Main Verbs and Helping Verbs
pages 130–135

Underline the helping verb once and the main verb twice.

16. Scientists can predict an earthquake.
17. They can't always be right, though.
18. An earthquake could hit unexpectedly.
19. You should know about fault lines.
20. Then you can have an emergency plan ready.

Language Use

Read the passage and decide which type of mistake, if any, appears in each underlined section. Mark the letter for your answer.

The <u>city of Bruges in belgium</u> is one of <u>Europes most beautiful places.</u> It is full of <u>canals and beautiful bridgs.</u> You don't need a car to see Bruges. You can <u>walk or you can ride a boat</u> through the canals. There are <u>museums, churches, and lace shops</u> to see. If you are traveling in <u>Belgium, you shouldnt miss Bruges.</u>

(1) (2) (3) (4) (5) (6)

1 A Spelling

  B Capitalization

  C Punctuation

  D No mistake

2 F Spelling

  G Capitalization

  H Punctuation

  J No mistake

3 A Spelling

  B Capitalization

  C Punctuation

  D No mistake

4 F Spelling

  G Capitalization

  H Punctuation

  J No mistake

5 A Spelling

  B Capitalization

  C Punctuation

  D No mistake

6 F Spelling

  G Capitalization

  H Punctuation

  J No mistake

Written Expression

Use this paragraph to answer questions 1–4.

---

(1) Start by sitting quietly for a few minutes. (2) Rest your index finger and middle finger on your pulse. (3) You also have a pulse in your neck. (4) Then find your pulse in your wrist. (5) Count the number of heartbeats you feel in thirty seconds. (6) Multiply the total by two to find out how many times your heart beats per minute.

---

1 Choose the best opening sentence to add to this paragraph.

 A You can take your pulse by following a few simple steps.

 B Don't use your thumb to take your pulse.

 C Do you exercise a lot?

 D Everyone needs a healthy heart.

2 Which sentence should be left out of this paragraph?

 F Count the number of heartbeats you feel in thirty seconds.

 G Start by sitting quietly for a few minutes.

 H You also have a pulse in your neck.

 J Rest your index finger and middle finger on your pulse.

3 Where is the best place for sentence 4?

 A Before sentence 6

 B Before sentence 2

 C Before sentence 4

 D After sentence 6

4 Choose the best sentence to conclude this paragraph.

 F If the number seems high, rest and check again.

 G Now you can work out.

 H Your heart rate goes up when you exercise.

 J Be sure to get enough rest.

Unit 3

Grammar More About Verbs

Writing Persuasive Writing

The
Roxbury School
Winter Play
will take place
December 14 at 8:00 p.m.

Come and support your school!
You and your family
will enjoy a great evening!

Tickets are available at the school office

163

Verb Tenses

The tense of a verb tells the time of an action.

Verbs have different tenses. A verb tense may show past, present, or future time.

Examples:

Present Tense: The painter **works** on her painting.

Past Tense: Yesterday, she **worked** all afternoon.

Future Tense: She **will work** hard to finish in time for the show.

The present-tense verb tells about something that is happening now. The past-tense verb tells about something that happened in the past. It ends in *ed*. The helping verb *will* tells that the verb is in the future tense.

Vocabulary Power

can•vas [kan′vəs] *n.* A cloth surface specially prepared for a painter to use. The painting itself also may be called a *canvas*.

Guided Practice

A. Identify the tense of each underlined verb as *present*, *past*, or *future*. Tell how you know.

Example: Ms. Campos <u>teaches</u> art to our class.
present, action is happening now

I. Each child <u>shows</u> things he or she has made.
2. Zack shows the animals that he <u>carved</u> out of soap.
3. Julio <u>molded</u> statues of people.
4. Tammi <u>draws</u> pictures of her friends.
5. Sometimes she <u>copies</u> paintings from a book.
6. Lupe <u>wants</u> to be an artist someday.
7. She <u>will go</u> to special classes at the museum.
8. She <u>will try</u> many different kinds of art.
9. Last year she <u>learned</u> how to draw with pastels.
10. This year she <u>will learn</u> how to use watercolor.

Independent Practice

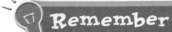
Remember

that **verb tenses** tell the time of an action. The tense can be present, past, or future.

B. Write the tense of the underlined verb.

Example: Maya <u>makes</u> collages on paper.
present

11. Yesterday she <u>selected</u> a large sheet of heavy paper.
12. Maya now <u>pastes</u> glitter on the paper.
13. Next, she <u>brushes</u> watercolors over the glitter.
14. Soon, she <u>will cut</u> shapes from colored paper.
15. She <u>will put</u> the shapes in her collage.

C. Write the sentence. Use the verb in parentheses that makes the most sense.

Example: Last week our class (studies, studied) art.
Last week our class studied art.

16. Last Monday, we (looked, look) at an art film.
17. In the film, an artist (carved, carves) masks.
18. He (hopes, will hope) that he (sell, will sell) them.
19. Last Tuesday, we (watched, will watch) a film about artists at work.
20. In one part of the film, a Mexican painter (stretched, will stretch) a canvas.

Writing Connection

Technology Working in small groups, take a virtual class trip to an art museum by exploring its website on the Internet. After you return from your Internet visit, write three sentences about the museum. Use the three verb tenses to tell something about the museum's history, something about what it is or has now, and something about its future plans.

Present-Tense Verbs

A verb in the present tense tells about action that is happening now or happens over and over.

Happening Now: The painter paints a picture.

Happening Over and Over: I always use blue paint.

Add *s* to most present-tense verbs when the subject of the sentence is *he, she, it,* or a singular noun.

When a present-tense verb ends in *ss, sh, ch, or x,* add *es.* When a present-tense verb ends in *y,* change the *y* to *i,* and add *es.* Do not add *s* or *es* to present-tense verbs when the subject is *I, you, we, they,* or a plural noun.

Subjects	Present-Tense Verbs
He, She, It, or singular noun	paints and sculpts.
The student	watches the artist.
The paint	dries quickly.
I, You, We, They	paint and sculpt.

Examples:

Sal **likes** bright colors.

He **mixes** red and yellow and **gets** orange.

I **paint** pictures on canvas.

Guided Practice

A. Identify the present-tense verb in each sentence.

Example: A sculptor carves shapes. *carves*

1. She uses a sharp tool called a chisel.
2. The sculptor taps the chisel with a hammer.
3. The chisel cuts the wood or stone.
4. This stone statue shows the face of a man.
5. Many sculptors make a clay model first.

Independent Practice

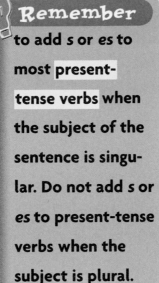
B. Rewrite the sentence. Underline the present-tense verb.

Example: My brother and I study the paintings and sculptures in museums.
My brother and I <u>study</u> the paintings and sculptures in museums.

6. We enjoy many different kinds of art.
7. Rory draws pictures of faces.
8. He molds figures out of clay.
9. He studies statues of people in the museum.
10. His sculptures look wonderful on his shelf.

C. Write each sentence. Use the correct present-tense form of the verb in parentheses.

Example: A painter (choose) something to paint.
chooses

11. She (pick) a scene of trees and flowers.
12. The scenes (show) the beauty of nature.
13. The young man (set) up his easel at the beach.
14. He (draw) a picture of the ocean.
15. Someone (watch) him at work.

Writing Connection

Writer's Journal: Evaluating Writing Artists can use their art to show beauty and to tell about their culture, time, and place. Does this statement reflect your ideas about art and creativity? Tell why you agree or disagree with the statement. Use present-tense verbs in your response.

Matisse was a famous French painter. He painted this picture, called *The Goldfish Bowl*.

USAGE AND MECHANICS

Subject-Verb Agreement

A verb must agree in number with the subject. If the subject is singular, use a singular verb. If the subject is plural, use a plural verb.

Verbs form their plurals differently from nouns. Notice that singular verbs, not plural verbs, end in **s** or **es**. Plural verbs take no special endings.

Subject	Present-Tense Verbs
Singular: he, she, it, singular noun	add *s* or *es*
Plural: I, you, we, they, plural noun	no ending added

Examples:

A sculptor **uses** clay to make a model.

Artists **create** many types of art.

Guided Practice

A. Identify the simple subject and the verb in each sentence. Tell if they are singular or plural.

Example: Artists use their imaginations.
subject: artists; verb: use; plural

1. A photograph shows horses.
2. Franz Marc imagines blue horses.
3. The painter expresses his feelings about the horses.
4. Colors stand for feelings in many paintings.
5. Dark paintings often feel mysterious or scary.

DID YOU KNOW?
The painter Franz Marc was born in Munich in 1880. He is best known for his paintings of animals. In 1911, he created this painting, called *The Large Blue Horses*.

Independent Practice

B. Write each sentence. Use the verb that correctly completes the sentence.

Example: Sculptors (create, creates) statues of people.
Sculptors create statues of people.

6. Some sculptures (show, shows) famous people.
7. Artists also (make, makes) portraits of ordinary people.
8. A portrait often (reveal, reveals) the artist's feelings about the person.
9. This statue (present, presents) a warrior.
10. The man (seem, seems) very brave and daring.

C. Write each sentence. Fill in the blank with the correct present-tense form of the verb in parentheses.

Example: I _____ mobiles. (like)
I like mobiles.

11. A mobile _____ from the ceiling of our classroom. (hang)
12. Another mobile _____ on a table. (stand)
13. We _____ mobiles from wire and cardboard. (make)
14. Students _____ the cardboard into shapes. (cut)
15. They _____ the pieces with poster paints. (color)

Remember

that a **verb agrees with** its subject. If the subject is singular, the verb must be singular. If the subject is plural, the verb must be plural.

Writing Connection

Writer's Craft: Strong Verbs Work with a partner to write a brief letter expressing your satisfaction or dissatisfaction with something you bought. Use strong verbs to tell how well (or poorly) the item works and why you are happy or unhappy with it. Try to convince the store or the manufacturer to do something about your situation.

Extra Practice

A. Write the verb in each sentence. Write whether the action is past, present, or future. *pages 164–165*

Example: These paintings will please many people.
will please, future

1. In past centuries, nature inspired many artists.
2. They painted pictures of beaches and oceans.
3. These pictures show the beauty of the outdoors.
4. A wave splashes on a beach.
5. Boats sail on the sea.
6. Some artists copied scenes in nature.
7. These artists tried to make objects look real.
8. They added light and shadows to objects on their canvases.
9. Light and shadow will make objects look three-dimensional.
10. Nature always will be a subject for artists.

B. Write the sentence. Underline the present-tense verb. Tell whether it is singular or plural. *pages 166–167*

Example: Art pleases many people.
Art <u>pleases</u> many people. singular

11. We learn many things from art.
12. An artist sometimes expresses happiness, sadness, or wonder through his or her work.
13. Many viewers understand the artist's feelings.
14. Paintings and drawings often tell about history.
15. Some paintings present scenes of everyday life.
16. We know about clothing and hair styles in the past from works of art.
17. We also see people at work and at play.
18. One scene shows tools used in the 1800s.
19. A room holds objects from olden times.
20. Art brings both enjoyment and information.

C. Write the sentence. Fill in the blank with the correct present-tense form of the verb in parentheses. *pages 168–169*

Example: A sculptor _____ to make a statue. (wish)
A sculptor wishes to make a statue.

21. The artist _____ the face of a woman. (study)
22. He _____ clay to make a model of her face. (mold)
23. He _____ to show her personality. (want)
24. The clay _____. (dry)
25. The artist _____ his work is good. (think)
26. The sculptor _____ to make a metal statue. (decide)
27. He _____ a plaster mold from the clay face. (make)
28. His helpers _____ metal in a furnace. (melt)
29. They _____ the melted metal into the mold. (pour)
30. The metal _____ hard. (become)
31. The statue _____ the artist. (please)
32. Another sculptor _____ metal together to make a sculpture. (weld)
33. The heat _____ the metal pieces. (join)
34. A third sculptor _____ objects together to make a sculpture. (patch)
35. She _____ everyday things such as bicycle parts and scraps of wood. (use)

Writing Connection

Art Suppose that you are a tour guide in an art museum. Describe a work of art that you have seen in this chapter. Write a few sentences about the painting or sculpture. Tell the name of the artist and why you think the work is interesting.

For additional practice with present-tense verbs, visit *The Learning Site:*

www.harcourtschool.com

Chapter Review

Read the passage, and choose the word that belongs in each space. Mark the letter for your answer.

STANDARDIZED TEST PREP

> Diana __(1)__ to become a painter. She __(2)__ at an art school. The school __(3)__ students with canvases, easels, and palettes for mixing paint. Each student __(4)__ his or her own brushes, paint, and drawing pencils. Diana __(5)__ the teacher as she __(6)__ how to make a drawing of a bowl with different fruits. The teacher __(7)__ the fruits with a charcoal pencil. Then the young artists __(8)__ to make a sketch on their own.

TIP Remember to use the correct forms of present-tense verbs with *he, she, it,* and singular nouns.

1 A wishs
   B wishes
   C wish
   D wishe

2 F study
   G studyes
   H studies
   J studys

3 A supplies
   B supples
   C supplys
   D supply

4 F buy
   G buyes
   H buys
   J bys

5 A watchs
   B watch
   C watchies
   D watches

6 F demonstrate
   G demonstrates
   H demonstrats
   J demonstraties

7 A sketch
   B sketchs
   C sketchies
   D sketches

8 F begin
   G begins
   H begines
   J beginn

For additional test preparation, visit *The Learning Site:*
www.harcourtschool.com

Listening for Facts and Opinions

You learn a great deal of information by listening. Sometimes speakers present information, or facts. They may also present their beliefs and feelings, or opinions. Speakers often try to persuade their audiences by supporting opinions with facts. Learning to identify facts and opinions will make you a better listener.

A fact is something that can be proved true.

Example:

The Pacific Ocean is bigger than the Atlantic Ocean.

An opinion is something that the speaker believes, thinks, or feels.

Example:

The Pacific Ocean is more beautiful than the Atlantic Ocean.

YOUR TURN

LISTEN FOR FACTS Read the following sentences aloud to a partner. Together, look at the painting, and decide whether each sentence is a fact or an opinion.

1. This painting was made in 1882.
2. The painter, John Singer Sargent, was very talented.
3. The painting shows four girls.
4. The girls look very happy.
5. Sargent should have done more paintings like this one.

The Daughters of Edward Darley Boit, by John Singer Sargent, 1882.

Past-Tense Verbs

A verb in the past tense shows that the action happened in the past. To form the past tense, add *ed* to regular verbs. Most verbs are regular.

Examples:

Present Tense
Each year a group **awards** the Newbery Medal to an author of children's literature.

Past Tense
The group **awarded** the first Newbery Medal to Hendrik van Loon for *The Story of Mankind*.

Guided Practice

A. **Identify the verb in each sentence. Tell whether the verb is past tense or present tense.**

Example: Author Elizabeth Speare received the Newbery award twice.
received; past tense

1. The Newbery committee also honored author Katherine Paterson twice.
2. She called her first winning book *Bridge to Terabithia.*
3. Readers enjoy her second winning book, *Jacob Have I Loved.*
4. Many authors create stories from the past.
5. Another winner, *The Door in the Wall*, describes the life of a boy in the Middle Ages.
6. *Johnny Tremain* takes place during the American Revolution.
7. The book tells about the life of a young boy.
8. He worked as a silversmith.
9. *A Gathering of Days* by Joan Blos received the Newbery Medal in 1980.
10. The book presents the diary of a girl.

Vocabulary Power

lit•er•a•ture
[li′tə•rə•chər] *n.*
Written work or works, especially writing that shows imagination and artistic skill.

Independent Practice

Remember

that a past-tense verb tells about something that happened in the past.

B. **Write the sentence, and underline the verb. Write whether the verb is past tense or present tense.**

> **Example:** The writer E. B. White lived in Maine.
> *The writer E. B. White <u>lived</u> in Maine. past tense*

11. E. B. White contributed literature to *The New Yorker* magazine.
12. Many readers enjoyed White's stories.
13. His writing covered topics such as baseball.
14. White published *Stuart Little* in 1945.
15. He created the main character, Stuart Little, as a mouse with human parents.

C. **Write the sentence. Change each underlined verb to past tense.**

> **Example:** Louisa May Alcott <u>calls</u> her best-known book
> *Little Women. called*

16. Louisa May Alcott <u>lives</u> in Boston, Massachusetts, in the 1800s.
17. She <u>talks</u> with many famous authors of the time.
18. Family friends <u>include</u> the writer Nathaniel Hawthorne.
19. Alcott <u>works</u> at an early age as a servant and a teacher.
20. She <u>nurses</u> soldiers during the Civil War.

Writing Connection

Writer's Craft: Strong Verbs Use the strongest verbs you can to make your writing vivid and interesting. Write three sentences about a book you especially enjoyed. Use strong past-tense verbs to tell about something that happened in the book.

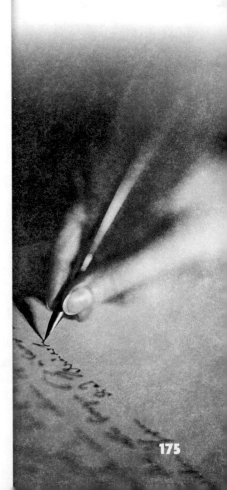

More About Past-Tense Verbs

Some verbs change spelling when *ed* is added to form the past tense.

- If a verb ends with *e*, drop the *e* before adding *ed*.

  Example:
  Edward Stratemeyer <u>used</u> the name Franklin Dixon.

- If a verb has one syllable and ends with a short vowel sound and a consonant, double the final consonant before adding *ed*.

  Example:
  He <u>planned</u> his mystery stories very carefully.

- If a verb ends with a consonant and *y*, change the *y* to *i* before adding *ed*.

  Example:
  He <u>tried</u> to write exciting pieces of literature.

Guided Practice

A. Tell the past-tense form of each verb in parentheses.

Example: Edward Stratemeyer (change) his name to Victor Appleton for other books.
changed

1. Victor Appleton (create) books about Tom Swift.
2. Stratemeyer (pen) the Bobbsey Twin books under another name, Laura Lee Hope.
3. These books (feature) two sets of twins.
4. Stratemeyer (name) the twins Flossie and Freddie and Nan and Bert.
5. He (use) a different name, Carolyn Keene, for the Nancy Drew series.

Independent Practice

B. **Write the past-tense form of each verb in parentheses.**

   Example: Beatrix Potter (illustrate) nearly thirty books.
            illustrated

   6. Potter (use) watercolors for her illustrations.

   7. She (live) in London in the late 1800s and early 1900s.

   8. The Lake District in England (provide) her with story ideas.

   9. She (jot) down notes on what she saw.

  10. She (study) animals very closely.

C. **Write the sentence. Use the correct past-tense form of the verb in parentheses.**

   Example: L. Frank Baum (describe) the land of Oz in his books.
            described

  11. He (name) his first book *The Wonderful Wizard of Oz.*

  12. The book (feature) a girl named Dorothy.

  13. Dorothy (carry) her dog, Toto, everywhere.

  14. A tornado (drop) Dorothy's house in the land of Oz.

  15. Dorothy (try) to get back home to Kansas.

Writing Connection

Writer's Journal: Reflecting on Writing

Think about your favorite story. Without giving too many details, write a few sentences telling what the story is about. Tell why you liked the story. Mention the main characters and what they did. Write your summary in the past tense, and read it to the class.

> ## Remember
> to change the spelling of some verbs before you add *ed.* You may have to drop an *e*, double a final consonant, or change a *y* to an *i*.

DID YOU KNOW?
The Newbery Medal was named after John Newbery, an eighteenth-century publisher and seller of children's books. The prize was established to improve the quality of children's books.

USAGE AND MECHANICS

Subject-Verb Agreement

Subjects and verbs always **agree**, even when the verb comes before the subject or when other words come between the subject and the verb.

Examples:

Rasha (subject) **comes** (verb) in with her favorite book.

She and her friend Nina (compound subject) **are** (verb) ready for the next book in the series.

In **comes** (verb) **Rasha** (subject) with her favorite book.

Are (verb) **she and her friend Nina** (compound subject) ready for the next book in the series?

Nina (subject), <u>together with her cousins</u> (words in between the subject and verb), **reads** (singular verb) mystery books.

Guided Practice

A. **Tell whether the subject and verb agree in each of the following sentences.**

Examples: In my backpack was a book and my lunch.
do not agree

My favorite book is now in the library.
agree

1. In the library is a book and two tapes of *Alice in Wonderland*.
2. Have Greg and Martha read *Stuart Little*?
3. Joan, unlike Ali and Jill, do not have a favorite book.
4. John's favorite book are *The Giving Tree*.
5. I, as well as Ann, thinks *Heidi* is good.

Independent Practice

B. Write the sentence, using the correct form of the verb in parentheses.

> **Examples:** (Is, Are) *Stuart Little* and *Charlotte's Web* your favorite books?
>
> *Are* Stuart Little *and* Charlotte's Web *your favorite books?*

6. On the Arable farm (lives, live) Fern and Avery.
7. In the litter of newborn pigs (is, are) a runt.
8. What (does, do) Fern and her father decide about the runt?
9. Fern, not her parents, (names, name) her pig Wilbur.
10. Wilbur, soon after his ten brothers and sisters, (gets, get) sold.
11. At the Zuckermans' house (lives, live) Templeton the Rat and Charlotte the Spider.
12. Flies and other bugs (is, are) what Charlotte eats.
13. (Do, Does) Fern and her family visit Wilbur?
14. Charlotte's web, with its beautiful patterns, (is, are) like a delicate veil.
15. The word *humble*, more than other words, (becomes, become) very important for Wilbur.

Writing Connection

Real-Life Writing: Write About a Job Imagine a job you might like to have as an adult. Would you like to do science experiments? Would you like to review literature? How would writing be important in your job? Write three ways you might use writing in the job you have chosen. When you finish, check to see that subjects and verbs agree. Then share your response with a partner.

Remember that the subject and verb in a sentence must agree.

179

Extra Practice

A. Identify the past-tense verb in each sentence.
pages 174–175

Example: The first U.S. children's magazines appeared before the American Revolution.
appeared

1. An early children's magazine, *St. Nicholas*, existed from 1873 to 1943.
2. It contained stories by children's authors.
3. The Boy Scouts organization started *Boy's Life* in 1911.
4. The Girl Scouts first published *American Girl* in 1917.
5. These early magazines helped children learn.
6. *My Weekly Reader* offered current events to children.
7. Educators founded this classroom newspaper in 1928.
8. Children in each grade used different newspapers.
9. *Scholastic* magazines followed *Weekly Reader* into classrooms.
10. Children discovered information in these magazines.

B. Write the past-tense form of each verb in parentheses. *pages 176–177*

Example: Hans Christian Andersen (create) *The Ugly Duckling* in 1843.
created

11. A mother duck in the story (stare) at a big egg.
12. Out (pop) a large baby bird.
13. The young bird (cry) "Peep, peep."
14. Another duck (believe) the little bird was a baby turkey.
15. The baby bird (surprise) them all.

Remember

that the past tense is used to show actions that happened in the past. Subjects and verbs must agree.

For more activities with past-tense verbs, visit *The Learning Site:*
www.harcourtschool.com

C. **Write the sentence, using the correct form of the verb in parentheses.** *pages 178–179*

Example: Among my favorite books (is, are) *Amelia Bedelia.*
Among my favorite books is Amelia Bedelia.

16. In the book (is, are) some very silly things.
17. What silly things (does, do) Amelia do?
18. Amelia Bedelia (has, have) a list of chores.
19. A list of many things (does, do) not sound funny.
20. Getting all things wrong (is, are) what she does.
21. On her list there (is, are) many things.
22. One of the chores (is, are) to dust the furniture.
23. Amelia Bedelia, unlike most people, (understands, understand) things in a funny way.
24. On the furniture she (sprinkles, sprinkle) dust!
25. Now everyone in my class (wants, want) to read that book!

D. **Each of the following sentences contains an error. Rewrite each sentence correctly.**
pages 174–179

Example: In the library is books and tapes.
In the library are books and tapes.

26. Do anyone remember the story of Jack and Jill?
27. Jack, together with Jill, go up the hill.
28. A pail of water are what they want.
29. Jack fall down and hurts himself.
30. Down the hill tumble Jill.

Writing Connection

Art Draw a picture of your favorite storybook character. Use your imagination to decide what the character looks like. Using past-tense verbs, write a caption that tells why you like the character. Give some examples from the story.

Chapter Review

Read the passage. Choose the correct word that belongs in each numbered space. Mark the letter for your answer.

> My grandfather __(1)__ to read to me when I was young. He always __(2)__ the best stories. He once __(3)__ a fairy tale. A man named Florio __(4)__ a princess in the story. The princess __(5)__ one day as she picked flowers in her garden. For years, the young man __(6)__ everywhere for her. One day, he entered the garden. Among the many beautiful flowers __(7)__ a forget-me-not. He picked the flower, and it __(8)__ into the lost princess.

STANDARDIZED
TEST PREP

TIP Remember that some verbs change their spelling when *ed* is added to form the past tense.

1 A like
  B likes
  C liked
  D likied

2 F picks
  G pick
  H picked
  J picking

3 A creatied
  B creates
  C create
  D created

4 F marry
  G married
  H marrys
  J marryed

5 A disappeared
  B disappear
  C disappeard
  D disappearied

6 F searched
  G searchd
  H search
  J searchied

7 A were
  B was
  C are
  D be

8 F turn
  G turned
  H turnied
  J turnes

For additional test preparation, visit *The Learning Site:*
www.harcourtschool.com

Using a Dictionary and Thesaurus

When you need to find out something about words, dictionaries and thesauruses are very useful.

The main purpose of a dictionary is to tell you information about words, such as meaning, pronunciation, number of syllables, and part of speech. Dictionaries list entry words in alphabetical order. When words all begin with the same letter, they are alphabetized by the second letter. When the first two letters are the same, words are alphabetized by the third letter, and so on.

Examples:

<u>ca</u>t

<u>ce</u>ment

<u>cen</u>ter

A thesaurus is a book that contains many synonyms, or words that have the same or nearly the same meanings. Entry words in a thesaurus are listed in alphabetical order. Thesauruses generally contain antonyms as well. Antonyms are words that have opposite or nearly opposite meanings.

Examples:

Synonyms of *happy*: joyful, cheerful, blissful

Antonyms of *dirty*: clean, cleansed, stainless

YOUR TURN

PICK A WORD With a group, play a game using a dictionary or thesaurus. From a dictionary or thesaurus, pick a word that you think most of the class might not know. Write the word in a sentence, making sure you have spelled it correctly. Every person in the group should try to guess the meaning of the word (5 points), the part of speech (5 points), and a synonym or an antonym (10 points). Each person in the group should get a chance to present a word. At the end of the last round, the person with the most points wins.

Writer's Craft

Effective Sentences

PERSUASION Did you ever **persuade** a friend to try a new food or to watch a movie with you? You use **persuasion** when you want someone to do something or to agree with you.

In *My Name Is María Isabel*, there are several girls named María in the class. The teacher decides to call María Lopez *Mary*. As a result, María doesn't recognize her name when it is called. Read the following passage. Notice how María tries to persuade her teacher.

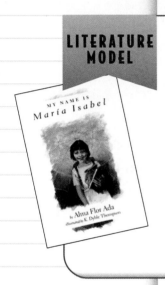

LITERATURE MODEL

> I think my greatest wish is to be called María Isabel Salazar López. When that was my name, I felt proud of being named María like my papá's mother, and Isabel, like my grandmother Chabela. If I was called María Isabel Salazar López, I could listen better in class because it's easier to hear than Mary López. Then I could have said that I wanted a part in the play.
>
> —from *My Name Is María Isabel* by Alma Flor Ada

Analyze THE Model

1. What does María want to persuade her teacher to do?

2. How does María try to persuade her teacher?

3. Why does María mention her grandmothers?

Using Effective Sentences

Persuasive writing is used to convince the reader to agree with the writer's ideas. To persuade successfully, you need to use **effective sentences**. Effective sentences keep readers interested in what you have written. Study the chart on the next page.

Vocabulary Power

op•por•tu•ni•ty
[op′ər•tyoo′nə•tē] *n.*
A right or convenient time, occasion, or circumstance.

Questions to Ask Yourself About Persuasive Writing

Strategies to Use

What do I want to persuade my reader to do or think?

- Write a strong **opening sentence.**
- Tell your reader the main idea.
- State your opinion clearly in the first sentence.

How can I persuade my reader?

- **Capture your reader's interest.**
- Vary your sentences. Include a question, an imperative sentence, or an exclamatory sentence where it fits.
- Combine sentences for greater interest and variety.

YOUR TURN

ANALYZE PERSUASIVE WRITING Work in a group with several classmates. Find examples of persuasive writing in newspaper editorials, letters to the editor, TV or movie reviews, or advertisements. Talk about how the writers used effective sentences in their writing.

Answer these questions:

1. What are you being persuaded to do?

2. Is the opening sentence effective? Why or why not?

3. How does the writer capture your interest?

4. Has the writer succeeded in persuading you? Why or why not?

Opening Sentences

A. Read each pair of sentences. On your paper, write the sentence that you think is a stronger opening sentence. Then tell why it is better than the other choice.

1. a. Our class must take better care of library books.
   b. I want to tell you my opinion about books.
2. a. I am a student in fourth grade at the Green Valley School.
   b. Wouldn't you like to improve our school without spending money?
3. a. I think we should make a special banner for Mr. Livingston.
   b. Mr. Livingston has coached our soccer team all year.

B. On your paper, write a good opening sentence for this paragraph. Remember that your opening sentence should tell what subject you are writing about and should state your opinion.

The door we have now is brown. It looks plain and dull. It doesn't fit the spirit of our school, which is inviting and fun. That's why I think the new school door should be bright red.

Capturing Reader's Interest

C. **Write four sentences about each of the following subjects. Write a declarative sentence, an interrogative sentence, an imperative sentence, and an exclamatory sentence about each one.**

  1. helping others
  2. taking care of pets
  3. your school media center
  4. your favorite snack
  5. setting aside space for bike paths

D. **Combine each pair of sentences into one sentence. Write the new sentence on your paper.**

  6. Keith paints with watercolors. Keith draws with charcoal.
  7. The sea is calm. The wind is still.
  8. Children ride bikes in the park. Children play ball in the park.
  9. Paintings hang on the walls. Statues stand in the hallways.
  10. The moon shines at night. The stars shine at night.

Writing and Thinking

Writer's Journal

Write to Record Reflections When you write, you want to capture your reader's interest. What kinds of things usually capture your interest when you read? In your Writer's Journal, write your reflections about ways that writers have captured your interest.

Persuasive Business Letter

In *My Name Is María Isabel,* María writes an essay in which she tries to persuade her teacher to call her by her real name. Jared is a student in the same grade as María. He wants to persuade the mayor of his town to attend a special event at his school. Read this business letter that Jared wrote to the mayor.

MODEL

heading

Willow Road School
Springville, TX 75082
November 5, 200_

inside address

Mayor Susan Ortiz
City Hall
Springville, TX 75082

greeting

Dear Mayor Ortiz:

opening sentence

body of letter

You are invited to a very special event. The students at Willow Road School are having a talent show in our school auditorium at 8:00 p.m. on January 10. Our parents and teachers are invited.

I know that you care about our school. That's why I think it would be a great idea for you to come to our show. You can show your support and have a good time, too.

I know you are very busy, but I hope you will mark this special date on your calendar. We would love to see you there, Mayor Ortiz!

closing

Sincerely,

signature

Jared Barnes

1. What is Jared's purpose for writing this letter, and who is his audience?
2. What reasons does Jared give to persuade his reader?
3. What information does he give in his opening sentence?
4. How does Jared capture his reader's interest?
5. How is a business letter different from a friendly letter?

YOUR TURN

WRITING PROMPT Imagine that a group in your community is planning an exhibit of work by local artists. Write a business letter to persuade the group to include art works by students. Use effective sentences.

STUDY THE PROMPT Ask yourself these questions.

1. What is your purpose for writing?
2. Who is your audience?
3. What writing form will you use?
4. What will you try to persuade your reader to do?

Prewriting and Drafting

Plan Your Business Letter Decide what you will say. Use a chart like this to help you plan your letter.

Opening Sentence
Write a sentence that states your opinion.

Write sentences that persuade your reader to agree with you. Write effective sentences that capture your reader's interest.

Restate your opinion in different words.

USING YOUR
Handbook

- Use the Writer's Thesaurus to find interesting words that will help you capture your reader's interest.

189

Editing

Read over the draft of your persuasive business letter. Do you see ways to make your sentences more effective and your letter more persuasive? Use this checklist to help you revise your business letter.

- ☑ **Is your opening sentence strong and direct?**
- ☑ **Have you used a variety of sentences?**
- ☑ **Will your sentences capture and hold your reader's interest?**
- ☑ **Will your letter persuade your reader to agree with you?**

Use this checklist as you proofread your paragraph.

- ☑ **I have used capitalization and punctuation correctly.**
- ☑ **I have used correct verb tenses.**
- ☑ **I have made sure that subjects and verbs agree.**
- ☑ **I have used a dictionary to check my spelling.**
- ☑ **I have used correct business letter form.**

Editor's Marks

✗	delete text
∧	insert text
♂	move text
¶	new paragraph
≡	capitalize
/	lowercase
◯	correct spelling

Sharing and Reflecting

Writer's Journal

Now make a final copy of your business letter. Share your work by trading letters with a partner. Discuss what you like best about each other's letters and what each of you could do better next time. Write your reflections in your Writer's Journal.

Persuasive Discussion

Have you ever taken part in a persuasive discussion? People have persuasive discussions for many different reasons. How is persuasive discussion like persuasive writing? How is it different? Study the Venn diagram.

Persuasive Writing
deals only with your own opinion; can be edited and revised

Both
use elaboration

Persuasive Discussion
two or more different opinions presented; need to listen to and analyze each other's opinions and reasons

YOUR TURN

Work with a small group to role-play a persuasive discussion. Follow these steps.

STEP 1 Choose a topic that many students have opinions about.

STEP 2 Decide what opinion each speaker will express.

STEP 3 Plan and practice your discussion. As you role-play, use the **Strategies for Listening and Speaking**.

STEP 4 Present your persuasive discussion to classmates.

STEP 5 Afterwards, ask your audience for comments about your persuasive discussion.

Strategies for Listening and Speaking

Use these strategies to help you have a good discussion:

• As you speak, choose your words and adjust your rate, volume, pitch, and tone to fit the audience and setting.

• As you listen, identify the speaker's main ideas and supporting details. Interpret the speaker's message, purpose, and perspective (viewpoint).

• As you respond, support your ideas with elaboration.

191

Future-Tense Verbs

A verb in the future tense shows that action will happen in the future.

You know that present-tense verbs show action that happens now or happens often. You also know that verbs in the past tense show actions that have already happened. Verbs in the future tense show action that will happen in the future. To form the future tense of a verb, use the helping verb *will* with the main verb.

Examples:
Future Tense
Chrissie **will dance** in tomorrow's show.

Tom **will perform** in the second half.

Examples:
Linda **listens** to the radio. ***present-tense verb***

Linda **listened** to the radio. ***past-tense verb***

Linda **will listen** to the radio. ***future-tense verb***

Vocabulary Power

cho•re•o•graph
[kôr′ē•ə•graf′] *v.*
To make up dance
movements.

Guided Practice

A. Identify the future-tense verb in each sentence.

Example: Our class will hear a concert tomorrow.
will hear

1. Everyone will gather in the gym for the concert.
2. A guitarist will perform for us.
3. She will play a regular guitar first.
4. This guitar will have six strings.
5. First, she will tune her instrument.
6. The guitarist will pluck one string at a time.
7. She also will strum a guitar with twelve strings.
8. Then she will explain electric guitars.
9. The electric guitar will make different sounds.
10. I think we will enjoy this concert.

Independent Practice

B. Write the sentence. Underline the future-tense verb.

Example: We will learn about wind instruments.
We <u>will learn</u> about wind instruments.

11. Andi will start clarinet lessons next week.
12. She will rent an instrument from the music store.
13. She promises that she will practice every day.
14. Before starting to play, she will buy some reeds.
15. Andi also will need a music stand.

C. Write the sentence. Use the future-tense form of the verb in parentheses.

Example: Jeff (learn) to play the violin.
Jeff will learn to play the violin.

16. He (play) a stringed instrument.
17. His sister (lend) him her small violin.
18. It (fit) him better than a large-size instrument.
19. He (buy) a new bow.
20. Jeff's playing probably (sound) squeaky at first.
21. He (need) several months of practice to play well.
22. He (practice) moving the bow over the strings.
23. His sister (help) him.
24. She (show) him how to hold the violin.
25. Perhaps he (join) an orchestra one day.

Writing Connection

Real-Life Writing: Advertisement Advertisers try to persuade you to buy something by making claims such as *When you use Product X, you will feel better.* Write an advertisement for an imaginary product that makes a promise about the future.

Remember

that a verb in the future tense shows action that will happen in the future.

More About Future-Tense Verbs

Sometimes other words may come between the parts of a future-tense verb.

You already know that *will* with the main verb makes a future-tense verb. Sometimes a word such as *often* or *also* comes between *will* and the main verb. When the word *not* comes between *will* and the main verb, it can make the contraction ***won't***. When you write a question, the subject comes between *will* and the main verb.

Examples:

I **will** probably **study** guitar this year.

When will you **study** guitar?

I **will not study** guitar. I **won't study** guitar.

Guided Practice

A. **Identify both parts of the future-tense verb in each sentence.**

Example: Won't Charlie want a new guitar case?
Will want

1. Will Charlie start classical piano lessons soon?
2. He won't wait until next year.
3. The piano will surely challenge him.
4. Won't he want a grand piano?
5. He will probably start with an upright piano.
6. He will surely learn about the instrument, too.
7. If he looks inside it, Charlie will see more than 220 strings.
8. Charlie won't tune them himself, though.
9. A piano tuner will come to his house.
10. She will use special tools.

Independent Practice

B. **Write each sentence. Then write both parts of the future-tense verb.**

> **Example:** Will you come with me to the square dance?
> *will come*

11. When will it start?
12. It will probably begin at eight o'clock.
13. I'm afraid that I won't know how to square dance.
14. You surely won't be the only one.
15. The caller will often choreograph the dance.

C. **Write each sentence. Underline the future-tense form of the verb. Then write the word or words that come between the two parts of the verb.**

> **Example:** <u>Will</u> the dancers <u>perform</u> other dances?
> *the dancers*

16. We will surely see many different dancers.
17. Dancers from parts of Africa will certainly dance.
18. Usually they won't dance alone or with a partner.
19. They will only dance in groups.
20. We won't arrive late for this exciting performance.

Remember
that the parts of a future-tense verb may be separated by other words.

Writing Connection

Writer's Journal

Writer's Journal: Effective Sentences
Imagine that you have an opportunity to study dance or a musical instrument. Write some good reasons to convince your parents or your teacher that you will be responsible and serious about your studies.

USAGE AND MECHANICS

Choosing the Correct Tense

Always choose the tense that tells when the action of the sentence happens.

For an action that happens now or over and over, use the present tense. For an action that happened in the past, use the past tense. For an action that will happen in the future, use the future tense. The spelling of the verb may change, depending on which tense is being used.

Examples: Jamie **plays** the drums in the band.
present tense

Her brother **played** violin in the orchestra.
past tense

Her sister **will play** in the orchestra soon.
future tense

Guided Practice

A. Identify the verb in each sentence. Then tell the tense of each verb.

Example: The kettledrum produces a mighty sound.
produces, present tense

1. A Russian composer wrote *Peter and the Wolf.*
2. Peter helps capture a dangerous wolf.
3. A narrator will tell the story.
4. Each character has an instrument.
5. You will learn how different instruments sound.

Independent Practice

Remember that a verb may be spelled differently, depending on which tense is being used.

B. Write each sentence and underline the verb. Then write the tense of each verb.

Example: Some singers write songs.
Some singers <u>write</u> songs. present tense

6. Aaron Copland was a composer.
7. Copland's work uses jazz and folk songs.
8. You will hear Copland's music in some movies.
9. Judges awarded Copland an important prize.
10. Audiences will enjoy Copland's music.

C. Write each sentence. Use the verb and the tense in parentheses to fill in the blank.

Example: Maybe you _____ a song. (write, future)
Maybe you will write a song.

11. People always _____ hearing many popular songs. (enjoy, future)
12. Songwriter Cole Porter _____ the violin. (play, past)
13. Porter _____ a musical in 1916. (compose, past)
14. Musicians _____ Porter's songs in performances. (play, present)
15. Porter's song lyrics _____ forever. (sparkle, future)

Writing Connection

Writer's Craft: Choosing Tenses Write a paragraph about your musical tastes. Tell what kind of music you enjoyed before, what you like now, and what you think you will like in the future. Use verbs with different tenses.

197

Remember

that a verb in the
future tense may
have words that
come between the
two parts of the
verb.

DID YOU KNOW?
Jazz is a type of music
that developed in the
United States in the late
1800s. Jazz combines
music from many
places, including African
rhythms, American
band instruments, and
European harmonies.

For more activities
using future-tense
verbs, visit
The Learning Site:

www.harcourtschool.com

Extra Practice

Independent Practice

A. **Write the future-tense verb in each sentence.**
pages 192–193

Example: The dancers will learn all the steps.
will learn

1. You will probably learn a lot about dance by watching.
2. This group of dancers will perform tonight.
3. How long will they practice?
4. They will definitely work all afternoon.
5. Serious dancers will practice for hours.
6. Without practice, dancers will feel stiff.
7. They won't bend their knees easily.
8. They won't jump gracefully.
9. The dancers will surely remember the choreography.
10. They will wear stage makeup and costumes.

B. **Write each sentence, and underline the verb. Write whether the verb is in the present tense, past tense, or future tense.** *pages 196–197*

Example: The Daring Dancers will perform *The Nutcracker* next week.
The Daring Dancers <u>will perform</u> The Nutcracker *next week. future tense*

11. *The Nutcracker* tells the story of a special toy.
12. Our friend Lupe will dance the part of Clara.
13. Another friend will take the role of the Snow Queen.
14. We will watch for them on stage.
15. Some of us attended last year's performance.

C. Write each sentence. Use the future-tense form of the verb in parentheses. *pages 194–195*

Example: We (do) the dance again.
We will do the dance again.

16. A production (require) many people backstage.
17. Stagehands (move) props between scenes.
18. Costume designers (prepare) fancy clothes.
19. Makeup artists (apply) powder and lipstick.
20. Painters (design) scenery.
21. Other people (sell) tickets.
22. The ballet (feature) a lovely waltz tune.
23. We (listen) to the music.
24. We (eat) dinner before the performance.
25. The dancers (practice) one last time.

D. Each sentence has a verb-tense error. Write the sentence correctly. *pages 196–197*

Example: The dancers practice hard yesterday.
The dancers practiced hard yesterday.

26. Dancer Ruth St. Denis tour Europe in 1909.
27. She start a school of dance in 1915.
28. Another one open in New York a year later.
29. Today, not many people remembered St. Denis.
30. A writer started a book about her next year.

Writing Connection

Art Pretend that your class will present a show of music and dance. Make a poster to advertise the show. Draw a picture and describe the acts. Use words and future-tense verbs that will persuade people to attend.

STANDARDIZED
TEST PREP

Chapter Review

Read the passage, and choose the verb that belongs in each space. Mark the letter for your answer.

My teacher taught us about traditional dances from around the world. Today, many people __(1)__ folk dancing. Folk dances __(2)__ in the past throughout the world. For example, Ireland long ago __(3)__ the Irish jig. People first __(4)__ the polka in Europe centuries ago. Many Italians still __(5)__ the tarantella. Early forms of the square dance __(6)__ in Europe in the 1400s. I __(7)__ an old English country dance at a talent show next week. My friends and I __(8)__ every day until the performance.

TIP If you have time, remember to check your answers after you finish the test.

For additional test preparation, visit *The Learning Site:*
www.harcourtschool.com

1 A enjoyed
   B will enjoy
   C enjoy
   D enjoys

2 F developed
   G develops
   H will develop
   J develop

3 A contributes
   B contributed
   C will contribute
   D contribute

4 F dance
   G will dance
   H danced
   J dances

5 A will like
   B like
   C liked
   D likes

6 F starts
   G started
   H start
   J will start

7 A performs
   B performed
   C will perform
   D perform

8 F practice
   G will practice
   H practiced
   J practices

Using Visual Media To Compare Points of View

Visual media, such as illustrations, advertisements, billboards, newspapers, television, and motion pictures, are used to communicate messages. As readers and viewers, we must learn how to interpret visual media.

A point of view, or an opinion about a topic, may be expressed using words and images. For example, the city council might display a billboard that says, "Let's work together." The picture on the billboard shows trash cans overflowing and the wind blowing litter around the neighborhood park. The city council uses this visual image to express its point of view that members of the community should help keep the neighborhood clean.

YOUR TURN

Write a few sentences about your favorite advertisement, billboard, or movie preview. Then interpret the artist's message or point of view. Do you agree or disagree? Now, design your own piece of visual media to express your point of view. Exchange with a partner. Think about what message your partner is trying to communicate. Discuss whether or not you interpreted your partner's point of view correctly.

Irregular Verbs

An **irregular verb** shows past tense by using a different form of the main verb.

You know that the past tense of regular verbs is formed by adding *ed* or *d*. An irregular verb does not end with *ed* in the past tense.

Irregular Verb	Present	Past
be	am, is, are	was, were
begin	begin, begins	began
break	break, breaks	broke
know	know, knows	knew
think	think, thinks	thought
wear	wear, wears	wore

Example:
Will that merry-go-round **break** down? It **broke** down last week.

Vocabulary Power

car•ou•sel [kar′ə•sel′]
n. A merry-go-round.

Guided Practice

A. Read each sentence. Identify the irregular verb.

Example: I thought about the carousel in the park.
thought

1. Carousels brought children joy for many years.
2. Folk artists began with horses.
3. These horses were the first carousel animals.
4. Then folk artists thought about other animals.
5. These animals became very popular as well.

Independent Practice

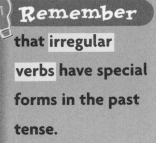

Remember

that irregular verbs have special forms in the past tense.

B. Write the correct past-tense form of the verb in parentheses.

> **Example:**   Edward Hicks (be) a famous folk artist.
>
> *was*

6. Edward Hicks (begin) as a carriage painter.
7. Then he (bring) his skill to sign painting.
8. In the 1800s, he (throw) aside his early work.
9. He (begin) a series of paintings of animals.
10. Hicks (throw) himself into his new work.
11. Art lovers (think) highly of his paintings.
12. He (be) famous for *The Peaceable Kingdom*.
13. People also (know) him for his paintings of farms.
14. In his paintings, people (wear) ordinary clothes.
15. His paintings (be) popular for years.
16. Eunice Pinney (begin) by painting scenes from her childhood.
17. People (think) she had copied other artists.
18. In one painting, a horse (throw) its rider.
19. The rider (wear) a soldier's uniform.
20. Her painting *Two Women* (be) very good.

Writing Connection

Writer's Journal: Recording Ideas Think about pictures or objects that decorate your home. Choose one picture or object, and write about it in your journal. Using some irregular past-tense verb forms, write words and phrases that describe the object.

More Irregular Verbs

Some irregular verbs use *n* or *en* to form the past tense with a helping verb.

Notice in the chart below that the past-tense form with a helping verb is different from the past-tense form without a helping verb.

Present	Past	Past + Helping Verb
blow(s)	blew	(have, has, had) blown
do(es)	did	(have, has, had) done
fall(s)	fell	(have, has, had) fallen
give(s)	gave	(have, has, had) given
ride(s)	rode	(have, has, had) ridden
speak(s)	spoke	(have, has, had) spoken
take(s)	took	(have, has, had) taken

Examples:

You **did** a good job on that cartoon.

You **have done** a good job on that cartoon.

Guided Practice

A. Identify the irregular verb and any helping verb in each sentence.

Example: My parents gave me a book of cartoons.
gave

1. The book fell open at a cartoon about a bird.
2. The bird has flown onto a flagpole.
3. The bird has spoken about people and politics.
4. A strong wind blew the bird off the flagpole.
5. Cartoonists have done their work well.

Independent Practice

B. Write the correct past-tense form of the verb in parentheses.

> **Example:** What have cartoonists (do) in the past?
> *done*

6. Cartooning has (grow) as an art.
7. The first cartoons (take) the form of rough drawings.
8. Artists (do) these drawings before making a painting.
9. Later the word *cartoon* was (give) a new meaning.
10. Cartoons had (fall) into use as jokes.

C. Write each sentence, using the correct form of the verb in parentheses.

> **Example:** How have cartoons (grew, grown) into stories?
> *How have cartoons grown into stories?*

11. Cartoons (grew, grown) into comic strips.
12. Heroes (rode, ridden) horses into battle.
13. Superheroes have (flew, flown) across the skies.
14. Winds (blew, blowed) ships across the sea.
15. Characters (spoke, spoken) to one another.

Remember

that some irregular verbs use *n* or *en* to form the past tense with a helping verb.

Writing Connection

Writer's Craft: Strong Verbs Choose a cartoon strip that you like from your local newspaper. Write a paragraph that tells what happens in the cartoon. Choose strong verbs that show action. Use as many different verbs as you can, including irregular verbs. When you finish, trade paragraphs with a partner. Draw a star next to your partner's strongest verb, and explain why it is important to the paragraph.

USAGE AND MECHANICS

Commonly Misused Verbs

Use the verbs *lie/lay*, *rise/raise*, and *sit/set* correctly.

The subject of a sentence can *lie* down, *sit* down, or *rise* up on its own. However, a subject *lays* down something, *sets* down something, or *raises* up something.

Present	Meaning	Past	Past + Helping Verb
lie(s)	recline	lay	(have, has, had) lain
lay(s)	put down	laid	(have, has, had) laid
rise(s)	get up	rose	(have, has, had) risen
raise(s)	bring up	raised	(have, has, had) raised
sit(s)	rest	sat	(have, has, had) sat
set(s)	place down	set	(have, has, had) set

Examples:

Subject does this on its own.

The dolls will **lie** in their boxes all night.

Subject does this to something else.

You **lay** the dolls in their boxes.

Guided Practice

A. Choose the correct verb in parentheses.

Example: She moved the dolls so she could (lie, lay) down on the bed. *lie*

1. The dolls (set, sit) on the shelf.
2. Doreen (set, sat) them there this morning.
3. She wanted to (raise, rise) the shelf a bit higher.
4. She (laid, lay) the dolls on the bed.
5. They have (laid, lain) there since this morning.

Independent Practice

B. Write each sentence, using the correct form of the verb in parentheses. Underline the verb.

> **Example:** Doll makers (sit, set) down and draw their ideas.
> *Doll makers <u>sit</u> down and draw their ideas.*

6. They (sit, set) their ideas down on paper.
7. The workers (lie, lay) out clay and mold it into a doll.
8. The clay doll (lies, lays) on a table.
9. The artist (rises, raises) the doll and looks at it.
10. She has made molds and has (sat, set) out plastic.
11. Hot air (rose, raised) as the plastic melted.
12. Then workers (laid, lain) out the parts from the molds.
13. They (sat, set) hats on the dolls' heads.
14. They have dressed the dolls and have (laid, lain) them in boxes.
15. The dolls (laid, lay) in the boxes until they were bought.

Remember that *lay* is the past tense of *lie* when that word means "recline." *Lay* is also the present-tense verb that means "put down."

Writing Connection

Art Cartoonists use pictures and captions to tell stories. Draw boxes for a three-panel cartoon about a doll or puppet that can walk and talk. Work with a partner to draw three scenes, one in each box, that show the doll or puppet doing three of the following actions: *lay, lie, raise, rise, set,* and *sit.* Tell your story by writing captions that use the verbs correctly.

Extra Practice

A. Write the correct past-tense form of the verb in parentheses. *pages 202–205*

> **Example:** Many people have (take) children to puppet shows.
>
> *taken*

1. People have (know) about puppets for many years.
2. In ancient Egypt, people (know) about puppets.
3. People (begin) telling stories with puppets.
4. Puppets (bring) folktales to the stage.
5. Many of these stories (grow) very popular.
6. Some puppets (be) as big as real people.
7. Folk artists often (give) puppets human features.
8. Some puppets (speak) about real events.
9. Puppets often (wear) brightly colored clothing.
10. Performers (raise) some puppets on strings.
11. These puppets were (knew) as marionettes.
12. Marionettes almost (fly) on the stage.
13. The strings had (give) the marionettes a way to move.
14. Children (think) the puppets were fun.
15. In many ways the puppets (be) like dolls.

B. Write the correct form of the verb in parentheses. *pages 202–205*

> **Example:** People have (gave, given) toys to their children for many years. *given*

16. Many girls (grew, grown) up playing with dollhouses.
17. Dollhouses have also (bring, brought) joy to boys.
18. The first dollhouses were (gave, given) to adults.
19. People (thought, thought) that some dollhouses looked like tiny, real houses.
20. Some dollhouses (were, been) quite large.

Remember

An irregular verb does not end with *ed* in the past tense.

For more activities with irregular verbs, visit *The Learning Site:*
www.harcourtschool.com

C. Write each sentence, using the correct verb in parentheses. *pages 206–207*

Example: Jack (sits, sets) and watches his aunt weave.
Jack sits and watches his aunt weave.

21. He watches her (sit, set) at her loom.
22. She has (sat, set) it up in the basement of her house.
23. This morning she (rose, raised) early to finish weaving a blanket for Jack.
24. She had (lay, laid) some patterns down on a table nearby.
25. Jack watches as she uses weaving tools to (rise, raise) threads in the loom.
26. The threads that she (rises, raises) and lowers form the blanket's design.
27. She has (sit, set) red and black triangles and squares into the pattern.
28. Prices of hand-woven blankets have (risen, raised).
29. Jack can't wait to (lie, lay) the blanket on his bed.
30. When he (lies, lays) down to rest, he will think of his aunt.

DID YOU KNOW?
In South Africa, a woman in the Mfengu tribe carries a doll until her first child is born. Then she gives the doll to the child.

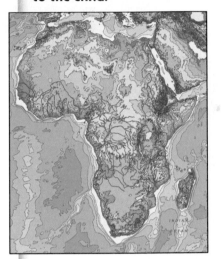

Writing Connection

Social Studies Think of art in your community. Perhaps you know someone who has made something out of fabric or wood. Perhaps you know someone who draws or paints. Write a paragraph that describes a special piece of artwork that someone in your family or community has made. Use descriptive words that allow readers to picture the art. Use correct verbs to explain how the art was made.

Chapter Review

Read the passage. Choose the correct irregular verb form for each sentence. Write the letter of your answer in the numbered space.

STANDARDIZED TEST PREP

I hope I __(1)__ a good job on my folk art project. I __(2)__ early Saturday to work on it. The idea __(3)__ from watching my grandpa make furniture. He __(4)__ how to use hand tools. He __(5)__ to me about the art of furniture making. Good furniture has always __(6)__ him pleasure. I liked to __(7)__ and watch him work. Grandpa always __(8)__ down his tools and talked to me awhile.

TIP Remember to read all of the answer choices before you select one.

1 A has did
   B does
   C did
   D done

2 F raised
   G rose
   H risen
   J rised

3 A growed
   B had grew
   C grown
   D grew

4 F has knowed
   G knows
   H knowed
   J known

5 A speaked
   B spoken
   C spoke
   D has speaked

6 F give
   G given
   H gives
   J gave

7 A set
   B sit
   C sat
   D have set

8 F lay
   G lie
   H lain
   J laid

For additional test preparation, visit *The Learning Site:*
www.harcourtschool.com

Prefixes and Suffixes

A **prefix** is a word part added to the beginning of a base word. A **suffix** is a word part added to the end of a base word. Adding a prefix or suffix affects the meaning of the base word.

Examples: re- + write = rewrite   friend + -ly = friendly

If a verb ends with *e*, drop the *e* before adding the suffix *-er* or *-able*.

Examples: write + -er = writer   love + -able = lovable

This chart shows how prefixes affect the meanings of words.

Prefix	Meaning	Base Word	New Word	New Meaning
re-	do again	read	reread	read again
un-	not	able	unable	not able
pre-	before	write	prewrite	before writing
dis-	not *or* opposite of	agree	disagree	not agree

This chart shows how suffixes affect the meanings of words.

Suffix	Meaning	Base Word	New Word	New Meaning
-er	one who does (something)	design	designer	one who designs
-less	without	use	useless	without use
-able	having the quality of	like	likable	being liked

YOUR TURN

On index cards, write the prefixes *re-, un-, pre-,* and *dis-* and the suffixes *-er, -less,* and *-able.* Then write the words *read, use, like, heat, aim, agree, do, tie, build,* and *test* on index cards. Match each prefix or suffix card with one of the word cards to make a new word.

TIP Make sure that all your combinations are real words. Look them up in a dictionary.

Persuasive writing tries to convince someone to believe or do something. In this selection, Annie's letter persuades others to give money to the Statue of Liberty pedestal fund. As you read, think about Annie's strong feelings and her reasons for writing the letter.

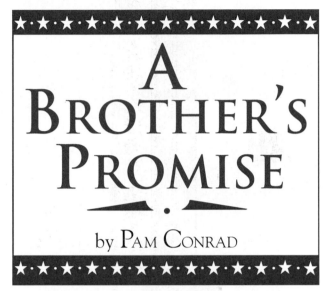

A BROTHER'S PROMISE

by PAM CONRAD

The people of France gave the Statue of Liberty to the United States as a symbol of friendship. In this selection, the torch is already in New York City, but the Statue of Liberty will not be sent to America until a pedestal is built for her to stand on. Annie and her brother, Geoffrey, who has recently died, had a tradition of viewing the city together from the torch. When the torch is sent back to Paris for final assembly, Annie is afraid that the entire statue will never be sent to America.

New York City, 1885

A few weeks after Geoffrey's death, Annie wrote this letter to the publisher of the *New York World* newspaper.

Dear Mr. Pulitzer,

I am sending this money for the Statue of Liberty Pedestal Fund. I live near Madison Square, and I used to visit the torch with my older brother, Geoffrey. Geoffrey was an art student in Paris, and he told me all about the statue and how the man who built the Eiffel Tower in Paris also built the foundation of the Statue of Liberty. He told me how the statue towers over the buildings in Paris, and how he used to look at it and imagine it in New York Harbor. We even made a solemn promise to meet in the torch when it was finally here again. He was always completely certain that she would be here one day.

I want to make sure of it. You see, my brother died this year, and although he can't keep his promise to me, I can still keep mine. I've been to see a local pawnbroker, and I sold Geoffrey's rare antique spyglass made of silver and wood that we used for looking around New York City, from up inside the torch. I'm sad to sell it, but I'm sure he'd understand. Please take this money in Geoffrey Gibbon's memory, and please build a pedestal.

Respectfully yours,
Annie Gibbon

Annie's letter was published in the *New York World*, and its heartfelt message touched off a series of contributions in memory of beloved relatives. Annie was proud to see the fund grow bigger every week until, finally, Joseph Pulitzer declared the fund to be complete, and the construction of the pedestal on Bedloe's Island was to begin at last.

Bedloe's Island, 1886

The Statue of Liberty has arrived in America, and Annie goes to the opening celebration. Joseph Pulitzer is conducting the ceremony.

Then, just when it seemed he was through, he looked over the crowd thoughtfully and shouted out, "By the way, is Annie Gibbon here today?"

"Here I am!" Annie cried, waving from her place in the crowd.

"Come up here, Annie!" He laughed, and the crowd parted for her. Mr. Pulitzer reached out his hand and guided her up the steps. He kept her at his side and spoke to the crowd.

"Well, I'm so glad you're here. You see," he said, turning back to his audience, "Annie lost her brother last year, a brother who loved the Statue of Liberty. He'd actually seen it in Paris, and Annie sold his special spyglass and sent the money to the Pedestal Fund in his memory. That led many others to do the same thing."

A few people clapped, and Annie looked down at their faces.

"Annie, I have a surprise for you." He turned around, and someone handed him a long, thin wooden box. "When I read your letter, I sent my people out to all the pawnshops in your area. I said to myself, 'Joseph, when the statue comes over, that little girl is going to have her spyglass back. Yes, she is.' Now you take this spyglass and climb to the top of that lady and take a good look around, Annie."

Analyze THE *Model*

1. What is the purpose of Annie's letter?
2. How does Annie persuade her readers?
3. What details strengthen Annie's main point?

READING — WRITING CONNECTION

Parts of a Persuasive Essay

Writers sometimes try to convince people to take an action or change the way they think. Study this essay, written by a student named Pearl. Pay attention to the parts of her persuasive essay.

MODEL

statement of opinion

first reason

details

second reason

details

third reason

Seeing Is Believing

Art is everywhere in our world. Copies of works of art are shown on posters, on T-shirts, in books, and on the Internet. Our field trip showed me, though, that copies aren't the same as the real thing. Seeing original works of art in a museum is something we should all try to do.

You can learn a lot about art in a museum. Sometimes you can look at more than one painting by the same artist. An exhibit might show sketches the artist made before doing a painting. It's amazing to see the different stages a work of art goes through before it is a finished painting or sculpture.

In addition, you can learn about the works of art as you look at them. Our tour guide explained how some artists changed their style of painting during a certain time period. It is so much easier to understand these ideas if you can see the original art!

The most important reason for seeing art

in a museum is that you can see it in more than one way. We could see brushstrokes from up close, but we had to step back to view the picture as a whole.

Art museums teach us about artists and how they work. They allow us to see works of art in different ways. If you get a chance to go to an art museum, don't miss it!

details

restatement of opinion

call to action

Analyze THE Model

1. What is Pearl's purpose for writing?

2. Who is Pearl's audience?

3. What is Pearl's most important reason? How does she support this reason?

Summarize THE Model

Write Pearl's opinion and reasons in a web like the one shown here. Use the web to write a summary of her persuasive essay.

opinion

reason   reason   reason

Writer's Craft

Capturing Your Reader's Interest

You can keep your audience's attention by writing different kinds of sentences. For example, start sentences with different words, ask questions, and make some sentences short and others long. Write three sentences from Pearl's essay that have different constructions.

Prewriting

Purpose and Audience

Writing is one way to share an opinion. In this chapter, you will share an opinion with your classmates by writing a persuasive essay.

WRITING PROMPT Write an essay to persuade your classmates to try an art-related hobby or to follow an art-related interest. State your opinion. Follow it with strong reasons to persuade your readers to agree with you. Conclude with a call to action.

Before you begin, think about your purpose for writing and your audience. Who will your readers be? What do you want to persuade them to do?

MODEL

Pearl decided to encourage her classmates to visit an art museum to see original works of art. She used this web to organize her thoughts:

Strategies Good Writers Use

- Determine your purpose and audience.
- State your opinion.
- List as many reasons as you can to persuade your audience.

My audience: classmates

My purpose: persuade my classmates to visit art museums

My Opinion: People should go to art museums.

learn about art

learn about how artists work

look at art in different ways

YOUR TURN

Choose an art-related hobby or interest. Use a web to organize your ideas.

Organization and Elaboration

Use these steps to help you organize your essay:

STEP 1 Capture Your Reader's Interest

Start with an interesting idea or fact about your topic.

STEP 2 State Your Opinion

State your opinion clearly and directly.

STEP 3 Give Reasons

Give each reason, followed by details that support it. Group your reasons in separate paragraphs, saving the strongest reason for last.

STEP 4 Conclude with a Call to Action

Restate your opinion. Suggest something for your reader to do.

MODEL

Read the first paragraph of Pearl's essay. How does she make you want to keep reading? Which sentence states her opinion?

> Art is everywhere in our world. Copies of works of art are shown on posters, on T-shirts, in books, and on the Internet. Our field trip showed me, though, that copies aren't the same as the real thing. Seeing original works of art in a museum is something we should all try to do.

YOUR TURN

Now draft your essay. Use your ideas from prewriting to help you organize your paragraphs. Use the models by Pam Conrad and Pearl to give you ideas.

Strategies Good Writers Use

- Write an interesting opening sentence to get your audience's attention.
- Give reasons with details and examples to persuade your audience to agree with your opinion.
- Save your strongest reason for last.
- End by restating your opinion and urging your audience to take action.

 Use the computer to draft your essay. The Insert feature lets you go back and add ideas as they occur to you.

Revising

Organization and Elaboration

Read your first draft. Think about these questions:

- How interesting is my opening sentence?
- How clear are my reasons? How well do the details support the reasons?
- Are there any details that don't belong?

MODEL

Look at the changes Pearl made. Notice how she added variety. Why do you think she deleted the detail about Winslow Homer?

You can learn a lot about art in a museum. Sometimes You can look at more than one painting by the same artist. ~~My favorite artist is Winslow Holmer.~~ An exhibit might show ~~You can see~~ sketches the artist made before doing a painting. It's amazing ~~interesting~~ to see the different stages a work of art goes through before it is a finished painting or sculpture.

In addition, You can learn about the ~~artworks~~ of art as you look at them. Our tour guide ~~told us~~ explained how some artists changed their style of painting during a certain time period. It is so much easier to understand these ideas if ~~because~~ you can see the original art!

YOUR TURN

Revise your persuasive essay. Make your sentences as interesting as you can. Add details, and take out any ideas that don't relate to your topic.

Strategies
Good **W**riters **U**se

- Revise sentences that begin the same way.
- Add details to support your reasons.
- Keep to the topic.

If you delete something by mistake, you may be able to get it back. Try using the Edit Undo feature.

Proofreading

Checking Your Language

Mistakes can make your writing less convincing. Always proofread your work. Look for mistakes in spelling, capitalization, punctuation, and grammar.

MODEL

Pearl proofread her revised essay carefully. See how she corrected her spelling errors. Where did she correct her punctuation? What grammar errors did she correct?

> The most (important) reason for seeing
> art in a museum is that you can (sea) it
> in more than (won) way. We could see
> brushstrokes from up close, but we had to
> step back to (veiw) the picture as a hole.
> art museums teaches us about artists
> and how they work. They allow us to
> (sea) works of art in (diffrent) ways. If you
> get a chance to go to a art museum, don't
> miss it!

YOUR TURN

Proofread your revised essay. Proofread your essay three times, using this checklist to

- check spelling, especially of irregular verbs.
- check punctuation of contractions, titles, and sentences.
- look for errors in grammar, such as subject-verb agreement.

Strategies Good Writers Use

- Check for subject-verb agreement.
- Check for irregular verbs.
- Look up spellings if you are unsure of them.

Editor's Marks

ℰ	delete text
∧	insert text
⟲	move text
¶	new paragraph
≡	capitalize
/	lowercase
◯	correct spelling

Publishing

Sharing Your Work

Your persuasive essay is now ready to be published. Answer these questions to help you decide on the best way to share it:

1. Who will read or hear your essay? Will it be read aloud in a classroom or in an auditorium? Will it be printed in a newspaper?

2. Should you print your essay in manuscript or write it in cursive?

3. Would illustrations or computer graphics make your essay more persuasive?

4. Should you give a speech based on your essay? To give a speech, use the information on page 225.

USING YOUR
Handbook

- Use the rubric on page 508 to evaluate your persuasive essay.

Reflecting on Your Writing

 Using Your Portfolio What did you learn about your writing in this chapter? Write your answer to each question below.

1. Does your opening paragraph grab the reader's interest? Why or why not?

2. What was your purpose for writing? Did you meet it? Explain your answer.

Add your answers and your essay to your portfolio. Now review your portfolio. Write one sentence about something you do well as a writer. Write one sentence about something you would like to do better. Use what you have written to help you set a goal for becoming a better writer.

Giving a Speech

Pearl made a speech to her class based on her essay.
You can use your essay to make a speech, too.

STEP 1 List the main ideas from each paragraph on separate note cards. Keep them short and easy to read. Number your cards.

STEP 2 Think about what multimedia aids, such as pictures, models, or music, would strengthen your reasons. If you use an aid, mark the point when you want to use it.

STEP 3 Underline your best reasons. Underlining will remind you to emphasize them.

STEP 4 Practice your speech. Speak slowly and clearly. Don't let your voice get too high.

STEP 5 Take a deep breath to help you relax. Smile. Talk directly to your classmates. Make eye contact.

Strategies for Listeners

As your classmates give their speeches, use these tips to help you gain information:

- Watch the speaker.
- Listen for the opinion and main reasons in the speech.
- Wait until the speaker is finished before you make up your mind.

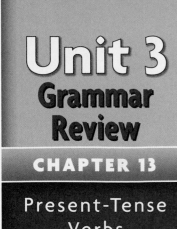

Verb Tenses *pages 164–165*

Write the sentence. Choose the correct tense of the verb in parentheses.

1. Yesterday Mark (finishes, finished) his art project.
2. Mark (works, worked) all last week on his project.
3. He (painted, will paint) a series of colorful outdoor scenes.
4. Mark (likes, will like) bright colors.
5. He (handed, will hand) in his artwork tomorrow.
6. Yesterday Mark (plans, planned) a new art project.
7. When he (starts, will start) a new project, Mark (made, makes) some rough sketches first.
8. He (worked, will work) with a partner in the future.
9. Mark never (needs, needed) help before.
10. Mark (hopes, hoped) that the new project (took, will take) less time.

Present-Tense Verbs *pages 166–167*

Write the sentence. Underline the present-tense verb.

11. Keisha and I like the sculpture behind the new building.
12. The sculptor always works with iron.
13. She makes heavy pieces of sculpture.
14. Her largest sculpture weighs almost a ton.
15. Her sculptures look great outdoors.

Subject-Verb Agreement *pages 168–169*

Write the sentence. Use the verb that agrees with the subject to complete the sentence.

16. Artists (buys, buy) new supplies for their work.
17. Painters (need, needs) new brushes and paint.
18. Some painters (keep, keeps) their supplies in neat piles.
19. One artist (stores, store) supplies for six months.
20. Many suppliers (give, gives) artists a discount.

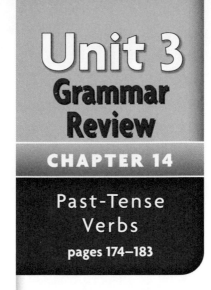

Past-Tense Verbs *pages 174–175*

Write the sentence, and underline the verb. Write whether the verb is past tense or present tense.

1. The writer Patricia MacLachlan lived in Wyoming as a child.
2. This author now lives in Massachusetts.
3. First she worked as an English teacher.
4. Then she started a writing career.
5. Her book *Sarah, Plain and Tall* tells about a New England woman who moves to the prairie.

More About Past-Tense Verbs
pages 176–177

Write the past-tense form of the verb in parentheses.

6. Maurice Sendak (illustrate) *Where the Wild Things Are.*
7. Sendak's career (soar) because of this book's success.
8. The book (earn) the Caldecott award in 1964 for best illustrations in a children's book.
9. First Sendak (study) art at night and (work) during the day.
10. Sendak later (design) costumes for an opera.

Subject-Verb Agreement *pages 178–179*

Write the sentence, using the correct form of the verb in parentheses.

11. Folktales, unlike other stories, sometimes (has, have) talking animals.
12. Among many examples (is, are) "Little Red Riding Hood" and "The Three Little Pigs."
13. Talking animals (appears, appear) to be like people.
14. An animal character in a folktale, like people, (has, have) feelings.
15. Do readers really (thinks, think) talking animals, fish, and birds exist?

225

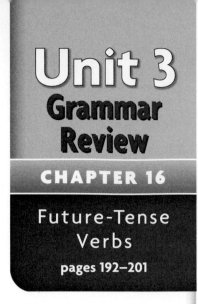

Unit 3
Grammar Review

CHAPTER 16

Future-Tense Verbs

pages 192–201

Future-Tense Verbs   *pages 192–193*

Write the sentence, and underline the future-tense verb.

1. The school band will march in the parade tomorrow.
2. The band will travel to the parade grounds on a bus.
3. The students will carry their own instruments.
4. The band members will wear colorful uniforms.
5. They will march in three rows along the parade route.
6. The drummers will form the first row.
7. The trombone players will follow in the second row.
8. Many people will hear the band tomorrow.
9. The band members will practice for several hours today.
10. Their teacher will conduct the band.

More About Future-Tense Verbs

pages 194–195

Write the sentence. Underline both parts of the future-tense verb.

11. Will the band members march in the Thanksgiving Day parade?
12. They will probably need permission from their parents.
13. Many school bands will enthusiastically perform in this parade.
14. The mayor will surely attend this year.
15. Where will people watch the parade?

Choosing the Correct Tense

pages 196–197

Write the sentence. Use the tense shown of the verb in parentheses to complete the sentence.

16. The orchestra (perform, *present*) on stage at the theater every night.
17. This orchestra (have, *present*) 92 members.
18. It (play, *past*) here last year, too.
19. Students (attend, *future*) a concert next week.
20. The students always (enjoy, *present*) the music.

Irregular Verbs *pages 202–203*

Write the sentence, using the correct past-tense form of the verb in parentheses.

1. I (begin) riding the merry-go-round years ago.
2. I (be) fond of merry-go-round rides as a child.
3. My parents often (take) me to the merry-go-round.
4. At first I (think) the horses were real.
5. After I rode them, I (know) they were not.

More Irregular Verbs *pages 204–205*

Write the correct past-tense form of the verb in parentheses.

6. Folk art has (take) many forms.
7. Folk artists have often (speak) about their crafts.
8. One scene in a painting shows leaves that have (blow) away.
9. This scene also shows that the leaves have (fall) on the ground.
10. The birds that (fly) from the trees looked real.
11. Some folk artists (do) excellent work on carved animals.
12. Many children have (ride) these animals on merry-go-rounds.
13. Most children never (fall) off these animals.
14. The rides (give) children joy.
15. Merry-go-rounds have (grow) very popular again.

Commonly Misused Verbs
pages 206–207

Write the sentence, using the correct form of the verb in parentheses.

16. Let's (sit, set) and watch the merry-go-round.
17. The ticket (lies, lays) in Blanca's hand.
18. Her parents (sit, set) her on the horse.
19. Her parents decide to (lie, lay) on the grass and watch.
20. The horse will (rise, raise) and fall with the music.

Make a Case for Art

Why should art be taught in schools? How is it important to your life? Work with a group to list reasons. Then present your case in a class debate. Follow the steps below.

Brainstorm Your Case

- With a group, brainstorm reasons to support your case.

- Why is art important to you?

- How does it help you in school and in life?

- What does art teach you about yourself and about other people?

- Why is art important to your community?

- Search the Internet or art magazines for more reasons to support your case.

Write a Group Essay

- Each group member should write a paragraph to support one of the reasons, including examples from real life to support it.

- Combine the paragraphs in a folder, or paste them into an e-mail message and send them to your teacher.

Have a Debate

- With your group members, present your reasons to your classmates. When you have finished, let the audience challenge your reasons. Then explain why you think your reasons are good, or give more reasons why art is important.

The Hundred Dresses
by Eleanor Estes
REALISTIC FICTION
The ordinary Wanda Petronski is suddenly the center of attention when she announces her collection of one hundred dresses.
Newbery Honor

The Kids' Multicultural Art Book
by Alexandra M. Terzian
NONFICTION
Art is important to cultures from all over the world, as shown by the many crafts and activities in this book.

Unit 4

Grammar Pronouns, Adjectives, and Adverbs

Writing Informative Writing: Classification

What I Like About Winter

- sledding
- ice-skating
- hot chocolat

What I Don't Like About Winter

- cold toes
- shoveling snow

233

Pronouns and Pronoun Antecedents

A **pronoun** is a word that takes the place of one or more nouns. Some common pronouns are *I, me, you, he, him, she, her, it, we, us, you, they,* and *them*. The **antecedent** of a pronoun is the noun or nouns that the pronoun replaces. A pronoun should agree with its antecedent in number and gender.

Examples:

María likes rain because **she** thinks puddles are fun.

Dan and Karen say that **they** do not like rain.

Pronouns	
Singular	**Plural**
I	we
me	us
you	you
he	they
she	
it	
him	them
her	
it	

Guided Practice

A. Read each sentence. Identify the pronoun and its antecedent. Tell whether the pronoun and its antecedent are singular or plural.

Examples: When Sue arrived, she checked the maps.
she, Sue, singular

Weather maps show rainfall, and they are helpful.
they, maps, plural

1. Amy's brothers, Will and Mike, went with her to visit Seattle, Washington.
2. Amy said that she enjoyed the visit.
3. Seattle can be gloomy in January because it gets about 6 inches of rain during that month.
4. "We like Seattle," said Will and Mike.
5. People in Seattle claim they like the weather.

Vocabulary Power

at•mos•phere
[at′məs•fir] *n.* The air surrounding the earth.

Independent Practice

B. Write each sentence. Underline the pronoun and its antecedent. Write whether the pronoun and its antecedent are singular or plural.

Examples: Matt said that he saw a double rainbow. *singular*

Rainbows are beautiful because they contain many colors. *plural*

6. "I saw a rainbow over the bay," said Amber.

7. "When did you see that rainbow, Amber?" asked Tom.

8. "The students saw the rainbow when we went on a picnic Sunday," answered Amber.

9. Amber said that she took a picture of the rainbow.

10. "Would you like to see that picture, boys and girls?" asked the teacher.

11. A rainbow has seven colors. They are red, orange, yellow, green, blue, indigo, and violet.

12. When you put the first letters of the colors together, they form the name Roy G. Biv.

13. A rainbow is really a perfect circle since it reflects the sun's rays.

14. When conditions are right, they can cause a double rainbow.

15. Marcos and María said that they would love to see a double rainbow.

Remember

that the **pronoun** *you* can have either a singular or a plural **antecedent**.

Writing Connection

Writer's Craft: Description Think about the kinds of rain you have seen, from light drizzles to downpours. Write a paragraph describing one of these events. Use pronouns when possible to add variety to your sentences. Exchange your paragraph with a partner, and check each other's use of descriptive words.

Pronouns	
Subject Pronouns	**Object Pronouns**
I	me
you	you
he, she, it	him, her, it
we	us
they	them

Always capitalize the pronoun *I*.

Subject and Object Pronouns

Pronouns can be subjects or objects in sentences.

A subject pronoun takes the place of one or more nouns in the subject of a sentence.

Examples:
I like to play in the snow.
We play outside when the weather is warm.

An object pronoun follows an action verb, such as *see* or *tell*, or a preposition, such as *at*, *for*, *to*, or *with*. The arrows in the following examples point from the action verb or preposition to the object pronoun.

Examples:
Veda *asked* **her** to come out to play.
Veda and Matt threw a snowball *at* **me**.

Guided Practice

A. **Read the sentence. Find the pronoun. Tell whether it is a subject pronoun or an object pronoun.**

Examples: We like to play in the snow.
We, subject pronoun

Mark liked playing in snow but not shoveling it. *it, object pronoun*

1. John "Snowshoe" Thompson did not let a blizzard stop him.
2. He carried letters in the 1800s.
3. Thompson always delivered them.
4. Thompson carved heavy skis and wore them.
5. I think Thompson had courage to deliver mail then.

Independent Practice

B. Write the sentence, and underline the pronoun. Write whether the pronoun is a subject pronoun or an object pronoun.

Remember
that the pronouns *you* and *it* can be either subject pronouns or object pronouns.

Example: <u>You</u> can find a book called *Snowflake Bentley*.
subject pronoun

6. Bentley said, "Mother taught me at home."

7. Bentley said that he first went to school at fourteen years of age.

8. There were books in the Bentley home, and Bentley read lots of them.

9. Bentley's mother was once a teacher, and she helped Bentley.

10. Bentley's mother let him use a microscope.

11. Bentley looked at things under it.

12. He enjoyed learning and studying.

13. Bentley was interested in snowflakes and put them under the microscope.

14. Bentley was fascinated by the patterns he saw.

15. However, they melted too quickly.

16. Bentley then got a camera with a microscope and used it.

17. He took the first photo of a snowflake.

18. We know that snowflakes have six sides.

19. Do you want to know more?

20. Articles give more facts about him.

Writing Connection

Health Write a short paragraph to tell how you and your family might prepare for bad weather. Put the sentences in order of what you would do first. Continue the sequence, including items for survival that you would store and your reasons for the items. Use both subject pronouns and object pronouns in your writing.

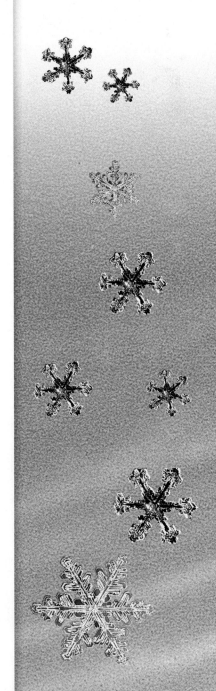

CHAPTER 19

Pronouns

USAGE AND MECHANICS

Using *I* and *Me*, *We* and *Us*

I and *we* are subject pronouns. *Me* and *us* are object pronouns.

When using *I* and *me* with nouns and other pronouns, place *I* and *me* last.

Examples:
I would like to know about the atmosphere.
Erica and **I** are going sailing today.
Tell Erica and **me** what the weather report says.
We will take the radio with **us** on the boat.

In the last example sentence, the antecedent of *us* is the subject pronoun *we*.

Guided Practice

A. Read the sentence. Study the pair of pronouns in parentheses. Decide which pronoun is correct. Tell whether it is a subject pronoun or an object pronoun.

Example: A local man has a story about last night's tornado to tell (we, us). *us; object pronoun*

  1. Mary and (me, I) heard a strange noise.
  2. The loud roar frightened (us, we).
  3. It sounded to (I, me) like a freight train.
  4. (I, Me) hope never to hear that sound again!
  5. Mary and (I, me) held onto each other tightly.

236

Independent Practice

B. Read the sentence. Decide which pronoun in parentheses is correct. Write the sentence, using the correct pronoun.

Example: Please tell (I, me) about your trip.
Please tell me about your trip.

6. An avalanche slid down beside (us, we).
7. A rainbow appeared in front of a friend and (I, me).
8. A classmate and (I, me) watched a flood.
9. Light rain cooled off Tom and (I, me).
10. Lightning struck a tree above (we, us).
11. Mom and (I, me) were camping by the hillside.
12. We could see the rain coming toward (we, us).
13. The wind blew toward (I, me).
14. A downpour gave (we, us) some trouble.
15. (I, Me) was walking on a very dusty trail.
16. (We, Us) had seen floodwater in the river.
17. Later (we, us) heard about a hurricane.
18. Mom and (I, me) watched fog cover the bridge.
19. While boating, (we, us) ran into heavy fog.
20. Friends and (I, me) built a huge snowman.

Writing Connection

Writer's Journal: Writing Idea What do you and your friends like the most and the least about storms or snowstorms? Using the pronouns *I*, *we*, *me*, and *us*, write a short paragraph describing these likes and dislikes. Give reasons why you like or dislike storms.

Remember

Check your usage by saying the sentence aloud, using the pronoun instead of the noun. Let your ear be your guide.

DID YOU KNOW?
Haze is the result of a still atmosphere that contains a lot of water particles. Only when the hazy air is washed out by rain or blown away by wind does the air become clear again.

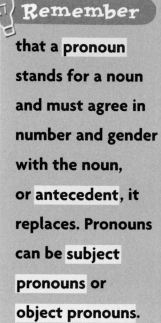

Remember

that a **pronoun** stands for a noun and must agree in number and gender with the noun, or **antecedent**, it replaces. Pronouns can be **subject pronouns** or **object pronouns.**

For more activities with pronouns and pronoun antecedents, visit *The Learning Site:*

www.harcourtschool.com

Extra Practice

A. Read the sentence. Write the pronoun and its antecedent and whether they are singular or plural. *pages 234–235*

Example: Ms. Evans knows a lot about the atmosphere, and she is teaching the class about clouds. *she, Ms. Evans, singular*

1. Ms. Evans asked, "Trish, do you know why clouds change shape?"
2. "I think clouds change shape because of the wind," Trish answered.
3. "The wind does move clouds, and that is one reason they change," said Ms. Evans.
4. "A cloud also changes shape when it runs into drier air," said Ms. Evans.
5. "We never knew that!" exclaimed James and John together.
6. "You should read more about clouds, boys," replied Ms. Evans.
7. Charlie asked, "Do you know if there are many kinds of clouds, Ms. Evans?"
8. Melinda said that she likes cumulus clouds best.
9. Stratus clouds are lower, and people can find them just above ground level.
10. Julio said the big, white clouds are most interesting to him.

B. Write each sentence. Underline the pronoun. Write whether it is a subject pronoun or an object pronoun. *pages 236–237*

Example: The weather forecaster has some good news, so listen to <u>her</u>. *object pronoun*

11. San Franciscans, you are in for some beautiful weather tomorrow.

12. The sun will rise early, and it will chase away the fog.

13. As for the clouds, do not worry about them.

14. By midmorning, they will be gone.

15. Tomorrow already looks perfect to me.

16. We will all want to have picnics on the beach.

17. The people thank you, Nature, for the nice day!

18. Iowans, you will have a chilly day.

19. Call the forecaster and speak with her.

20. Maybe she knows what weather to expect.

C. Read the sentence. Decide which pronoun in parentheses is correct. Write the sentence, using the correct pronoun. *pages 238–239*

Example: The desert is a beautiful place for (we, us) to visit.

The desert is a beautiful place for us to visit.

21. (We, Us) must be careful in a dry creek bed.

22. You and (I, me) have to be aware of flash floods.

23. A sudden downpour far away could sweep you and (I, me) away.

24. Some people have learned the hard way what you and (I, me) know.

25. Careful travelers like (we, us) should be safe.

Writing Connection

Real-Life Writing: Safety Brochure You can inform people of ways to be safe during a severe thunderstorm. In a small group, discuss some ideas to include in a brochure about weather safety. List at least three safety tips. Include drawings and photos to make the brochure interesting. Use pronouns in your brochure only if they can replace nouns and still remain clear.

cumulus clouds

stratus clouds

Chapter Review

Read the passage, and choose the correct pronoun that belongs in each space. Write the letter of your answer.

> Watching the television report about the hurricane made __(1)__ think about being prepared. __(2)__ told Mom and Dad that __(3)__ needed to store some food and water. I live with __(4)__ in a house in Florida. __(5)__ have been lucky. __(6)__ can never be sure what path a hurricane will take. A storm could hit __(7)__ anytime. Last month my friend's town was hit by a hurricane. __(8)__ damaged many homes.

TIP When taking a test, cross out answers you know are wrong. Then choose the correct answer from those remaining.

1 A we
  B me
  C it
  D they

2 F Me
  G It
  H I
  J Them

3 A us
  B me
  C them
  D we

4 F we
  G us
  H it
  J them

5 A Them
  B It
  C We
  D Us

6 F You
  G Them
  H Us
  J She

7 A I
  B we
  C us
  D they

8 F It
  G They
  H Them
  J I

For additional test preparation, visit *The Learning Site:*
www.harcourtschool.com

Conducting an Interview

Interviewing someone is a good way to gather information. Read the following interview.

> **Ethan:** How does the weather affect your work?

> **Mr. Siebert:** The climate affects my choice of crops to plant every year. Here, we usually have a warm, moist growing season, so I plant a lot of corn. Then, if there is too little rain, the plants don't have enough water to grow. Too much rain can also cause problems with insects.

> **Ethan:** How does temperature affect farming?

> **Mr. Siebert:** A late spring frost can damage the plants before they have a chance to grow.

> **Ethan:** What problems are caused by a heat wave?

> **Mr. Siebert:** During a heat wave, there usually is not much rain.

Notice that the interviewer asks questions that require more than *yes* or *no* answers. These are open-ended questions.

YOUR TURN

WORK WITH A PARTNER With a partner, plan an interview. Take turns playing the roles of people with jobs that depend on the weather. Write or talk about your answers to these questions.

1. What do you want to learn from the interview?
2. What are some open-ended questions you can ask that require more than *yes* or *no* answers?
3. Will you take notes, use a tape recorder, or both?

Possessive Pronouns

A possessive pronoun shows ownership.

It replaces a possessive noun. There are two kinds of possessive pronouns. One kind is used before a noun. The other kind stands alone.

Possessive Pronouns with Nouns	Possessive Pronouns That Stand Alone
my	mine
your	yours
his, her, its	his, hers
our	ours
their	theirs

Examples:

The sun's gravity is very strong. Its gravity is very strong.

This telescope belongs to Dr. Ortega and his helpers. This telescope is **theirs**.

Vocabulary Power

as•tron•o•mer
[ə•stron′ə•mər] *n.* A person who studies stars, planets, and other heavenly bodies.

Guided Practice

A. Read each sentence. Identify the possessive pronoun.

Example: Their telescope is used every night.
Their

1. Mrs. Green ordered a telescope for her class.
2. "This telescope is ours," Mrs. Green said.
3. Her hobby is studying the solar system.
4. "Your report on comets is due next week," Mrs. Green said.
5. "That library book about comets is mine," Stan said.

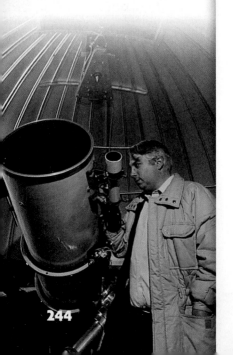

Independent Practice

B. Write each sentence, and underline the possessive pronoun. Draw an arrow from the pronoun to the noun that follows it. If the possessive pronoun stands alone, write *stands alone*.

Examples: *Stan read about the sun and learned that its diameter is 864,000 miles.*

I thought yours was the best report.
stands alone

6. Ken and Manuel used their notes to study.
7. Ken said, "Our sun produces energy."
8. "Its core is around 27,000,000 degrees!" Manuel said.
9. "Which model of the sun is yours?" Denise asked.
10. "This model is mine," Ken said.
11. "Your notes state that the layers of the sun rotate at different speeds," Ken said.
12. Ken studied the photo of the solar eclipse in his book.
13. "Last year my father saw an eclipse," Ken said.
14. The poster showing the layers of the sun is his.
15. Mine is a poster showing a partial eclipse.

Remember that a possessive pronoun shows ownership. It takes the place of a possessive noun.

Writing Connection

Science The lights of a city can prevent people from seeing some kinds of stars at night. Write three sentences describing your view of the night sky. Use at least three different possessive pronouns as you describe what you see.

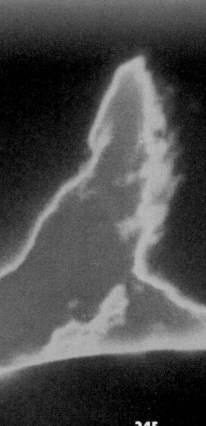

Contractions with Pronouns

Subject pronouns are often used with forms of helping verbs to make contractions.

Do not confuse a possessive pronoun such as *its* with a contraction such as *it's*.

Examples:

They are watching the space shuttle take off. **They're** watching the space shuttle take off.

I would like to watch it, too. **I'd** like to watch it, too.

Some Contractions with Pronouns		
Pronoun	**Helping Verb**	**Contraction**
I	have	I've
you	will	you'll
he	would	he'd
she	is	she's
it	would	it'd
we	have	we've
they	are	they're

Guided Practice

A. **Read each sentence. Replace the underlined words with one contraction.**

Example: <u>It is</u> exciting to see films about outer space.
It's

1. <u>We are</u> studying about flights to outer space.
2. <u>I am</u> writing a report about Neil Armstrong.
3. <u>He is</u> a famous astronaut.
4. Today <u>I will</u> see a film about Mars.
5. Then <u>we will</u> talk about the film in class.

Independent Practice

B. Write each sentence. Replace the underlined words with one contraction.

Example: <u>You will</u> learn about gravity.
You'll learn about gravity.

6. Mr. Dean says <u>it is</u> certain that the former Soviet Union and the United States had competing space programs.

7. <u>It is</u> a fact that the first launch of a liquid fuel rocket took place in 1926.

8. <u>I will</u> always remember that an American named Robert Goddard invented the rocket.

9. As for people in Russia, <u>they are</u> proud that the first satellite to orbit Earth was *Sputnik I*.

10. Paul says <u>he has</u> read about *Sputnik I*.

C. Write the two words that make up the contraction in each sentence.

11. We're learning about the space station called *Mir*.

12. Marcel says he's going to be an astronomer.

13. Kim says, "I'm going to study space, too."

14. Students say that they're surprised that no astronaut has been to Mars yet.

15. Maybe we'll be the first to walk on Mars.

Writing Connection

Writer's Journal: Story Beginning Suppose you have been chosen to go on a space mission. You will live aboard a spaceship for six days. Write a short paragraph describing your first hour on a spaceship. As you write about what you see and feel, use at least three contractions with pronouns.

Remember

that **contractions** with pronouns often contain a pronoun and a form of a helping verb.

Some Homophones	
its	it's
your	you're
their	they're
	there

USAGE AND MECHANICS

Homophones

Homophones, such as *its* and *it's*, sound the same but have different spellings and different meanings. Here are some tips for using the correct homophone in your writing.

- Think about the meaning of the word.
- Think about how the word is used in the sentence.

Examples:

Incorrect: Its my turn to look through the telescope.

Correct: It's my turn to look through the telescope.

Incorrect: Your going to take notes about what I see.

Correct: You're going to take notes about what I see.

Incorrect: Their are billions of stars in the sky.

Correct: There are billions of stars in the sky.

Guided Practice

A. Read each sentence. Study the homophones in parentheses. Decide which word belongs in the sentence.

Example: (Your, You're) going to study the moon. *You're*

1. "Tomorrow (you're, your) going to talk with Lin, an astronomer," Mr. Hall said.
2. "(They're, There) are science books that can help you to get ready," Mr. Hall said.
3. Denise asked Lin, "What is (your, you're) favorite part about being an astronomer?"
4. "(It's, Its) fun to look at the moon," Lin said.
5. "(Your, You're) work sounds interesting," Denise said.

Independent Practice

B. Read each sentence. Write the sentence, using the correct word from the parentheses.

Example: The asteroid belt moves on (it's, its) path.
The asteroid belt moves on its path.

6. When planets ran into each other, (their, they're) pieces may have become asteroids.
7. (It's, Its) still not proven.
8. (There, They're) are three kinds of asteroids.
9. (Your, You're) science book may tell about an asteroid that came near Earth in 1989.
10. (Its, It's) a good thing that it came no closer!

C. Write each sentence below correctly, using a word from the box. Use capital letters as necessary.

its	it's	your	you're
their	they're	there	

Example: The asteroid is huge, but _____ not a planet.
The asteroid is huge, but it's not a planet.

11. In space _____ is solar wind.
12. _____ speed is about 1,116 feet per second.
13. Solar wind is harmful to _____ health.
14. Cosmic rays are in space, and _____ energy is harmful, too.
15. _____ important to protect astronauts.

Writing Connection

Writer's Craft: Clear Pronouns Suppose that you are one of a group of six space scientists. You have just landed on Mars. Tell about the ways each scientist reacts. Use at least three of the following words: *its, it's, your, you're, their, they're,* and *there.*

Remember that homophones, like *its* and *it's,* sound the same but have different spellings and different meanings.

Remember

that possessive
pronouns show
ownership. Subject
pronouns are
often used
with forms of
helping verbs in
contractions.
Homophones, such
as *its* and *it's*,
sound the same
but have different
spellings and dif-
ferent meanings.

Extra Practice

**A. Write each sentence, and underline the posses-
sive pronoun. If the possessive pronoun is used
before a noun, circle the noun. If the possessive pronoun is not used before a noun, write
stands alone.** *pages 244–245*

Example: My book from the library is about Mercury.
My book from the library is about Mercury.

1. Your notes state that Mercury is covered with craters.
2. The closest planet to the sun is Mercury, and its surface is rocky.
3. Our planet has a moon, but Mercury does not.
4. *Mariner 10* was a space probe, just like our *Viking 1*.
5. From 1974 to 1975, *Mariner 10* flew by Mercury, and its mission was a success.
6. Photographs show that Mercury's poles may be covered in ice, as ours are.
7. That chart of yours explains that Mercury makes one rotation in about 59 days.
8. My book shows that Venus is the second planet from the sun.
9. Her picture of Venus shows it covered with clouds.
10. Venus is very hot, and its atmosphere is poison- ous to humans.
11. Those notes of yours explain that Venus has volcanoes.
12. Her plan is to read more about Venus in an encyclopedia.
13. Mine is to interview an astronomer.
14. That chart of Venus's rotations is his.
15. Astronomers watch Venus three hours before sunrise through their telescopes.

For more activities
with possessive
pronouns, visit
The Learning Site:
www.harcourtschool.com

B. **Write each sentence, replacing the underlined words with a contraction.** *pages 246–247*

16. <u>We have</u> learned that Mars has two moons.
17. <u>I will</u> learn more about Mars today.
18. Mars is next to Earth, and <u>it is</u> the fourth planet from the sun.
19. <u>You will</u> see in the chart that Mars is about 142 million miles from the sun.
20. <u>I am</u> interested in Mars because it has volcanoes.

C. **Write each sentence, making corrections where they are needed. If the sentence is correct, write** *correct.* *pages 248–249*

Example: Their looking at pictures of planets.
They're looking at pictures of planets.

21. Your supposed to be with the group that is studying Saturn.
22. There studying Saturn at that table.
23. Bring your book about Saturn to class tomorrow.
24. Saturn is pretty because its surrounded by colorful rings.
25. Saturn is made of gas, and it's rings are made of ice and tiny rocks.

DID YOU KNOW?
Scientists believe that black holes are places in space where gravity is so strong that light cannot escape.

Writing Connection

Art Work with a partner. Suppose that you and your partner have discovered a new star and must choose a name for it. Design a poster with a picture of the star. Use possessive pronouns and contractions with pronouns to describe its unusual qualities.

Chapter Review

Read the passage. Choose the best way to write each sentence, and mark the letter for your answer. If the sentence needs no change, mark the choice _No mistake_.

STANDARDIZED
TEST PREP

> (1) Me interest is stars. (2) A star begins its life as gases and dust. (3) When a star is young, its called a protostar. (4) Then stars can produce they're energy. (5) Theyll cool when they lose hydrogen. (6) They collapse when there cool.

TIP First, answer the test questions that you know. Then go back to answer the questions that you need to think about.

1 A My interest is stars.
 B Mine interest is stars.
 C I'm interest is stars.
 D No mistake

2 F A star begins it's life as gases and dust.
 G A star begins it life as gases and dust.
 H A star begins it is life as gases and dust.
 J No mistake

3 A When a star is young, its's called a protostar.
 B When a star is young, it called a protostar.
 C When a star is young, it's called a protostar.
 D No mistake

4 F Then stars can produce they energy.
 G Then stars can produce their energy.
 H Then stars can produce there energy.
 J No mistake

5 A Them'll cool when they lose hydrogen.
 B They're cool when they lose hydrogen.
 C They'll cool when they lose hydrogen.
 D No mistake

6 F They collapse when their cool.
 G They're collapse when they cool.
 H They collapse when they're cool.
 J No mistake

For additional test preparation, visit _The Learning Site:_
www.harcourtschool.com

Using a Library's Electronic Resources

Libraries now have electronic resources, such as databases, the Internet, or CD-ROMs. CD-ROMs and many informational Websites on the Internet contain the following:

- Table of contents
- Main text
- Spoken words or music
- Illustrations and photographs
- Highlighted or underlined words that take you to other sections

- Help and Search buttons
- Home button, which takes you back to the beginning
- Quit button, which stops the program

If you have a topic to research, you use the Search button and type in a keyword. If there is no Search button, look in the table of contents for the topic.

As you read the computer screen, you may want to save some information for later use. You can jot down your notes in a notebook or on index cards.

YOUR TURN

EXPLORE OUTER SPACE Work with a partner to plan and conduct research on a topic related to outer space. Use an electronic resource such as an informational CD-ROM, and take notes about the information you find. Write a paragraph based on your notes. When you have finished your paragraph, share it with the rest of the class.

TIP Most websites and CD-ROMs contain a Help button that you can use if you are confused.

Writer's Craft

Elaboration

When you write to inform, you might tell how two things or ideas are different. Noting differences between things is called **contrasting**.

Read the following passage. Notice how the writer contrasts different types of animals.

LITERATURE MODEL

Creatures of the night depend on sharpened senses to survive where there is little or no light. Most night animals, such as mice, can see much better than you can in very dim light. Extra-sensitive whiskers help guide a mouse as it feels its way through the dark. High up in a tree, an owl hearing the faintest squeak can tell the mouse's exact location. From another direction, a skunk eating an earthworm picks up the scent of mouse and follows its nose toward more dinner. Just as the owl takes to the air, the mouse, startled by a moth, scurries to safety. It was unaware of the real danger—the owl and the skunk.

—from *One Small Square Backyard*
by Donald M. Silver

Analyze THE *Model*

I. How does the writer contrast creatures with humans?

2. What details does the writer give?

3. How do strong words like *extra-sensitive* and *faintest* help you understand the information?

Using Elaboration

Elaboration means using powerful words and adding reasons and details to explain your ideas. Study the chart on the next page.

Vocabulary Power

ex•tra–sen•si•tive
[ek'strə-sen'sə•tiv] *adj*.
Especially capable of
feeling or reacting
quickly or easily.

Elaboration Strategies	How to Use Strategies	Examples
Use powerful words.	• Use strong words to make your explanation more effective.	• **High** up in a tree, an owl hearing the **faintest** squeak can tell the mouse's **exact** location.
Include reasons and details.	• Support your ideas with facts.	• The details, which tell how different animals use their sharpened senses, support the idea that the animals depend on their senses to survive.

YOUR TURN

ANALYZE REASONS AND DETAILS Work with two or three classmates. Look through your science textbook to find several examples of statements that are supported by reasons and details. Discuss each example with your group.

Answer these questions:

1. What main idea or statement is the writer supporting?

2. What reasons and details does the writer offer to explain the idea?

3. How do the reasons and details help you understand the main idea?

4. What powerful words does the writer use to emphasize the reasons and details?

Powerful Words

A. **Find five examples of powerful words in the following paragraph. Write the words on your paper, and explain why you think each of them is powerful.**

Hurricanes are violent windstorms that can cause widespread damage. A hurricane forms when a low-pressure center develops and winds begin swirling around it. The winds are at their maximum strength nearest the center, which is also called the eye of the storm. Gale-force winds often spread out for 300 miles or more around the eye. The most ferocious hurricanes have winds that can exceed 155 miles per hour.

B. **Read the paragraph. Choose a powerful word from the box to fill in each blank. Write the completed paragraph on your paper.**

detect	sharp	minute	keen	fierce

Most sharks have _____ senses and rows of _____ teeth that allow them to hunt and feed on nearly every kind of large animal in the sea. Their sense of smell is particularly good. Sharks can _____ even the most _____ hint of a wounded animal in the water. Despite their _____ reputation, however, shark attacks on humans are relatively rare.

Reasons and Details

C. Read the statement and then read the reasons and details. Choose the reasons and details that support the statement. Then, write the statement and supporting reasons and details on your paper in paragraph form.

Statement: Sir Isaac Newton, born in the 17th century, was one of the greatest scientists of all time.

Reasons and Details: Newton studied motion and developed the three laws that explain it.

Albert Einstein was one of the best-known scientists of the 20th century.

From the laws of motion, Newton drew conclusions that led him to discoveries about gravitation, or gravity.

Newton left college for two years because he was afraid of catching the plague.

Modern scientific methods, including a reliance on planned experiments, first appeared in the 17th century.

Many of Newton's writings deal with religion and other interests not connected to his work in science.

A great deal of scientific progress since Newton's time has been based on his discoveries and ideas.

Writing and Thinking

Writer's Journal

Write to Record Reflections Some words are powerful because people have strong reactions to them. For example, people tend to have positive feelings about words like *liberty* and *freedom*. What words create strong feelings in you? Write your reflections in your Writer's Journal.

Paragraph That Contrasts

Donald M. Silver, the author of *One Small Square
Backyard*, contrasted the excellent night vision of mice
with the poorer night vision of humans. Nikki knows
that mice are rodents. Gerbils and guinea pigs are
rodents, too. Read the paragraph Nikki wrote contrasting gerbils and guinea pigs. Notice how she uses elaboration in her writing.

MODEL

main idea	Guinea pigs and gerbils are both rodents,
powerful words	but they are different in many ways. A
reasons/ details	guinea pig is a small, stout animal with little
	round ears and no tail. Gerbils are generally
contrast	smaller and have long tails. There are
reasons/ details	many different colors of guinea pigs, includ-
powerful words	ing solid white, black, tan, or light colors with
contrast	streaks or blotches of darker colors. Gerbils, on
	the other hand, have light tan fur. Guinea
contrast	pigs originally came from South America,
reasons/ details	while gerbils are native to western Asia and
	Africa.

Analyze THE Model

1. What contrasts does Nikki make in this paragraph?

2. What reasons and details does she give to explain
   the contrasts?

3. What powerful words does Nikki use, and how do
   they emphasize her reasons and details?

WRITING PROMPT Choose two animals, plants, or other objects. Write a paragraph that contrasts the two items you have chosen. Elaborate by giving reasons and details and by using powerful words. You may want to use a reference source for additional information.

STUDY THE PROMPT Ask yourself these questions:

1. What is your subject?

2. What is your purpose for writing?

3. Who is your audience?

4. What writing form will you use?

USING YOUR
Handbook

- Use the Writer's Thesaurus to find powerful words to use in your paragraph that contrasts.

Prewriting and Drafting

Plan Your Paragraph After you have decided on the items you want to contrast, list ways in which they are different from each other. Then use a chart like this one to organize your information.

Begin the paragraph with a sentence that names the items you are contrasting.

⬇

Give a reason or detail that supports or explains the contrast.

⬇

Give additional reasons and details to support or explain the contrast.

Editing

Read over your paragraph that contrasts. Can you revise your paragraph to make it more informative? Use this checklist to help you revise your work:

- ☑ Will your reader understand how the two items are different from each other?
- ☑ Can you add reasons and details to explain or support the contrast?
- ☑ Are there details you should omit because they do not relate directly to your topic?
- ☑ Can you add powerful words to emphasize the differences?

Use this checklist as you proofread your paragraph:

- ☑ I have used pronouns and pronoun antecedents correctly.
- ☑ I have used possessive pronouns correctly.
- ☑ I have used apostrophes correctly in contractions.
- ☑ I have used the words *their, they're, there, your, you're, its,* and *it's* correctly.
- ☑ I have used a dictionary to check my spelling.

Editor's Marks

✄	delete text
∧	insert text
↻	move text
¶	new paragraph
≡	capitalize
/	lowercase
◯	correct spelling

Sharing and Reflecting

Writer's Journal

Make a final copy of your paragraph that contrasts, and share it with a partner. Tell what you like best about your partner's paragraph. Point out reasons and details that help you understand the contrasts in the paragraph. Discuss how to use elaboration to improve your writing. Write your reflections in your Writer's Journal.

Words That Signal Contrast

Speakers and writers often use signal words or phrases that tell you they are contrasting something. Can you can pick out signal words and phrases in the conversation among this group of friends?

My soup is hot, but my milk is cold.

Tomato soup is smooth, while vegetable soup has vegetables in it.

The meat in this sandwich tastes good. On the other hand, the bread is too dry.

Unlike desserts that are full of sugar, an apple is good for you.

YOUR TURN

Work in a small group to find examples of words or phrases that signal contrasts in your classroom. Here are some places you might look:

- library books
- magazine articles
- newspapers
- textbooks
- messages and notices

Keep a list of the words and phrases you find. Then compare your list with those of other groups. Challenge classmates to create original sentences using signal words from the lists.

Adjectives

An **adjective** is a word that describes, or modifies, a noun or pronoun.

Adjectives can tell what kind, how many, or which one. An adjective can come before the noun it modifies, or it can follow a linking verb, such as *is*, *seems*, *appears*, or *feels*. More than one adjective can describe the same noun.

> **Examples:**
> **What Kind:** I drew a **large green** plant.
> **How Many:** **All** plants must adapt to their locations.
> **Which One:** **This** plant needs water.

An adjective formed from a proper noun is called a proper adjective. Proper adjectives are always capitalized.

> **Example:** Leaves fall off **Japanese** maples.

The adjectives *a*, *an*, and *the* are called articles. *The* refers to a specific person, place, or thing. *A* and *an* refer to any person, place, or thing. Use *a* before a consonant sound and *an* before a vowel sound.

> **Example:** **The** botanist used **a** plant in **an** experiment.

Guided Practice

A. Identify the adjectives, including proper adjectives and articles. Draw an arrow from each adjective to the noun or pronoun it describes.

Example: *Many plants are large.*

1. Some plants are bushy.
2. The cactus survives on little water.
3. The national flower of this country is the rose.
4. Some states have different official flowers.
5. The stems of these plants support thick leaves.

Independent Practice

B. Write the adjectives in each sentence, including articles and proper adjectives. Write the noun or pronoun each adjective describes.

Example: The stems of some ivies are climbers.
The (stems); some (ivies)

6. The stem of a tree is the thick trunk.
7. Hairy roots absorb water.
8. Most fruits grow on trees.
9. Sweet blossoms bloom this spring.
10. Oriental cherries are showy.
11. These trees come in many different sizes.
12. Botanists found special plants in Asian forests.
13. These plants also grow in Australia.
14. *Rose* is a common name for one family of plants.
15. Most roses need warm weather.
16. Roses come in many beautiful colors.
17. Long-stemmed roses are very popular.
18. A hard coating protects seeds.
19. One seed can create a new plant.
20. The redwood is a giant tree.
21. These three seeds are small.
22. The huge redwood was named for Sequoia, the inventor of the Cherokee alphabet.
23. A giant sequoia is ancient.
24. The bark of this tree is spongy.
25. It is a grand evergreen tree.

Writing Connection

Science Think of three plants grown for food. What do they look like? How do they taste? Write two sentences about each plant. Include an article, an adjective, or a proper adjective in each sentence. Circle each one, and draw an arrow to the noun or pronoun it modifies.

Adverbs

An adverb is a word that describes, or modifies, a verb.

You already know that a verb is a word that describes action or being. An adverb may tell *where*, *when*, or *how*. Adverbs that tell *how* often end with *ly*. Notice that an adverb is not always right next to the verb it modifies.

Examples:

Where: A giant sequoia tree <u>grows</u> **nearby**.

When: We <u>learned</u> about giant sequoia trees **yesterday**.

How: A sequoia tree <u>grows</u> **slowly**.

Guided Practice

A. Identify the adverb in each sentence. Tell what verb each adverb modifies.

Example: Builders commonly use wood from oak and pine trees.
commonly, use

1. Sugar maples often live for many years.
2. Our family hikes weekly in the woods.
3. We saw wonderful maple trees yesterday.
4. Their leaves change beautifully in autumn.
5. Softwood is frequently used as lumber.
6. Many people greatly enjoy plants.
7. Some people tend their plants carefully.
8. Tropical plants grow poorly in cool climates.
9. Cold weather can easily kill these plants.
10. Tropical plants really need warm weather.

Independent Practice

B. **Write the adverb in each sentence. Then write the verb it modifies.**

> **Example:** Rain frequently falls on the trees in my yard.
> *frequently, falls*

11. A good water supply greatly helps tree growth.

12. Most trees grow easily with water.

13. Tree roots actively drink water under the ground.

14. Some tree roots reach deeply under the ground.

15. The environment often affects a tree's health.

16. Some scientists study trees carefully.

17. A tree grows rings yearly.

18. You can usually tell a tree's age by its rings.

19. The trees in the park bloom early.

20. They have aged gracefully.

C. **Write each sentence. Underline the adverb. Then write whether the adverb tells *where*, *when*, or *how*.**

> **Example:** Some plants grow <u>indoors</u>. *where*

21. Some plants grow quickly in sunlight.

22. African violets grow nicely in indirect light.

23. I keep my cactus inside.

24. I bought plant food yesterday.

25. I keep an aloe plant nearby.

Remember
that an adverb modifies a verb and tells *where*, *when*, or *how*. Adverbs that tell *how* often end with *ly*.

Writing Connection

Science Think about some different kinds of animals you might see in a tree. Using vivid adverbs, write four sentences that describe these animals and what they might be doing. Then, trade papers with a partner and underline the adverbs in each other's sentences.

USAGE AND MECHANICS
Adjective or Adverb?

Be sure to use an adjective to modify a noun and an adverb to modify a verb.

Certain adjectives and adverbs are commonly confused. *Good* and *bad* are always adjectives. *Well* is an adverb, except when it means "in good health." *Badly* is always an adverb.

Examples:

adjective
The cherries looked **good**.

adverb
The cherries grew **well** last season.

adjective–health
The patient is not **well**.

adverb   adjective
I wanted **badly** to go out, but the weather was **bad**.

Guided Practice

A. Identify the adjectives and adverbs in each sentence.

Example: I went on an enjoyable trip yesterday.
an, enjoyable (adjectives); yesterday (adverb)

1. We always go to see the colorful cherry trees in Washington, D.C.
2. We strolled slowly among the beautiful trees.
3. The fruit looked good to eat.
4. Japan generously gave them to the American people.
5. The trees sway gently in the cool breeze.

Independent Practice

B. Choose the word in parentheses that correctly completes each sentence.

Example: Many plants grow (good, well) indoors.
well

6. Home gardeners plant their flowers in (good, well) soil.
7. Cold temperatures are (bad, badly) for many house plants.
8. Frost can damage plants (bad, badly).
9. African violets bloom (good, well) in small flowerpots.
10. Fresh air is (good, well) for plants.

C. Rewrite each sentence, adding the adjective and the adverb in parentheses.

Example: Mr. Lorca cares for his plants during the winter months. (cold) (patiently)
Mr. Lorca patiently cares for his plants during the cold winter months.

11. He builds frames for his plants. (special) (often)
12. These frames have a glass top. (clear) (always)
13. The frames hold the sun's warmth. (wooden) (usually)
14. During the months, Mr. Lorca plants seeds in the frames. (cold) (carefully)
15. The seedlings rise. (little) (upward)

> ### Remember
> that **adjectives** describe nouns and **adverbs** modify verbs.

Writing Connection

Writer's Craft: Vivid Adjectives and Adverbs Write three sentences about your favorite plant, using vivid adjectives and adverbs. Trade sentences with a partner, and circle all the adjectives and adverbs. Proofread to make sure they are used correctly.

Extra Practice

A. Write the adjectives in each sentence. Include articles and proper adjectives. *pages 262–263*

Example: African violets can have pink, white, or purple flowers.

African, pink, white, purple

1. Violets have thin stems and five petals.
2. Many carpenters use hard wood for building fine furniture.
3. In autumn, the leaves of many trees change colors.
4. An English daisy grows to about six inches.
5. The white flowers have yellow centers.
6. A rhododendron is an evergreen tree or shrub.
7. *Rhododendron* is a Greek word meaning "red tree."
8. These plants have pretty flowers in different colors.
9. The flowers can be red, white, and rose.
10. These lilacs are a lovely shade of purple.

B. Write the adverb in each sentence. Then write the word that the adverb modifies. *pages 264–265*

Example: I recently learned a valuable lesson about grass.

recently, learned

11. Gardeners sometimes use grass to make a field pretty.
12. It often saves loose topsoil from wear.
13. Grass survives well in wet swamps and dry deserts.
14. Grass can actually grow short or tall.
15. I was certainly surprised to learn that rice is a type of grass.

Remember

that **adjectives** describe, or modify, nouns and that **adverbs** describe, or modify, verbs.

DID YOU KNOW?
Some plants are heroes. A plant that is attacked by insects can warn other plants of the danger. The wounded plant gives off a special gas.

For more activities with adjectives and adverbs, visit *The Learning Site:*

www.harcourtschool.com

C. Write each sentence. Tell whether the underlined word is an adjective or adverb. Circle the word that the adjective or adverb modifies. *pages 262–267*

Example: I learned a lot from a <u>local</u> gardener.
I learned a lot from a local (gardener.) *adjective*

16. She taught me about <u>harmful</u> weeds.
17. Weeds damage a garden <u>badly</u>.
18. I remove weeds <u>completely</u> now.
19. Weed removal is <u>important</u> for a garden's health.
20. The gardener showed me some <u>handy</u> tricks.
21. Some of her tricks work <u>well</u>.
22. I sprinkled some straw on the soil <u>yesterday</u>.
23. Straw <u>often</u> stops weeds completely.
24. Straw does not look <u>bad</u> on the ground.
25. The gardener gave me <u>good</u> advice.

D. Write each sentence. Correct the errors.
pages 266–267

Example: I found a well place to plant begonias.
I found a good place to plant begonias.

26. These flowers grow good in this soil.
27. They grew quick in indirect light.
28. The cherries on these trees are wonderfully.
29. My garden is in a well location.
30. The flowers are safely from the wind.

Writing Connection

Writer's Journal

Real-Life Writing: Captions Browse through a magazine about gardening. Cut out pictures of several kinds of plants that you think are beautiful, and paste them onto a piece of drawing paper. Use adjectives and adverbs to write captions describing the beauty of the plants. Put all of the pictures together to make a classroom collage.

STANDARDIZED
TEST PREP

TIP Check twice to make sure you have marked the correct answer.

Chapter Review

Each of the following numbered items is a complete sentence. Read each sentence. If you see a mistake, mark the letter of the line with the mistake. If the whole sentence is correct, choose *No mistakes*.

1 A A lilac's rich colors
   B make a splendidly addition
   C to any backyard.
   D No mistakes

2 J Lilac bushes
   K usually require
   L little attention.
   M No mistakes

3 A Many kinds of lilacs
   B grow really good
   C in northern climates.
   D No mistakes

4 J Common South-eastern european
   K lilacs grow about
   L twenty feet tall.
   M No mistakes

5 A An lilac has
   B purple, white, or
   C red flowers.
   D No mistakes

6 J Some gardeners
   K usual pot their lilacs
   L indoors in the spring.
   M No mistakes

7 A They put the
   B lovely plants
   C outdoors in warm weather.
   D No mistakes

8 J Lilacs' cheerful colors
   K real brighten
   L many gardens.
   M No mistakes

9 A Nothing is
   B more wonderfully than
   C a garden with lilacs.
   D No mistakes

10 J Many people say that
    K lilacs smell
    L as well as they look.
    M No mistakes

For additional test preparation, visit *The Learning Site:*
www.harcourtschool.com

Using Context and Structural Clues

VOCABULARY

When you read, you can often figure out the meanings of unknown words by using **context clues** and **structural clues**.

Using a **context clue** means looking at how a word is used in a sentence. You probably know *bark* means either (1) the outer covering of a tree or (2) the short, gruff sound made by a dog. Those two meanings do not make sense in these sentences:

> He saw the *bark* come into the bay. The bark had a large rip in its sail. The sailors looked happy to see land.

How is the word *bark* being used? The words *bay*, *sail*, and *sailor* are context clues. From these context clues, you know that *bark* has another meaning. In this context, *bark* means "a type of sailing ship."

Using **structural clues** means looking at the different word parts, or structures, such as the base word, the word's **prefix**, or its **suffix**.

Prefix	Base Word	Suffix
dis (not)	trust	ful (full of)

Using structural clues helps you figure out that *distrustful* means *not full of trust*.

YOUR TURN

Work with a partner to use context clues and structural clues to figure out the meanings of the underlined words. After you have finished, explain how you used the context clues and structural clues.

1. The cowboy drove the cattle across miles of open <u>range</u>.

2. The strong, old oak tree was <u>unshakable</u> in the storm.

3. The gardener <u>prunes</u> the dead branch off the tree.

Other Kinds of Adverbs

Adverbs sometimes modify adjectives and other adverbs.

You already know that an adverb describes, or modifies, a verb. An adverb can also modify an adjective or another adverb.

Examples:

adverb adjective

A **really bad** storm was approaching.

Really modifies the adjective *bad.*

adverb adverb

Temperatures dropped **very quickly**.

Very modifies the adverb *quickly.*

Vocabulary Power

e•ro•sion [i•rō′zhən]
n. The wearing away
of soil or rock by
water or wind.

Guided Practice

A. Tell what word each underlined adverb modifies. Then tell if that word is an adjective or another adverb.

Examples: The wind was <u>quite</u> strong.
modifies strong, *adjective*

The weather changed <u>quite</u> suddenly.
modifies suddenly, *adverb*

1. Wind plays a <u>very</u> big part in soil erosion.
2. Strong winds pick up <u>fairly</u> loose soil from the ground.
3. Winds can wear away rock <u>very</u> slowly.
4. <u>Swiftly</u> blowing sand can wear away rock.
5. Wind carries sand easily because sand is <u>so</u> light.

Independent Practice

B. Write the word that each underlined adverb modifies. Then write whether that word is an adjective or another adverb.

Example: These <u>highly</u> unusual forms were eroded.
unusual, adjective

6. The Grand Canyon formed <u>very</u> slowly.
7. The Colorado River has cut <u>quite</u> deeply into the canyon.
8. <u>Swiftly</u> running water wore through the rocks.
9. Wind, too, eroded rocks to form the <u>unusually</u> beautiful Grand Canyon.
10. Many visitors hike <u>very</u> bravely to the bottom of the Grand Canyon.
11. The hiking trail is <u>extremely</u> narrow.
12. The trail drops <u>quite</u> steeply.
13. Rocks along the trail are <u>richly</u> striped.
14. Erosion has polished these <u>brightly</u> colored rocks.
15. Some hikers seem <u>too</u> tired to climb back to the top.

Writing Connection

Science Think about some things you use every day (a telephone, a car or bus, an electric light). How do these things help you? How are they important in your life? Write a short sentence that explains what one of these things does. Make your sentences especially clear by using adverbs to modify adjectives and other adverbs.

Comparing with Adjectives and Adverbs

Adjectives can be used to compare two or more people, places, or things.

Examples:

The water is **colder** than the glass. *(Add er to short adjectives when comparing two things.)*

The ice is the **coldest** of all. *(Add est to short adjectives when comparing two or more things.)*

Adverbs can be used to compare two or more actions.

Examples:

Chris walks more **slowly** than Avi. *(Use more and most with some adjectives or adverbs that compare.)*

Beth sang **loudest** of all.

Guided Practice

A. Read each sentence. Tell if the underlined adjective or adverb is comparing two things or actions or more than two.

Example: This river flows <u>faster</u> than that one.
two actions

1. The <u>loudest</u> waves are down by the cliffs.
2. Waves are <u>bigger</u> during storms.
3. Beach cliffs may erode <u>faster</u> than other cliffs.
4. Erosion happens <u>fastest</u> when waves crash against cliffs.
5. Even the <u>calmest</u> seas can cause beach erosion.

Independent Practice

B. Write the sentence, using the correct form of the adjective or adverb in parentheses.

Examples: This stream flows _____ in the fall than in the spring. (gently)
This stream flows more gently in the fall than in the spring.

Floods uproot _____ trees than rains do. (big)
Floods uproot bigger trees than rains do.

6. Rivers are _____ than streams. (large)

7. When it rains, rivers move _____ than usual. (quickly)

8. The upper part of a river moves _____ than the lower part. (fast)

9. Gentle rivers move boats _____ than fast rivers do. (slowly)

10. It's _____ to swim downriver than upriver. (easy)

11. Some rivers are _____ than others. (deep)

12. Matter at a river bottom is _____ than usual during floods. (heavy)

13. In a storm, rivers run _____ than usual. (rapidly)

14. Riverbanks change the _____ when water carries away soil. (more)

15. Flooded rivers can wash away _____ amounts of soil than they leave. (great)

Remember

that an adjective or adverb that compares may end in *er* or *est*. Use *more* or *most* for adjectives and adverbs that have more than two syllables. Never use both *er* and *more* together or *est* and *most* together.

Writing Connection

Writer's Journal: Writing Idea Think about how you have changed since you started going to school. In your Writer's Journal, write three sentences telling how you do things differently now that you are older. Use adjectives and adverbs that compare to help you describe yourself and your actions.

Adjectives	Adverbs
good	well
bad	badly

Comparing Two Things	
better	better
worse	worse

Comparing More Than Two	
best	best
worst	worst

USAGE AND MECHANICS

Special Forms

Some adjectives and adverbs have special forms
for comparing.

Examples:
Adjectives That Compare

The rain yesterday was **good** for the crops.

More moisture would have been **better** for the corn.

A light, steady drizzle would have been **best** of all.

Adverbs That Compare

The garden grew **well** last fall.

It grows **better** in the spring.

It will grow **best** in the summer.

Guided Practice

**A. Identify the correct form of the adjective or
adverb in parentheses.**

Example: Erosion damage has been (bad, worse) than
flood damage. *worse*

1. Erosion can ruin the (better, best) farmland.
2. A long drought is one of the (worse, worst)
   things for the land.
3. (Fewer, Fewest) plants grow on prairies than in
   forests.
4. Planting trees and shrubs may be the (better,
   best) way to stop wind erosion.
5. Planting trees works (well, better) to keep city
   air clean.

Independent Practice

B. Write the sentence, using the correct form of the adjective in parentheses.

Remember that some adjectives and adverbs used for comparing have special forms.

6. There are _____ hazy days now than before the parks were built. (few)

7. The shade is _____ here than I remember. (good)

8. You probably get the _____ shade at the beach. (little)

9. You have a _____ chance of getting sunburned at the beach than in the city. (good)

10. Wind from the sea is _____ here than in the city. (bad)

C. Write the sentence, using the correct form of the adverb in parentheses.

11. Temperature changes can _____ erode rock surfaces. (badly)

12. Salt can erode surfaces _____ than other minerals. (badly)

13. Erosion is _____ studied by looking at rock surfaces. (well)

14. Some rocks last _____ than others. (well)

15. These rocks have eroded _____ than others. (little)

Writing Connection

Writer's Craft: Lively Adjectives and Adverbs What changes have you noticed in your community? Write a short letter to a friend describing how something has changed over time. Use lively adverbs and adjectives to make comparisons between the past and now. When you are finished, trade letters with a partner. Proofread to check that your partner has used the correct comparative forms.

Remember

to use the correct
form of an adjec-
tive or adverb
when making
comparisons.

Extra Practice

A. Write the word that each underlined adverb modifies. Tell whether that word is an adjective or an adverb. *pages 272–273*

Example: Geologists work <u>quite</u> hard to identify rock surfaces.

hard, adverb

1. Geologists look for <u>highly</u> interesting rock forms.
2. They may spend <u>fairly</u> long hours studying.
3. Geologists know <u>really</u> good places to study rock surfaces.
4. Geologists also know that some sites are <u>much</u> better than others.
5. Areas with <u>almost</u> no plants are good for studying rocks.
6. Scientists work <u>rather</u> steadily to get information.
7. Sand dunes are <u>very</u> interesting places to study rock forms.
8. Geologists can study rocks formed <u>quite</u> far back in time.
9. Some ideas are not understood <u>too</u> easily.
10. Rocks at the bottom of a canyon are <u>usually</u> older than rocks at the top.
11. Geologists <u>very</u> closely examine the soil in beaches and streams.
12. Sand and gravel are <u>most</u> often found along streams.
13. You may learn <u>rather</u> interesting facts about stream or river bottoms from sand or gravel.
14. You can <u>almost</u> certainly collect sand or gravel in a jar.
15. A baking pan and a magnifying glass are <u>also</u> necessary.

For more help with adjectives and adverbs, visit *The Learning Site:*

www.harcourtschool.com

278

B. Read the sentence. Write the term that compares, and tell whether it is an adjective or an adverb. *pages 274–275*

Example: Put a mixture of clay, sand, and pebbles in your largest jar.
largest, adjective

16. Add the cleanest water you have, tighten the lid, and shake the jar forcefully.
17. Which element settles most quickly?
18. The highest layer will be clay or mud.
19. Pebbles will settle most frequently on the bottom.
20. A real streamed forms more slowly.

C. Write the sentence, using the correct form of the adjective or adverb in parentheses. *pages 276–277*

Example: You can see these things even (good, better) when they are dry.
better

21. The experiment works (good, best) when a teacher heats the materials in an oven.
22. Which pieces are the (darker, darkest)?
23. Are some pieces (less, least) shiny than others?
24. Rocks may come from nearby or (farther, farthest) away.
25. Rocks are (more, most) movable than we thought!

Writing Connection

Technology With a partner, compare a bound volume of an encyclopedia with a similar volume of an electronic encyclopedia. Using comparing adjectives and adverbs, write a few sentences that tell how the two kinds of encyclopedias are similar and different.

CHAPTER 24

Writing Workshop

Advantages
and
Disadvantages
Essay

You know that one reason for writing is to give information. This selection is about two kinds of weather. As you read, think about how the information is organized.

WILD, WET AND WINDY

by Claire Llewellyn

Hurricanes and tornadoes are two of Earth's most powerful storms. In many ways hurricanes and tornadoes are similar, but they also have differences.

STORMY WEATHER: HURRICANES

Hurricanes are among the most dangerous storms on Earth. They can flatten forests, smash houses, and overturn cars. They can even tear the clothes off your back.

They bring towering waves which surge up the shore, wrecking boats and beach huts, flooding shops, cafés, and people's precious homes.

Hurricanes start over warm tropical seas to the north and south of the equator. Hot, steamy air rises quickly from the water, forming thick clouds that start to spin.

283

Day by day the storm grows bigger and more powerful. Within a week, it's hundreds of miles wide. It's a mass of swirling winds, moving slowly but surely toward land.

The hurricane hits the coast with devastating force. On dry land there's no damp sea air to feed it, and hour by hour it slowly blows itself out. It can take as long as 18 hours for a hurricane to pass by completely. As soon as it's all over, everyone goes outside to check the damage. Then it's time to start cleaning up the mess.

In some parts of the world, hurricanes are called cyclones, typhoons, or Willy-Willies. They're all the same sort of storm, and they all spell trouble!

WHIRLING WINDS: TORNADOES

Long and gray like an elephant's trunk, a tornado screams past at more than 35 miles per hour.

It's a giant vacuum cleaner, pulling up everything in its path, including trees, barns, tractors, and animals.

Tornadoes are whirling winds that form when a column of cold air sinks down from a thundercloud while lighter warm air rises up around it. The warm air rises so quickly that it starts to spin, sucking up dirt from the ground and forming a dark whirling funnel that twists its way back to the cloud.

Some tornadoes start over lakes and seas. These whirling winds are called waterspouts, and they suck up soaking wet funnels of spray. Waterspouts spin more gently than tornadoes, but they're still strong enough to pick a boat clean up out of the water.

WATERSPOUT

SIZE AND SPEED OF STORMS

Many tornadoes are only 300 or so feet wide across the base and last for less than an hour. They're much smaller than hurricanes and over much more quickly.

Don't be fooled. The winds in a tornado whiz around at more than 350 miles per hour. They're twice as fast as hurricane winds, and twice as powerful, too!

Analyze THE Model

1. What information does the author present in the sections Stormy Weather and Whirling Winds?

2. How is the last section different from the Stormy Weather and Whirling Winds sections?

3. What are some of the powerful words and phrases that help the reader picture the storms or feel their strength?

READING — WRITING CONNECTION

Parts of an Advantages and Disadvantages Essay

Claire Llewellyn gives information about two kinds of storms. Tamara, a student, thinks that storms have some good points. Look for Tamara's strong thoughts, both good and bad, about thunderstorms.

MODEL

introduction of topic

statement of main idea

disadvantages

advantages

Thunderstorms: Foes or Friends?

Lightning flashes, thunder booms, and people dash for cover. A thunderstorm is soaking the town. Some people talk about thunderstorms as if they only had disadvantages. I disagree. I think that thunderstorms have advantages as well.

It's true that thunderstorms can be really bad news. Some thunderstorms bring so much rain that floods happen. The flood we had here eight years ago damaged people's homes. Lightning strikes branches, causing them to fall and block roads or crush cars. In addition, a strong thunderstorm can cause the power to go out. To me, no power means no fun!

Thunderstorms, however, do some good. They are especially good news for plants. Plants need the rain that thunderstorms bring. Lightning makes the air release nitro-

gen, and rain carries the nitrogen to the ground. Nitrogen makes the soil rich, and plants grow better in rich soil.

The next time you hear a clap of thunder, take shelter. A thunderstorm can be dangerous. Don't let it ruin your day, though. Remember that a thunderstorm is a necessary part of nature. It even can be a friend!

conclusion

restatement of main idea

Analyze THE Model

1. What is the main idea in Tamara's essay?

2. What does she add to show that thunderstorms have disadvantages?

3. How is the conclusion of Tamara's essay similar to the introduction? How is it different?

Summarize THE Model

Write Tamara's main ideas in a chart like the one shown here. Then write a summary of the essay. Include the important points, but leave out the details.

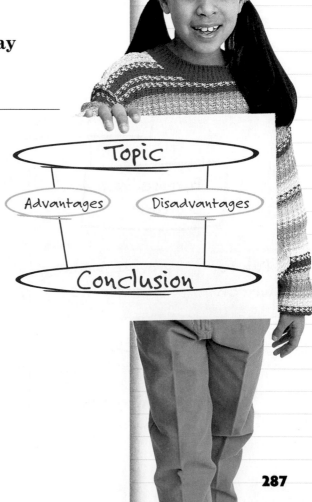

Topic

Advantages   Disadvantages

Conclusion

Writer's Craft

Elaboration Tamara used powerful words to give her reasons and details extra strength. List some of Tamara's powerful words and phrases.

Advantages and Disadvantages Essay

Prewriting

Purpose and Audience

In this chapter, you will give information by writing an essay that explores the good and bad results of a decision that many families make.

WRITING PROMPT Write an advantages and disadvantages essay for your family about getting a pet. Tell about some of the good results of having a pet, and tell about some problems. Let the main idea show which you think are stronger: the advantages or the disadvantages.

Before you begin, think about your audience and purpose. Who will your reader be? What information should your essay give them?

Strategies
Good Writers Use

- Briefly state your purpose for writing.
- Identify the audience for the essay.
- Write a main idea that goes along with the purpose.

MODEL

Tamara began by imagining thunderstorms that she had seen or heard other people describe. She made this web to organize her thoughts.

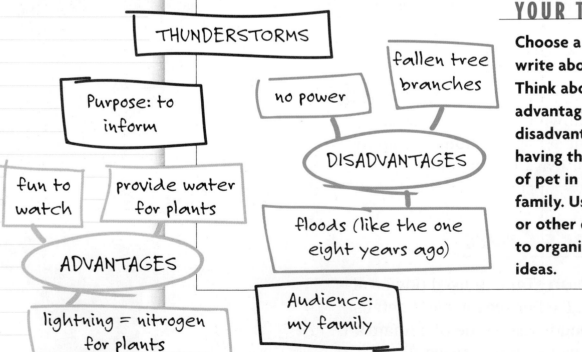

THUNDERSTORMS

Purpose: to inform

no power

fallen tree branches

DISADVANTAGES

fun to watch

provide water for plants

floods (like the one eight years ago)

ADVANTAGES

lightning = nitrogen for plants

Audience: my family

YOUR TURN

Choose a pet to write about. Think about the advantages and disadvantages of having that kind of pet in your family. Use a web or other diagram to organize your ideas.

Drafting

CHAPTER 24

Advantages and Disadvantages Essay

Organization and Elaboration

Follow these steps to draft your essay:

STEP 1 Introduce Your Topic and Main Idea
Introduce your topic in a catchy way.

STEP 2 Organize Your Ideas
Decide which are stronger: the advantages or the disadvantages. Save the strongest argument for last.

STEP 3 Provide Details
State the advantages and disadvantages clearly. Give details for each reason.

STEP 4 Have a Strong Conclusion
Restate your main idea, using different words. Then, let readers know which argument you think is stronger.

MODEL

Here is the beginning of Tamara's essay. How does she make the introduction catchy? Why doesn't she state her main idea in the first sentence?

> Lightning flashes, thunder booms, and people dash for cover. A thunderstorm is soaking the town. Some people talk about thunderstorms as if they only had disadvantages. I disagree. I think that thunderstorms have advantages as well.

YOUR TURN

Use the steps above to draft your essay. Organize your information and look for ideas in your prewriting diagrams and in Tamara's essay.

Strategies Good Writers Use

- Introduce the topic and the main idea in a catchy way.
- Write about the advantages in one paragraph and the disadvantages in another.
- Conclude by reminding the audience of your main idea.

Use a computer to draft your essay. Choose a font that is easy to read.

289

Revising

Organization and Elaboration

Carefully reread your draft. Think about these questions.

- Does the order of my information make sense?
- Have I said enough about the advantages and the disadvantages? Do I need more details?
- Have I used transitions to help my audience follow my thoughts? Some transition words are *first, then, in addition, however,* and *finally.*
- Have I used powerful words to keep my writing lively?
- Is my conclusion strong? How could it be better?

MODEL

Here is part of Tamara's essay. Notice that she has added an example, stronger words, details to support the disadvantages, and a transition.

It's true that thunderstorms can be ^really bad news. Some thunderstorms bring so much rain that floods happen. Lightning strikes branches, causing them to fall and ~~mess up~~ block roads or, ^crush ~~hurt~~ cars. ^In addition, A strong thunderstorm can cause the power to go out. To me, no power means no fun!

The flood we had here eight years ago damaged people's homes.

YOUR TURN

Revise your essay. Add details if they are needed. Add transitions if they will help connect ideas and make them clear. Make sure that your essay is presented in an order that makes sense.

Strategies
Good **W**riters **U**se

- Make sure that your information is in an order that makes sense.
- Add details to make your points stronger and more interesting.
- Use strong and precise words.
- Add transitions to connect ideas.

Print two or more copies of your draft. Make different changes on each copy. Choose the changes that you like best.

Checking Your Language

Good ideas are important for a good essay. A good essay should also have as few mistakes as possible. Make sure that grammar, spelling, and punctuation are correct. Have a classmate double-check your work.

MODEL

After Tamara revised her essay, she proofread it. Here is another part of her essay. Why did Tamara change some of her verbs? Where did she correct spelling errors? What other errors did she fix?

> Thunderstorms however, does some
> (they are) (especially)
> good. (There) (espesally) good news for
> plants. Plants need the rain that
> thunderstorms bring. Lightning makes
> release   carries
> the air (relese) nitrogen, rain (carry) the
>   and.
> nitrogen to the ground. Nitrogen
>   and   better
> makes the soil rich, plants grow weller
> in rich soil.

Strategies Good Writers Use

- Make sure that subject and object pronouns are used correctly.
- Spell all contractions correctly.

YOUR TURN

Proofread your revised essay. You may want to proofread several times:
- **Once to check grammar**
- **Once to check spelling**
- **Once more to check punctuation and capitalization**

Trade essays with a partner, and look for mistakes with object pronouns, possessive pronouns, adjectives, and adverbs.

Editor's Marks

ℛ	delete text
∧	insert text
◊	move text
¶	new paragraph
≡	capitalize
/	lowercase
◯	correct spelling

Advantages and Disadvantages Essay

Publishing

Sharing Your Work

Answer these questions to help you decide how to share your essay.

1. Who is your audience? What method of publishing would interest them the most? For example, should you read your essay aloud to your family?

2. How should the essay look? Will your audience read it? You might write it in cursive or use a computer's word processing program. For more information about word processing programs, see page 293.

3. Would illustrations make your ideas clearer? For example, would a chart of advantages and disadvantages help?

USING YOUR
Handbook

• Use the rubric on page 509 to evaluate your essay.

Reflecting on Your Writing

 Using Your Portfolio What did you learn about your writing in this chapter? Write your answer to each question below.

1. Did your essay meet its purpose? Why or why not?

2. Was it easier to write about advantages or disadvantages? How easy was it to figure out which points were stronger?

3. Using the rubric from your Handbook, what score would you give your essay? Explain your answer.

Add your answers and your essay to your portfolio. Then look over the pieces in your portfolio. Describe yourself as a writer, such as *organized* or *has interesting beginnings*.

Using a Word Processing Program

After Tamara finished her essay, she decided that she wanted other people to read it. She used a word processing program to type it on a computer. After Tamara read her essay, she wanted to make a few more revisions.

Word processing programs make it easy to revise and edit your writing. For example, to move a sentence to a new position, you should:

STEP 1 Place the **cursor** at the beginning of the sentence.

STEP 2 Then, **click and drag** the mouse to highlight the sentence.

STEP 3 Next, use the **cut button** on the tool bar to cut the highlighted text.

STEP 4 Place the **cursor** where you want the text to go.

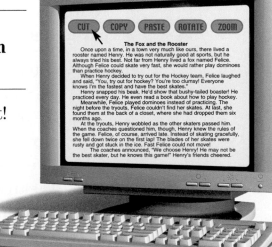

STEP 5 Finally, click on the **paste button** on the tool bar.

The text should appear where you want it!

TIP **Computer Strategies** Each computer or word processing program is different. If your program doesn't have the buttons you need in the tool bar, check the File and Edit menus.

Pronouns and Pronoun Antecedents *pages 234–235*

Write the sentences. Underline each pronoun and its antecedent. Tell whether they are singular or plural.

1. The weather forecasters said they think the storm will be bad.
2. The tide will be high at 6:30. It may cause flooding.
3. Mrs. Jameson says that she will drive inland.
4. Some people say they want to stay.
5. Some families ask neighbors to help them.

Subject and Object Pronouns
pages 236–237

Write the sentence and underline the pronoun. Write whether the pronoun is a subject pronoun or an object pronoun.

6. Alex and Amir heard a thunderstorm coming near them.
7. They were frightened and ran for cover.
8. The rain poured down on them.
9. The thunder roared, but it did not last long.
10. Alex wished he had brought a raincoat.

Using *I* and *Me*, *We* and *Us*
pages 238–239

Write the sentence. Choose the correct pronoun in parentheses to complete the sentence.

11. Mitch and (I, me) were walking in the woods after an ice storm.
12. My brother Stan met Mitch and (I, me) at the maple grove.
13. (We, Us) kept slipping on the ice.
14. The trees around (we, us) were covered with ice.
15. Stan gave Mitch and (I, me) some icicles.

Possessive Pronouns   *pages 244–245*

Write the sentence. Underline the possessive pronoun.

1. Leslie looks at the night sky through her telescope.
2. The planets can be seen in their orbits.
3. Leslie wants to see Saturn and its rings.
4. She says, "I wish my telescope were stronger."
5. Her father listens to her.
6. A nearby college has a telescope in its science building.
7. Professor Klein allows the family to use his telescope.
8. "Hold your hands very steady," said Professor Klein.
9. He showed Leslie the moon and its craters.
10. Leslie asked if her class could visit the college.

Contractions with Pronouns
pages 246–247

Write the sentence. Replace the underlined words with the correct contraction.

11. We will go watch the meteor shower tonight.
12. I will bring a blanket to sit on.
13. You will bring the telescope.
14. I have been reading about meteors at school.
15. I know that you have studied about them, too.

Homophones   *pages 248–249*

Write the sentence, using the correct word in parentheses.

16. (There, Their) are several kinds of meteors.
17. Some meteors are known for (they're, their) brightness.
18. (There, They're) called fireballs.
19. Tell me what else (you're, your) studying in (you're, your) science class.
20. We're learning about a shooting star and (it's, its) light.

Unit 4
Grammar Review

CHAPTER 22

Adjectives and Adverbs

pages 262–271

Adjectives *pages 262–263*

Write the sentence. Underline each adjective, including articles and proper adjectives.

1. A florist raises or sells different flowers and plants.
2. The modern florist arranges flowers into attractive designs.
3. Florists use many types of flowers for new displays.
4. One florist studied design at a famous school in Boston.
5. This florist opened two shops in busy areas.
6. She kept the flowers fresh in a huge refrigerator.
7. The first customer bought red roses.
8. The florist tied a white bow on the blue wrapping paper.
9. The next customer had an unusual request.
10. He asked for a floral arrangement of tiny African violets.

Adverbs *pages 264–265*

Write the sentence. Underline the adverb.

11. Plants usually need plenty of water to grow.
12. Plants in pots must be watered carefully.
13. Seeds grow quickly with the right amount of water.
14. After spring rains, grass seeds soon become tall blades.
15. Plants without water slowly droop and lose color.

Adjective or Adverb? *pages 266–267*

Write the sentence. Use the correct word in parentheses to complete the sentence.

16. Some regions produce (good, well) apples.
17. McIntosh apples grow (good, well) in the Northeast.
18. A late frost can damage apple blossoms (bad, badly).
19. Green apples taste (good, well) to me.
20. Mice and rabbits can (serious, seriously) damage apple trees.

Other Kinds of Adverbs *pages 272–273*

Write the word that the underlined adverb modifies.
Then write whether that word is an adjective or
another adverb.

1. Yosemite Valley is a <u>very</u> beautiful place.
2. The ancient glaciers cut <u>very</u> deeply into the rock.
3. Water has worn away <u>particularly</u> hard granite.
4. <u>Immensely</u> tall rocks tower high into the air.
5. Sometimes they are covered <u>fairly</u> lightly with snow.

Comparing with Adjectives and Adverbs *pages 274–275*

Write the sentence. Fill in the blank with the correct
form of the adjective or adverb in parentheses.

6. El Capitán is one of the _____ rocks in the world.
(breathtaking)
7. El Capitán is _____ than Half Dome. (tall)
8. The granite rock face of El Capitán is one of the _____
in the United States. (smooth)
9. Half Dome is the _____ point in the valley. (high)
10. Waterwheel Falls is the _____ of all the waterfalls in
Yosemite National Park. (famous)

Special Forms *pages 276–277*

Write the sentence. Fill in the blank with the correct
form of the adjective or adverb in parentheses.

11. There has been _____ rain this year in the Sierras than
last year. (little)
12. There will be _____ floods than before. (few)
13. It was the _____ year for skiing in a long time. (bad)
14. However, the year has been _____ than last year for
farmers. (well)
15. When the snow on the mountains melts, it brings
_____ needed water to the valley. (bad)

Unit 4
Grammar Review

CHAPTER 23

More About
Adjectives and
Adverbs
pages 272–281

Two Sides to the Issue

Imagine that someone wants to build a new shopping mall in your community. What would be the advantages or disadvantages of building the mall? Work with a team to do research. Here are some steps to help you.

Select an Area

- Choose an area you know that does not already have buildings on it.

Analyze the Area

- What plants and animals live there?

- Does the area contain creeks or streams? If so, do they lead to larger bodies of water?

- Are there other important resources in the area?

Research the Advantages and Disadvantages

- Research how building in undeveloped areas affects the environment. Contact an environmental group or visit its website to get information.

- List the ways a new mall would be good or bad for your community.

Write a TV News Report

- Write a news report discussing the advantages and disadvantages of building the mall. Watch the news to get ideas about how to organize a report. Write a part for a reporter. Write another part for someone who has an opinion about whether the mall should or should not be built.

- With a partner, act out your report for your classmates.

Will We Miss Them?
by Alexandra Wright

NONFICTION

Colorful pictures accompany interesting facts about many endangered animals and what humans can do to help them.

Disaster at Parsons Point
by Susan Saunders

REALISTIC FICTION

Dana, her cousin Tyler, and many other volunteers pull together to save the land, air, and sea animals when an oil tanker crashes nearby.

Award-Winning Author

Waterman's Boy
by Susan Sharpe

REALISTIC FICTION

Ben and his friends discover oil in the bay where many families make their living fishing.

Sentences *pages 24–29*

Write the sentence. Write whether it is *declarative*, *imperative*, *interrogative*, or *exclamatory*.

1. Our neighborhood has a picnic every summer.
2. Will you ask your grandparents to come this year?
3. All of the neighbors bring their favorite foods.
4. What a variety of dishes we will have!
5. Bring one of your great salads this time.

Subjects/Nouns *pages 34–39*

Write the sentence. Underline the complete subject.

6. Ellie wants to be a professional skater.
7. She and her coach work out every morning.
8. Ellie's skates are always in perfect condition.
9. Her feet move quickly.
10. Ellie and her family have worked hard for her career.

Predicates/Verbs *pages 52–57*

Write the sentence. Underline the complete predicate.

11. Mrs. Gardner decorates for every holiday.
12. She carves pumpkins at Halloween.
13. She displays turkey cutouts at Thanksgiving.
14. Valentine's Day remains her favorite holiday.
15. She makes and displays dozens of lacy hearts.

Simple and Compound Sentences *pages 62–67*

Write the sentence. Then identify it as a *simple sentence* or a *compound sentence*.

16. Emmett gets up before dawn each day.
17. He milks the cows, and then he feeds the chickens.
18. On cold days, he cuts wood for the wood stove.
19. All the animals must be fed, or he cannot go to school.
20. He likes school, but he prefers working on the farm.

Nouns *pages 92–97*

Write the nouns in each sentence. Label each one as *common* or *proper* and as *singular* or *plural*.

1. People can strain their muscles.
2. Joanie does gentle stretches first.
3. The body should warm up before exercise.
4. After workouts, Joanie takes a walk to cool down.
5. Use ice and then heat on a sore muscle.

Possessive Nouns *pages 102–107*

Write the sentence, using the correct possessive noun in parentheses.

6. The (Amazon's, Amazons') forests are amazing.
7. Many (tree's, trees') branches are homes to monkeys.
8. The (river's, rivers') waters hold strange fish.
9. Their (tooth's, teeth's) edges are sharp.
10. Amazon (explorer's, explorers') lives are adventurous.

Action and Linking Verbs *pages 120–125*

Write the sentence. Underline each verb and label it as an *action verb* or a *linking verb*.

11. An exploding volcano sends lava down its sides.
12. Lava is a boiling hot substance.
13. Everything in the path of lava burns.
14. Ash flows out of the volcano.
15. Sometimes the sun seems dark because of the ash.

Main and Helping Verbs *pages 130–135*

Write the sentence. Underline each helping verb once and each main verb twice.

16. Earthquakes can cause tidal waves in the ocean.
17. A tidal wave could destroy coastal buildings.
18. People do know about tidal waves.
19. Those in coastal communities should leave.
20. They can return when the danger has passed.

Cumulative Review Unit 2

More About Nouns and Verbs

301

Present-Tense Verbs pages 164–169

Write the sentence, using the correct verb in parentheses.

  1. A sculpture of an eagle (sit, sits) on our school lawn.
  2. Everybody (look, looks) at it while walking by.
  3. Few people (notice, notices) the baby eagle.
  4. The sculptor (is, am) a local woman.
  5. Her works (is, are) very famous.

Past-Tense Verbs pages 174–179

Write the sentence, using the correct verb in parentheses.

  6. Marcia (studyed, studied) to become a ballet dancer.
  7. She (tried, tryed) very hard to master each movement.
  8. Marcia (lovved, loved) ballet.
  9. In February she (competed, competted) in a contest.
  10. Her instructor (huged, hugged) her when she won.

Future-Tense Verbs pages 192–197

Write the sentence. Underline each future-tense verb.

  11. Our school will once again host an international dance show.
  12. Will the Guatemalan dancers appear?
  13. The Nigerian group will come.
  14. People in my class will sell tickets.
  15. Will the show be a success?

Irregular Verbs pages 202–207

Change the underlined verb to the past tense. Write the sentence with the past-tense verb.

  16. Mr. Guillermo <u>gives</u> guitar lessons.
  17. All four McManus girls <u>take</u> lessons from him.
  18. They only <u>know</u> four chords at first.
  19. Then they <u>become</u> very good at playing the guitar.
  20. They <u>go</u> to the city to take more lessons.

Pronouns *pages 234–237*

Write the sentence. Underline the subject pronouns once and the object pronouns twice.

1. Diana and I were near a tree when lightning hit it.
2. We were startled.
3. The storm got worse, worrying us and the horses.
4. She and I led them to the barn.
5. They followed her and me safely inside.

More About Pronouns *pages 244–247*

Write the sentence. Underline each possessive pronoun. Write the words that make up any pronoun contractions.

6. My mother is an astronomer.
7. She'd rather ride in a space shuttle than spend time in her office.
8. She's always looking through her telescope, which she keeps at our house.
9. We'd be excited if she commanded her own space shuttle.
10. Traveling in space has been a dream of hers because she thinks it's exciting.

Adjectives and Adverbs

pages 262–265, 272–275

Write the sentence. Underline each adjective once. Underline each adverb twice.

11. I planted a huge garden last summer.
12. The vegetables grew quickly, but the weather became very dry.
13. I watered the garden often, and most plants grew fairly well.
14. The tomatoes grew best of all, and they became bigger and juicier than the other vegetables.
15. In August, the tomatoes were ripe, and I sold them.

Language Use

Read the passage and decide which type of mistake, if any, appears in each underlined section. Mark the letter for your answer.

> An astronomer, <u>dr. Watson, told</u> our class
> (1)
> about the planets. We asked him <u>if people</u>
> <u>would ever live on other planets?</u> "<u>Your'e</u>
> (2)
> <u>descendants</u> may live on Mars," <u>he replyed,</u> "but
> (3)
> it would be very different from Earth." <u>Its very</u>
> (4)   (5)
> <u>strange</u> to imagine <u>living on another planet.</u>
> (6)

1 A Spelling

  B Capitalization

  C Punctuation

  D No mistake

2 F Spelling

  G Capitalization

  H Punctuation

  J No mistake

3 A Spelling

  B Capitalization

  C Punctuation

  D No mistake

4 F Spelling

  G Capitalization

  H Punctuation

  J No mistake

5 A Spelling

  B Capitalization

  C Punctuation

  D No mistake

6 F Spelling

  G Capitalization

  H Punctuation

  J No mistake

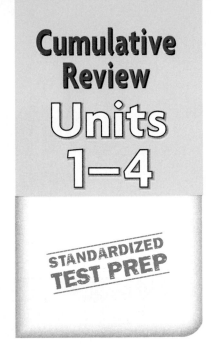
Written Expression

Read the paragraph and the questions that follow it. Write the letter for the correct answer.

> If you take music lessons, you can enjoy the music you play. You can learn a lot about music, and learning about it will help you appreciate music more. Studies even show that taking music lessons makes you smarter!

1 Why was the paragraph written?

  A To give facts

  B To persuade the audience

  C To tell a story

  D To describe something

2 Which would be the best topic sentence for the paragraph?

  F The violin is hard to learn.

  G Many people take piano lessons.

  H Music lessons can enrich your life.

  J People can learn to sing if they're willing to work a little.

3 Which sentence would not belong in the paragraph?

  A Most people find music lessons rewarding.

  B Some people think that music is like math.

  C Learning to sing can open up the world of music to you.

  D You even can join an orchestra or chorus.

4 Which sentence would best conclude the paragraph?

  F Increase your brainpower, and take music lessons!

  G Practice, practice, practice every day!

  H There are many wind instruments.

  J Some people prefer singing to playing an instrument.

Unit 5

Grammar Phrases and Clauses

Writing Informative Writing: Research Report

The Rain Forest

Most rain forests are near the Equator and are warm all year. A tropical rain forest is a forest of tall trees that gets plenty of rain. Th largest tropical rain fo

Prepositions

A **preposition** is a word that shows how a noun or a pronoun is related to other words in the sentence.

You already know and use many prepositions. You use prepositions such as *in*, *near*, and *across* to tell where something is. Prepositions can provide many kinds of information.

Examples:

The first towns **in** the United States were small.

Some towns grew **into** large cities.

Many people moved **to** them.

Common Prepositions

across	near
after	of
at	on
before	over
by	to
for	under
from	up
in	upon
into	with

Vocabulary Power

ur·ban [ûr′bən] *adj.* Having to do with cities; about city life.

Guided Practice

A. Identify the preposition or prepositions in each sentence.

Example: Many people live *in* urban areas.

1. The first American cities were near the ocean.
2. European ships brought goods to American cities.
3. Ships also took goods from them.
4. Americans traded with Europeans.
5. More and more Europeans sailed across the ocean to American cities.
6. Many workers arrived in New York City.
7. The city grew quickly in 1850.
8. Most people lived in small buildings.
9. Carriages went through the streets.
10. Many people worked in factories.

Independent Practice

Remember that a **preposition** is a word that shows how a noun or a pronoun relates to other words in a sentence.

B. Write each sentence. Underline the preposition.

Example: *Many people enjoy life _in_ clean cities.*

11. People have kept cities clean for many years.
12. Fresh water is brought into cities.
13. The water flows under the ground.
14. Dirty water is taken from cities.
15. Garbage is collected from the streets.
16. Workers clean the streets with brooms.
17. Sometimes they spray water over the streets.
18. People build parks for play.
19. Urban parks are filled with trees.
20. Flowers and grass grow through the summer.

C. Write each sentence. Choose a preposition from the chart on page 308 to complete each sentence correctly.

Example: The railroad carried products _____ the nation.
The railroad carried products across the nation.

21. Western cities were different _____ eastern cities.
22. Chicago was an urban market _____ cattle.
23. It was also a center _____ railroad lines.
24. The railroad brought people _____ the east.
25. Cities grew _____ the coming of the railroad.

Writing Connection

Writer's Journal: Writing Idea Imagine that you have just returned from a trip to a busy city. Write a short paragraph describing your experience. What did you do? Where did you go? Use prepositions in your writing, such as *before, after, with, in, off, from,* and *to.*

Object of the Preposition

The **object of the preposition** is the noun or pronoun that follows the preposition. A **prepositional phrase** is made up of a preposition, the object of a preposition, and any words between them.

The words between a preposition and its object are words that tell about the object. In the following examples, the prepositional phrase is underlined once and the object of the preposition is underlined twice.

Examples:

Millions of people live <u>in large <u>cities</u></u>.

Cities contain one-third <u>of the world's <u>people</u></u>.

The city spreads <u>across many <u>miles</u></u>.

Guided Practice

A. **Identify the prepositional phrases in these sentences. Some sentences may contain more than one prepositional phrase.**

Example: Trains travel to big cities.
to big cities

1. The oldest part of most cities is the center.
2. Newer parts grow around the city center.
3. Most city buses run along the streets.
4. In many cities subways run under the ground.
5. Airports are near major cities, but not in them.

Independent Practice

B. Write these sentences. Underline each prepositional phrase once and the object of the preposition twice. Some sentences may contain more
than one prepositional phrase or object of the
preposition.

Example: *Walking <u>through a big <u>city</u></u> is fun.*

   6. You can see people from many places.
   7. New York City has a zoo in a large park.
   8. San Francisco has cable cars that run up the hills.
   9. Los Angeles has beaches that stretch for miles.
  10. The arch in St. Louis rises into the sky.
  11. You can visit the White House in Washington, D.C.
  12. Washington, D.C., is the capital of the United
         States.
  13. The Lincoln Memorial is close to the Potomac
         River.
  14. President Lincoln sits on a huge chair.
  15. There is a large building around his statue.

Writing Connection

Real-Life Writing: Conversation With a partner, take
turns discussing where you would prefer to live. Would
you prefer a city, a small town, or the country? What
would you enjoy about living there? Take notes while
your partner speaks. Write a few sentences telling why
your partner would choose one place over another. Use
prepositions in your writing.

USAGE AND MECHANICS

Using Prepositional Phrases

Use **prepositional phrases** to expand sentences.

You can use a prepositional phrase to make a sentence clearer and to add more details.

Notice how the prepositional phrases in the examples tell more about what happened.

Examples:

Francis saw the buildings.	Francis saw the buildings **in Mexico City.**
Smoke was rising.	Smoke was rising **from the volcano.**
The volcano was close.	The volcano was close **to the city.**

Guided Practice

A. **Read the sentences. Add a prepositional phrase to each one, using the word in parentheses as a guide. Then write the new sentence. Your prepositional phrases can tell when, where, or how.**

Example: Jason rode the bus. (where)
Jason rode the bus into the city.

1. He got off. (where)
2. Then he walked. (where)
3. He had to meet Ellen. (when)
4. Then she arrived. (how)
5. They walked together. (where)

Independent Practice

B. Rewrite each sentence. Add more details with prepositional phrases. Underline each preposition.

> **Example:** New York is not the biggest city.
>
> *New York is not the biggest city <u>in</u> the world.*

6. There are many jobs.
7. Cities need many workers.
8. Garbage workers take trash.
9. Cooks make food.
10. Firefighters fight fires.
11. Police keep the streets safe.
12. Teachers help students.
13. Truck drivers bring goods.
14. Workers build subways.
15. Bus drivers drive buses.
16. There are different kinds of buildings.
17. Some buildings have apartments.
18. There are houses.
19. Skyscrapers rise high.
20. Many cities have bridges.

> **Remember** that you can add details to a sentence with a prepositional phrase.

Writing Connection

Art Think about a busy street in the largest city you have ever seen. What is in the shop windows? What are people doing? Where are they going? How much traffic is in the streets? Work in a small group to create a drawing of a city street. Make pictures of buildings, people, and activities. Then write a caption for each picture that uses prepositional phrases to describe the street scene.

313

Extra Practice

A. Write the prepositions in these sentences. Some sentences may have more than one preposition. *pages 308–309*

Example: There are many jobs in large cities. *in*

1. Some city neighborhoods have people from one country.
2. You can hear people talking in other languages.
3. Different kinds of restaurants are popular in these neighborhoods.
4. Wonderful smells are often in the air.
5. Living in a city can be full of surprises.

B. Write the prepositional phrase in these sentences. *pages 310–311*

Example: Across the United States, cities have grown.
Across the United States

6. The first large cities were in the Northeast.
7. Next, big cities grew across the Midwest.
8. During the 1900s, western cities grew quickly.
9. The biggest city in the West was Los Angeles.
10. Other cities were growing at a fast pace.
11. Cities throughout the Southwest became larger.
12. People moved to Phoenix, Houston, and Dallas.
13. Many people were attracted by the warm, sunny climate.
14. Las Vegas is one of the fastest-growing cities.
15. People can find jobs in these cities.

Remember

that a **preposition** is a word that shows how a noun or a pronoun is related to other words in the sentence. A **prepositional phrase** is made up of a **preposition, the object of the preposition,** and any words between them.

For more activities with prepositions, visit *The Learning Site:*

www.harcourtschool.com

C. Write the sentences. Underline each prepositional phrase once and each object of the preposition twice. Some sentences may have more than one prepositional phrase. *pages 310–311*

Example: *Many cities are located <u>near water</u>.*

16. Denver citizens can look at high mountains.
17. The city is a mile above sea level.
18. The sun shines most days of the year.
19. Sometimes it is buried under heavy snowfall.
20. You can easily go snow skiing from Denver.
21. Chicago is on the shore of Lake Michigan.
22. A chilly wind often blows from the lake.
23. Some cities have mountains near them.
24. Mt. Rainier towers above Seattle.
25. You can see it on clear days.

D. Read the sentences. Add a prepositional phrase to each one, using the word in parentheses as a guide. Then write the new sentence. *pages 312–313*

Example: Most cities have suburbs. (where)
Most cities have suburbs around them.

26. Many Americans moved. (where)
27. Suburbs became crowded. (how)
28. People liked life. (where)
29. Many people stayed. (where)
30. Some people moved back. (where)

Writing Connection

Social Studies Write a paragraph about a city you would like to visit. Be sure you include sentences with prepositional phrases. Write why you would like to visit the city. Tell about things you might see there. Then, exchange your paragraph with a partner. Write a paraphrase of your partner's paragraph.

Chapter Review

Read the group of words in the box. There may be a mistake in sentence structure. If you find a mistake, choose the answer that is written most clearly and correctly. If there is no mistake, choose *Correct as is*.

TIP Read each possible answer carefully before you make your final choice.

1 | Frank's family is taking a vacation. In San Francisco.

   A Frank's family in San Francisco is taking a vacation.

   B Frank's family is taking a vacation in San Francisco.

   C Frank's family is taking in San Francisco a vacation.

   D Correct as is

2 | They ride the cable cars. Up the steep hills.

   F They ride up the steep hills the cable cars.

   G Up the steep hills they ride them. The cable cars.

   H They ride the cable cars up the steep hills.

   J Correct as is

3 | At Fisherman's Wharf, they go there to look at the boats.

   A They go to Fisherman's Wharf to look at the boats.

   B They go to look at the boats. At Fisherman's Wharf.

   C At the boats, they go to look at Fisherman's Wharf.

   D Correct as is

4 | The masts of the sailboats rise into the blue sky.

   F Into the blue sky, the masts rise of the sailboats.

   G The masts of the sailboats rise. Into the blue sky.

   H On the sailboats the masts rise into the blue sky.

   J Correct as is

For additional test preparation, visit *The Learning Site:*
www.harcourtschool.com

Reading Strategies

You can use reading strategies to help you find and use information more easily. The next time you are doing some research, try these strategies:

Skimming is reading a passage very quickly. You can often skim the Table of Contents of a book to see how it is organized. Skimming the first and last chapters can help you learn the book's main idea.

Scanning is looking over a passage to find certain information. When you scan, you do not read every word. You look through the passage for key words that relate to your topic. Scanning will help you know when to look at a source more closely.

Self-Questioning is asking yourself questions about what you've read. You can pause occasionally while you are reading to ask yourself questions. When you self-question, you check your understanding of what you are reading.

Rereading is reading something more than once. When you are reading about a new topic, there may be parts that are unclear. It is important that you reread sections that are unclear to you. Make sure that you understand any new information before you continue reading.

YOUR TURN

RESEARCH A TOPIC Use the reading strategies on this page to write a short report about a topic you want to learn more about. Follow these steps:

1. Skim through an article or a book to learn what it is about and how it is organized.
2. Scan the article to decide if it tells about your topic.
3. As you read, check your understanding of new information by self-questioning.
4. Reread the parts of the article that are unclear.

Independent Clauses

A clause is a group of words that has both a subject and a predicate.

An **independent clause** expresses a complete thought and can stand alone as a sentence. A **phrase** is a group of closely related words that work together. A phrase does not contain a subject and a predicate.

Examples:

Independent Clause:

subject   predicate

America's heritage is different in each region.

Phrase: in each region

Guided Practice

A. Tell whether each group of words is a phrase or an independent clause. Tell how you would make each independent clause into a complete sentence.

Examples: traditions are customs *Traditions are customs.*

According to tradition *phrase*

1. of many different regions
2. the United States has different regions
3. one region is known as the Southwest
4. of the Northwest
5. from the Southeast
6. the people shape a region
7. they give a region its character
8. each region has its own heritage
9. with different kinds of festivals
10. each has its own environment

Independent Practice

B. Write whether each group of words is a phrase or an independent clause. Write each independent clause as a complete sentence.

Example: each region has different festivals
independent clause; Each region has different festivals.

11. the climate in each region is different
12. in the West's dry region
13. it shows the mountains of a region
14. parts of the West are very dry
15. the Northeast has a lot of rain
16. for the rainy Southeast
17. it stretches from the Atlantic to the Pacific
18. Alaska is cold
19. in the cold Northeast
20. during the long winters
21. tornadoes are common in the central states
22. throughout the shorter summers
23. temperatures are milder on the west coast
24. with a high average rainfall
25. the weather forecaster knows the temperature

Writing Connection

Writer's Journal: Drawing Conclusions A conclusion is a statement based on facts. If someone said, "In Maine, the winters are long," you might conclude that Maine has a cold climate. List several facts about weather. Exchange lists with a partner. Look over your partner's list and write at least three conclusions based on your partner's facts. Identify the complete sentences, independent clauses, and phrases in each.

Dependent Clauses

A dependent clause is a group of words that has a subject and a predicate but cannot stand alone as a sentence.

A dependent clause cannot stand alone, because it does not express a complete thought. A dependent clause often begins with a connecting word, such as *after*, *because*, or *when*.

Examples:
Independent Clauses
Some Minnesota lakes are not used for transportation.
We have learned about Lake Erie.

Dependent Clauses
although some Minnesota lakes are deep
when you visit one of the Great Lakes

Guided Practice

A. Identify the dependent clause in each sentence. Then identify the connecting word that begins the clause.

Example: Many people visit Maine because the weather is often cool.
because the weather is often cool; because

1. The New England states are located in the northeast where the winters can be very cold.
2. Many New Englanders became sailors because they lived near the sea.
3. Shipbuilding was important until other industries developed.
4. The American Revolution began when colonists protested against British rule.
5. Boston became the capital of Massachusetts in 1632 when Massachusetts was still a colony.

Independent Practice

B. Write the dependent clause in each sentence. Then circle the connecting word that begins the clause.

Example: The South has been heavily farmed because it has a long growing season.

(because) it has a long growing season

6. This region is special because it has a rich heritage.
7. New Orleans, Louisiana, was founded in 1718 when French settlers began clearing the brush.
8. Because it sits on a river bend, New Orleans is called the Crescent City.
9. Before Louisiana belonged to Spain, it was a French settlement.
10. When people go there, they often eat tasty food.
11. Florida has many beaches because its coastline is long.
12. Although Florida is famous for its oranges, the state has other industries.
13. People can visit famous theme parks while they are in Florida.
14. Some Southern cities have important seaports because they are near major rivers.
15. Norfolk, Virginia, sits on a large harbor where many ships are built.

> **Remember**
> that a dependent clause cannot stand alone as a sentence. It often begins with a connecting word.

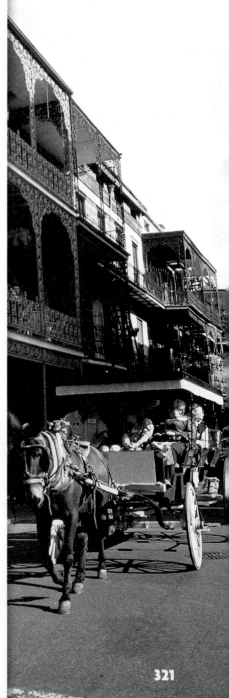

Writing Connection

Writer's Craft: Elaboration Brainstorm ideas for a paragraph about your region or community. Write a topic sentence for your paragraph. Trade sentences with a partner. Then write a paragraph elaborating on the idea your partner introduced in the topic sentence. Be sure to include some dependent clauses in your writing.

GRAMMAR – WRITING CONNECTION

Distinguishing Independent and Dependent Clauses

An independent clause can stand alone as a sentence, but a dependent clause cannot.

You know that a clause has both a subject and a predicate. A dependent clause cannot stand alone because it does not express a complete thought.

Example:

The country's midsection is called the Heartland because it is in the middle of the country.

Guided Practice

A. **Identify which is the independent clause and which is the dependent clause in each sentence. Tell how you know.**

Example: When our country was young, it had only two major regions.
Independent Clause: it had only two major regions
Dependent Clause: When our country was young

1. The Midwest has different weather conditions because the region is large.
2. When disease ruined crops in Wisconsin, the farmers raised dairy cows.
3. Some farmers planted soybeans after they planted corn.
4. People can farm more land when they use machines.
5. If Iowa is known for any one crop, it is corn.

Independent Practice

Remember

that an independent clause can stand alone as a sentence but a dependent clause cannot.

B. Write each sentence. Underline the independent clause once and the dependent clause twice.

> **Example:** <u>When early settlers came to Nebraska</u>, <u>they built sod houses</u>.

6. They were called sod houses because the houses were made of earth.
7. Many early settlements were in eastern Ohio, where Fort Harmar was established in 1785.
8. This region is called the Midwest because it is in the center of the country.
9. When the settlers moved, they built log cabins.
10. Stone houses were built where the sod houses once stood.

C. Write each clause. Label it independent or dependent.

> **Example:** Some farm machines can plant crops.
> *independent*

11. Since the corn is used for hog feed.
12. Farmers also raise hogs.
13. Where the farmers' crops are sold.
14. When the price of corn is high.
15. They raised more hogs that year.

Writing Connection

Social Studies Locate your state on a map of the United States. List the names of the states that border your state, and tell what you know about their main industries. Which state's products or industries are the most similar to your state's? Which are the most different? Explain your answers. Be sure to use clauses correctly.

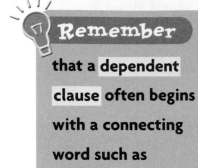

Remember

that a **dependent
clause** often begins
with a connecting
word such as
because, when,
or *if.*

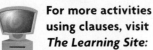

For more activities
using clauses, visit
The Learning Site:

www.harcourtschool.com

Extra Practice

A. **Write each group of words. Tell whether it is a
phrase or an independent clause. If the group
of words is an independent clause, underline
the subject once and the predicate twice.**
pages 318–319

Example: Another region is the Southwest.
<u>Another region</u> <u><u>is the Southwest.</u></u>
independent clause

 1. The Southwest includes the state of Arizona.
 2. On the New Mexico border.
 3. Six states border Oklahoma.
 4. The weather is dry in the Southwest.
 5. Along the Colorado River.
 6. Near the state of Oklahoma.
 7. In the time of Texas's independence.
 8. Along the shores of the Rio Grande.
 9. We read about their culture.
10. The Rocky Mountains continue into that state.

B. **Write the dependent clause in each sentence.
Then circle the connecting word that begins the
clause.**   *pages 320–321*

Example: The Rio Grande often floods when it rains
hard.
(when) it rains hard

11. It is beautiful in the Arizona desert where the
cactus grows.
12. After Alaska became a state, Texas became the
second–largest state.
13. When tourists come to Texas, they often visit
Dallas or Houston.
14. Before fall arrives, the wildflowers in central
Texas are alive with color.
15. The flowers bloom for a long time because the
Texas summer is very long.

C. Write each sentence. Underline the independent clause once and the dependent clause twice.

pages 316–323

Example: *When it is summer in Texas, the temperature is hot.*

16. Early settlers arrived there when they traveled along the Santa Fe Trail.
17. Since many people visit New Mexico, tourism is a big industry there.
18. Before it flows into Texas, the Rio Grande divides New Mexico.
19. Many farmers raise cattle instead of crops because the land is dry.
20. The Native American culture is active in Arizona because many Navajo people live there.
21. The Southwest also includes Texas and New Mexico, where the Spanish heritage is strong.
22. The people do not usually need warm clothing because the climate is hot and dry.
23. Dams provide water for other areas where water is needed.
24. Many tourists visit the Southwest because the deserts and hills are beautiful.
25. If you go to the Southwest, you will probably like it.

DID YOU KNOW?
Texas was a separate country for about nine years. Texas declared its independence from Mexico in 1836. Then it became part of the United States in 1845.

Writing Connection

Real-Life Writing: Requesting Information With a partner, write a brief letter to the tourism office in your state. Ask for travel tips and information about places of interest. Change some of your sentences to dependent clauses by adding words such as *when, because,* and *after.* Then combine the dependent clauses with independent clauses to make new, longer sentences.

Chapter Review

STANDARDIZED
TEST PREP

Look for mistakes in the sentences below. When you find a mistake, write the letter of the line containing the mistake. Some sentences do not have any mistakes. If there is no mistake, choose the letter beside *No Mistakes*.

1 A When limestone is
B mixed with
C grass. It forms a rich soil.
D No Mistakes

2 F Winters in northern Texas
G are cold. When north
H winds sweep down.
J No Mistakes

TIP Remember to read all of the choices before you select an answer.

3 A During the early spring.
B tornadoes often hit
C parts of Texas.
D No Mistakes

4 F Tornadoes can cause a
G lot of damage because
H they have such strong winds.
J No Mistakes

5 A Some fishermen head for
B the Texas coast. Where they
C can catch shrimp.
D No Mistakes

6 F Another popular catch
G is sea trout. When fishing
H in saltwater.
J No Mistakes

7 A Many people make their living
B in the oil business
C With rich oil deposits.
D No Mistakes

8 F When Texas led the nation
G in oil production. The state
H depended less on farming.
J No Mistakes

For additional test preparation, visit *The Learning Site:*
www.harcourtschool.com

Taking Notes and Making an Outline

When you are asked to listen or read for information, you should take notes to help you remember the most important points. Your notes might look like this:

States—Arizona, New Mexico, Texas, Oklahoma
mountains—Rocky Mountain range
rivers—Rio Grande, Red River, Pecos, Arkansas, Colorado
plains—Great Plains, Staked Plains
deserts—Painted Desert, Sonoran Desert

If you are writing a report, you can use your notes to organize the information in an outline. Outlines help you sort information according to categories. That means that you put subtopics under a main topic. In an outline, the first word of each topic and subtopic begins with a capital letter. Your outline might look like this:

Title: The American Southwest
I. Introduction to the American Southwest
   A. Early history of the region
   B. Geography of the region
II. The Southwest today
   A. Resources
   B. Economy
III. The future
   A. Challenges
   B. Solutions to problems

YOUR TURN

RECORDING YOUR RESEARCH Read a book about one of the states in the Southwest. Take notes as you read. Then create an outline of the major ideas in the book. Make sure that you have at least three main topics with subtopics in your outline.

Writer's Craft

Paragraphing

You can write to give directions, to explain something, or to contrast. You might also write to share facts.

Read the following passage from the chapter "Great Lakes" from the book *Rivers & Lakes*. Look at the details in each paragraph.

LITERATURE MODEL

The five Great Lakes, in North America, are the world's largest group of freshwater lakes. They formed when the glaciers that covered the region many thousands of years ago melted. Water filled the basins dug out by glaciers.

Canada and the United States share four of the lakes, including the largest, Lake Superior. Lake Michigan is in the United States. Together, the five Great Lakes form part of an enormous inland waterway.

—from *Rivers & Lakes*
by Neil Morris

Analyze THE Model

1. What is the topic of the first paragraph?

2. What details are given in the first paragraph?

3. Which event in the first paragraph happened first?

4. What is the topic of the second paragraph?

5. What details are given in the second paragraph?

Forming Paragraphs

If you have a lot of information, you may need to write more than one paragraph. The sentences in each paragraph tell about one main idea. Dividing information into paragraphs is called **paragraphing**. Study the chart on the next page.

Vocabulary Power

trans•con•ti•nen•tal
[trans′kon′tə•nen′təl]
adj. Stretching from
one side of a conti-
nent, or major land
mass, to the other.

Strategies to Use for Paragraphing	Applying the Strategies	Examples
Give information in the correct order, or sequence.	• Put steps or ideas in an order that makes sense. You may want to use signal words such as *first, next, after, before,* or *then,* or use dates.	• **First,** the settlers built shelters to keep them warm and dry. **After** that, they cleared the land and planted crops.
Write a topic sentence for each paragraph, and give details that relate to it.	• Begin each paragraph with a topic sentence. Give details in the other sentences of the paragraph.	• **Topic sentence:** A modern country needs a good system of transportation. • **Details:** Goods have to be moved from factories to stores. People need to get from place to place.

YOUR TURN

ANALYZE INFORMATIVE WRITING **Work with two or three classmates. Look for articles in magazines or newspapers that give information about a topic that interests you. Notice how the articles are organized.**

Answer these questions:

1. What does the writer explain or give information about?

2. What is the main idea of each paragraph?

3. What details does the writer include in each paragraph?

4. Does the writer present ideas and details in a sequence that makes sense? Explain.

Sequence Words

A. Write the following paragraph on your paper. Choose signal words from the box to fill in the blanks so that the paragraph makes sense. Remember to capitalize the first word of each sentence.

during	now	first	later

The _____ Aztecs to settle in Mexico lived on a very small island. _____, they built a great city called Tenochtitlán. The city was located where Mexico City is _____. As years passed, the power of the Aztecs grew. _____ that time, they built roadways and bridges to connect the island to the mainland.

B. Read the following sentences. Put them in time order. Then write the sentences in a paragraph on your paper.

Then came the first transcontinental railroad.
After the automobile came the airplane.
Today, jetliners fly from coast to coast in a matter of hours.
In pioneer days, people traveled slowly in covered wagons pulled by oxen.
The next great step after the railroads was the invention of the automobile.

Topic Sentence and Details

C. Read the details below for a paragraph about the Internet. Then choose the best topic sentence to begin that paragraph. Write the complete paragraph.

> **Details:**
> You can find information about almost any subject. You can communicate with people from all over the world. You can ask questions and get answers.

> **Topic Sentences:**
> The Internet can be a useful learning tool.
>
> You can buy books, clothing, and other items on the Internet.

D. Read the topic sentence. Choose three details that fit that topic sentence. Write the complete paragraph on your paper. Remember to indent the first line.

Topic Sentence: Our flag has changed over the years.

Details: The first American flag had thirteen stars. The flag of Great Britain is called the Union Jack. The stars represented the original thirteen states. In 1818, Congress voted to add a star for each new state admitted to the Union. Francis Scott Key wrote "The Star-Spangled Banner."

Writing and Thinking

Write to Record Reflections Sometimes events happen in a certain order, or sequence, because the first event causes the second one. Can you think of an important event in your lifetime that caused another important event to happen? Write your reflections about the events in your Writer's Journal.

Writing Paragraphs of Information

Neil Morris, author of *Rivers & Lakes*, tells facts about the Great Lakes. Have you ever written a paper for school to share information? Richard researched the Panama Canal for his social studies class. Read these paragraphs that Richard wrote to share the information he learned.

MODEL

Topic Sentence

Details in Sequence

    The Panama Canal connects the Atlantic and Pacific Oceans. It is located in the country of Panama in Central America and is about 40 miles long. Before the canal was built, ships had to sail all the way around the tip of South America to get from one ocean to the other.

Topic Sentence

Details in Sequence

    It took a long time to get the Panama Canal built. Explorers in Central America had suggested the idea all the way back in the 1500s. For hundreds of years, though, it was just a dream. Finally, in 1906, the United States Congress approved a plan, and workers began digging. The Panama Canal was completed in the summer of 1914.

Analyze THE Model

1. What is the topic of the first paragraph? How do the details relate to the topic?

2. What is the topic of the second paragraph? How do the details relate to the topic?

3. How does Richard show the sequence of events?

4. Do you think Richard's paragraphs of information tell facts in a clear and understandable way? Explain.

YOUR TURN

WRITING PROMPT Research a historical topic of interest to share with your classmates. Write two or three paragraphs of information. Begin each paragraph with a topic sentence and explain the sequence of events.

STUDY THE PROMPT Ask yourself these questions:

1. Who is your audience?

2. What is your purpose for writing?

3. What writing form will you use?

4. What information will you give your readers?

Prewriting and Drafting

Organize Your Ideas As you read different sources of information, take notes on your topic. Then use an outline like this one to plan your paragraphs.

I. Topic Sentence (main idea of paragraph)
   A. Detail (information that relates to the main idea)
   B. Detail
II. Topic Sentence
   A. Detail
   B. Detail

USING YOUR
Handbook

• Use the Writer's Thesaurus to find signal words that will help your reader understand the sequence of events.

Editing

Read over the draft of your paragraphs of information. Use this checklist to help you revise your paragraphs:

- ☑ Have you begun each paragraph with a topic sentence?
- ☑ Do all the details in each paragraph tell about the topic?
- ☑ Does the sequence of events make sense?
- ☑ Have you used signal words to help your reader understand the sequence?

Use this checklist as you proofread your paragraphs:

- ☑ I have used capitalization and punctuation correctly.
- ☑ I have used prepositional phrases and dependent clauses correctly.
- ☑ I have indented the first line of each paragraph.
- ☑ I have used a dictionary to check my spelling.

Editor's Marks

- ✗ delete text
- ∧ insert text
- ↻ move text
- ¶ new paragraph
- ≡ capitalize
- / lowercase
- ◯ correct spelling

Sharing and Reflecting

Writer's Journal

Make a final copy of your paragraphs of information, and share them with a partner. Tell what you like best about your partner's work. Discuss what each of you might do better next time. Write your reflections in your Writer's Journal.

Online Searches

Have you ever used a computer to search for information online? Look at this flowchart to get some ideas about doing an online search.

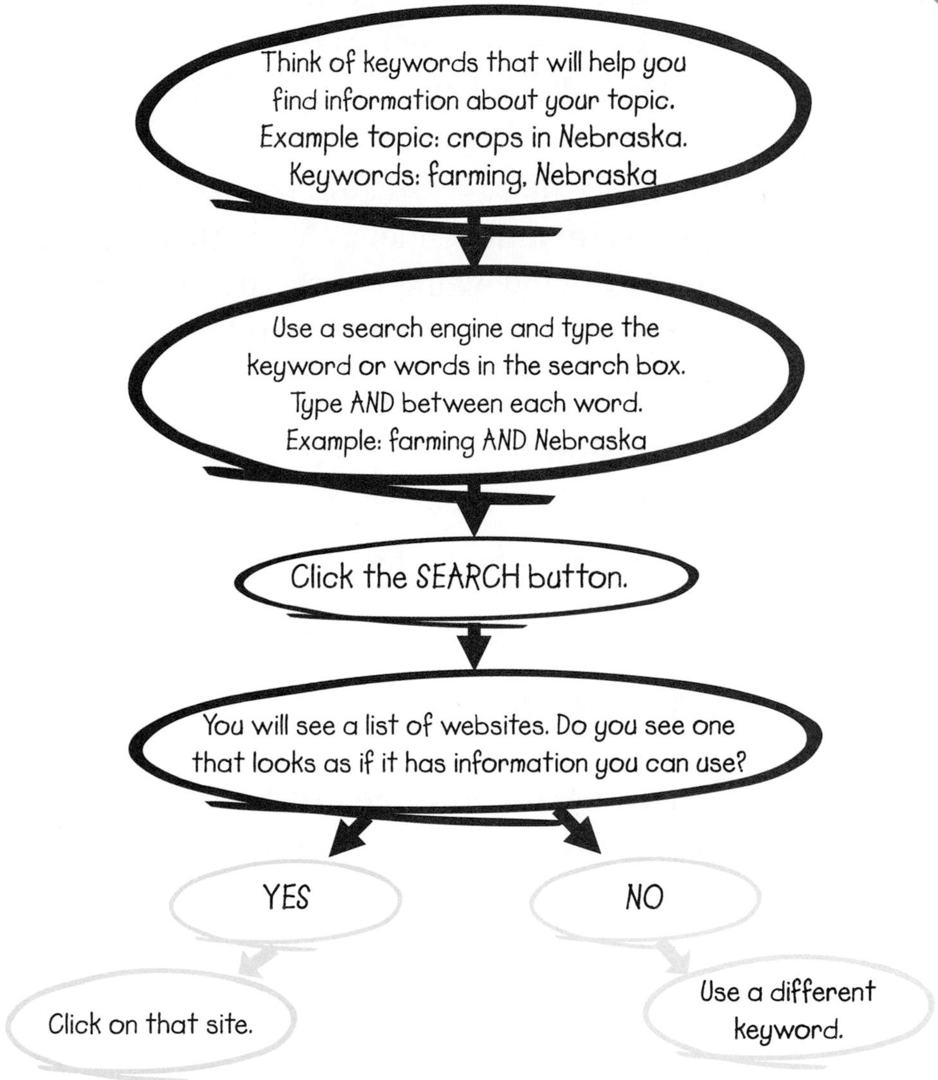

Think of keywords that will help you find information about your topic.
Example topic: crops in Nebraska.
Keywords: farming, Nebraska

↓

Use a search engine and type the keyword or words in the search box.
Type AND between each word.
Example: farming AND Nebraska

↓

Click the SEARCH button.

↓

You will see a list of websites. Do you see one that looks as if it has information you can use?

YES ← → NO

Click on that site.   Use a different keyword.

YOUR TURN

You and a partner can do research online. Follow these steps.

STEP 1 Choose a topic.

STEP 2 Carry out your search.

STEP 3 When you find information, take notes. Write down the website address, too.

STEP 4 Use your notes to write paragraphs of information. Share your work with classmates.

CHAPTER
28

Complex Sentences

Vocabulary Power

ir·ri·gate [irʹə·gāt] *v.*
To bring water to land by using pipes, ditches, or canals.

Complex Sentences

A **complex sentence** is made up of an independent clause and at least one dependent clause.

You know that a dependent clause cannot stand alone. It must be paired with an independent clause to form a sentence. A sentence with both a dependent and an independent clause is known as a complex sentence. In a complex sentence, dependent clauses often begin with *as*, *because*, *before*, *during*, *if*, and *while*. Put a comma after a dependent clause that begins a sentence. In the following examples, the independent clause is underlined once, and the dependent clause is underlined twice.

Examples:

If you water seeds, they will grow.

Seeds grow best when they get enough sun.

Guided Practice

A. **Read each sentence. Tell whether or not it is a complex sentence. Tell how you know.**

Example: When farmers water the wheat regularly, it grows rapidly.
complex; it is made up of a dependent clause and an independent clause

1. Farming is important because it produces food.
2. Before people began to farm, they ate wild plants.
3. After they learned to grow plants from seeds, they depended on farming.
4. Dairy farmers raise cows for milk.
5. They are called dairy farmers because they raise their animals for milk.

Independent Practice

B. Read each sentence. Write whether or not it is a complex sentence.

Example: The Great Lakes are important because they are shipping routes to the sea. *complex*

6. People go to the Great Lakes if they like fishing.
7. Lake Erie is one of the Great Lakes.
8. Lake Superior is the largest of the Great Lakes.
9. Although it doesn't rain much in Mexico, corn has always grown well there.
10. When there is little rain, farmers irrigate their crops.
11. Dry farming is a method of growing crops in dry regions.
12. Plants need water as they grow.
13. If plants don't get water, they won't grow well.
14. The farmer decides when he will pick his crops.
15. Farmers grow flowers because people buy them.

> **Remember**
>
> that a **complex** sentence consists of an independent clause and one or more dependent clauses.

Writing Connection

Writer's Craft: Writing Complex Sentences Do you live on a farm? Have you ever visited one? What animals live on a farm? Using some complex sentences, write a paragraph about what life on a farm is or might be like. Tell why you might like or dislike it. Exchange papers with a partner. Explain to each other the good points of the writing and the ways it could be better with more complex sentences.

More About Complex Sentences

An **independent clause** can stand alone as a sentence. A dependent clause cannot stand alone.

A dependent clause can come at the beginning or at the end of a complex sentence and often begins with a connecting word. The following words are often used to begin dependent clauses in complex sentences:

after	because	since	when
although	before	though	where
as	if	unless	while

Examples:

When the dam was opened, the water flowed out.
begins with a dependent clause

The water flowed out **when the dam was opened.**
ends with a dependent clause

Guided Practice

A. **Make each pair of clauses into a complex sentence. Use one word from the chart above to begin each dependent clause.**

Example: The crops will grow _____ there is rain.
The crops will grow <u>when</u> there is rain.

1. The crops will fail _____ rain doesn't come soon.
2. The farmer will sell the crop _____ the price rises.
3. He will not sell the crop _____ the price is low.
4. Pecans grow in the South _____ they need warmth.
5. He grew peaches _____ he lived in Georgia.

Independent Practice

B. Write each sentence. Underline the dependent clause.

> **Example:** The Great Lakes formed <u>after the last Ice Age ended</u>.

6. Because it is bordered by Lake Michigan, Chicago has become an important city.
7. The Great Lakes are used for shipping though they may be full of ice during the winter.
8. Although people are trying to clean up the Great Lakes, the water is still polluted.
9. Many cities are built near large lakes because water is necessary for life.
10. People first settled in towns near farms because food was available.
11. Farmers brought their crops to a market where they sold them.
12. Towns grew around markets since people came there for food.
13. Although it was a cold spring, fruit from the orchard was plentiful.
14. Fruit trees can be damaged when the weather is cold.
15. After the ground froze this winter, not much fruit grew in the spring.

Remember

that an **indepen-dent clause** can stand alone as a sentence. A **dependent clause** cannot stand alone.

Writing Connection

Health Suppose that for one week you could choose whatever you wanted to eat. However, you could not buy any food from a store. You could eat only food that comes directly from farms. What would you eat to stay healthy? Make a list of six possible meals. Using complex sentences, write a paragraph explaining your choices.

CHAPTER 28

Complex
Sentences

off

USAGE AND MECHANICS

Commas in Complex Sentences

A dependent clause that begins a sentence is followed by a comma.

You already know that a dependent clause can come at the beginning or at the end of a sentence. A dependent clause that comes at the end of a sentence is not usually preceded by a comma.

Examples: **Because our tap water tastes good,** I drink it often.
begins with a dependent clause; comma follows clause

I drink our tap water often **because it tastes good.**
ends with a dependent clause; no comma

Guided Practice

A. Read each sentence. If the sentence needs a comma, put it in the correct place. If the sentence does not need a comma, write *no comma*.

Example: After he planted the field the farmer watered it.
After he planted the field, the farmer watered it.

1. Although they grow up on farms many farmers study agriculture at college.
2. Because seeds cannot be planted in hard ground farmers must use plows.
3. Plows are helpful when farmers have to break the ground.
4. Plows can loosen soil if it has been packed hard.
5. If the soil is too dry the wind can blow it away.

Independent Practice

B. Write each sentence. If the sentence needs a comma, put it in the correct place. If not, write *no comma*.

Example: After the farmer attached the plow to the tractor he worked in the field.
After the farmer attached the plow to the tractor, he worked in the field.

6. The whole family worked in the field after they ate lunch.
7. Although wheat farms are large many vegetable farms are small.
8. When they have good weather many farmers earn money from their crops.
9. Although wheat is also grown in other places most wheat farms are on the Great Plains.
10. New York State has apple orchards because the climate is good.
11. Because orange trees need a lot of sunlight they grow well in Florida.
12. Orange trees cannot survive when it is very cold.
13. Beef cattle graze in areas where grass grows.
14. Plants need rich soil because it helps them grow.
15. Because fertilizer enriches soil farmers add it.

Remember that a comma follows a dependent clause that begins a sentence. A comma does not usually come before a dependent clause that ends a sentence.

Writing Connection

Writer's Craft: Writing Complex Sentences What plants and animals are raised in your region? Do you live near wheat fields or cattle farms? With a partner, choose one food plant or animal, and make a list of things that you know about it. Write several sentences, including some complex sentences, to explain what you know.

Extra Practice

A. Read each sentence. Tell whether the sentence is a complex sentence. *pages 336–337*

Example: After he harvests the apples, the farmer sells them by the bushel. *complex*

1. Some farmers use chemicals because they help plants grow.
2. When they are put on the soil, some chemicals prevent the growth of weeds.
3. The farmer puts chemicals in the soil every spring.
4. Farmers test their soil unless they already know it is rich.
5. Rich soil contains minerals, such as iron and calcium.

B. Combine each pair of sentences to make a complex sentence. Use the word in parentheses to make one of the sentences a dependent clause. Add a comma if necessary. *pages 338–339*

Example: Water is used for power. It is plentiful. (because)
Water is used for power because it is plentiful.

6. The water mill was invented about 2,000 years ago. People began using water power. (after)
7. Water mills were simple to make and use. They did not produce much power. (although)
8. Falling water turned the mill's wheels. The water mill was used only in the mountains. (because)
9. Coal and oil are used for energy. They rarely can be used again. (after)
10. Water cannot become steam. It is heated. (unless)

Remember

that complex sentences contain one independent clause and one or more dependent clauses. A dependent clause that begins a sentence is followed by a comma. A dependent clause that ends a sentence is not usually preceded by a comma.

For more activities with complex sentences, visit *The Learning Site:*

www.harcourtschool.com

C. **Write each sentence. If the sentence needs a comma, put it in the correct place. If no comma is needed, write *no comma*.** *pages 340–341*

Example: Because regions have different soils and climates farmers use different farming methods.
Because regions have different soils and climates, farmers use different farming methods.

11. When there is little rain many crops cannot grow.

12. People use dry farming methods in areas where little rain falls.

13. Since summers can be very dry in the Midwest dry farming is often used there.

14. Dry farming is sometimes used in other regions if they do not get enough rain.

15. When farmers plant in rows across hills rain gets trapped in these rows.

16. Because water cannot flow downhill it moistens the rows of plants.

17. Farmers expect a good crop when they dry farm.

18. Before the weather gets too hot barley is planted.

19. After barley is ripe it is ready to be picked.

20. The soil in an unplanted field becomes richer when crops are not drawing out minerals.

Writing Connection

Social Studies Think about a farmer's life and work. Write three questions to ask a farmer about the work that he or she does. Perhaps you can ask why the farmer likes farming or why he or she raises certain crops. Then write an answer that the farmer might give you. Use complex sentences in your writing.

Chapter Review

Read the passage, and choose the answer that belongs in each space. Mark the letter for your answer.

Some Native Americans planted corn in the region __(1)__ Mexico is today. They planted corn __(2)__ it grew well in a dry, hot climate. __(3)__ Native American farmers grew corn, it usually produced a lot of food. __(4)__ they did not use modern farming methods, Native Americans were successful farmers.

Before they __(5)__ Native American farmers used sticks to dig holes in the ground. After they put seeds in the __(6)__ the farmers covered them with soil. The farmers also cleared weeds with hoes.

TIP For each incomplete sentence, try the possible answers first. Then decide which one works best in the sentence.

1 A since
   B where
   C that
   D , where

2 F because
   G although
   H , because
   J except

3 A Before
   B Unless
   C When
   D Though

4 F For
   G Although
   H If
   J Where

5 A planted
   B , planted
   C planted.
   D planted,

6 F holes,
   G holes
   H holes.
   J , holes

For additional test preparation, visit *The Learning Site:*

www.harcourtschool.com

Planning a Video

Planning a video is similar to planning a real film or television show. A video is a good way to give people information. People often listen more carefully to things that they can see and hear.

YOUR TURN

LET'S PLAN A VIDEO

- **With a partner or in a small group, decide what information you want to share.**

- **After choosing the subject for your video, list the information you want to include. What characters would you include? Who would have some information about your subject? Could you interview that person? Decide how to present the information and the characters in your video.**

- **What pictures come to mind when you think about your subject? Make a storyboard. A storyboard is a series of pictures showing each scene in the video.**

- **Think of an interesting or exciting beginning for your video. Make sure that it tells the subject of your video.**

- **Think of a strong ending. For example, summarize the most important information in one or two sentences.**

- **Now you are ready to film. If possible, use a video camera and cassette. Shoot your video by following the scenes on your storyboard. If you do not have a video camera, act out the scenes on your storyboard.**

TIP You have to get permission from people to record them on videotape. You can tape them saying that they give their permission, or you can get their permission in writing.

345

DID YOU KNOW?
The Amazon River is longer than the distance between San Francisco and New York City!

Vocabulary Power

del·ta [del′tə] *n.* A flat plain at a river's mouth made of soil that the river has carried downstream.

Sentence Fragments

A sentence fragment is a group of words that does not express a complete thought.

Every sentence needs a subject and a predicate. In a sentence fragment, at least one of these parts may be missing.

Examples:

Sentence Fragment: The longest river in the Americas.

Complete Sentence: The Amazon is the longest river in the Americas.

Sentence Fragment: Longer or shorter than the Nile?

Complete Sentence: Is the Amazon longer or shorter than the Nile?

Guided Practice

A. Read each group of words. Tell whether it is a sentence fragment or a complete sentence.

Examples: The Amazon is the second-largest river in the world. *complete sentence*

Is the largest river in the world. *sentence fragment*

1. At busy ports along the river.
2. The air in the rain forest is warm and damp.
3. Many kinds of plants and animals.
4. In the rain forest a little sunlight.
5. Ships travel 2,300 miles up the wide river.

Independent Practice

B. Write whether each group of words is a sentence fragment or a complete sentence.

> **Examples:** Surrounded by beautiful forests.
> *sentence fragment*
>
> The Amazon River is surrounded by beautiful forests.
> *complete sentence*

6. The Amazon is incredibly wide.
7. More than 90 miles wide in the delta?
8. Thousands of plants in the rain forest are.
9. May be used for new medicines.
10. The river basin of the Amazon.

C. Read each group of words. If the sentence is complete, write *complete sentence*. If it is a sentence fragment, write *fragment* and name the missing sentence part(s).

> **Example:** Sometimes the Amazon River.
> *fragment, no predicate*

11. Alligators live in the Amazon.
12. In addition, the dangerous piranha fish.
13. An amazing variety of flowers.
14. Many ships and barges.
15. Rains most of the year.

Writing Connection

Writer's Journal: Recording Ideas Work with a small group to write at least five questions about rivers. Avoid using sentence fragments. Use complete sentences, such as these: What is the longest river in my state? Where does it begin and end? What songs have been written about it?

> **Remember**
> that every sentence must have a subject and a predicate. If one or both of these sentence parts are missing, or if the sentence does not express a complete thought, it is a sentence fragment.

Run-on Sentences

A **run-on sentence** is two or more sentences that are incorrectly joined by a comma or by nothing at all.

Change a run-on sentence to a compound sentence or to two separate sentences. A compound sentence is two complete sentences joined with a comma and the connecting word *and, or,* or *but.*

Examples:

Incorrect: The Nile River is in Africa it is the longest river in the world.

Correct: The Nile River is in Africa, and it is the longest river in the world.

Correct: The Nile River is in Africa. It is the longest river in the world.

Guided Practice

A. **Read each sentence. Tell if the sentence is correct or a run-on sentence.**

Example: The Nile River is long, it is about 250 miles longer than the Amazon River.
run-on sentence

1. Crops need water they also need sun.
2. Egypt is a hot, dry country in Africa.
3. The sea north of Egypt is called the Mediterranean, the Nile flows into this sea.
4. Part of the delta's soil is swampy, but some of it is very good.
5. The Nile carries fine soil Egypt's farms are along the banks of the river.

Independent Practice

B. **Rewrite each sentence correctly. Use a comma and the connecting word given in parentheses.**

Example: The Nile flows north it empties into the sea. (and)

The Nile flows north, and it empties into the sea.

6. The river has fresh water, the delta is salty. (but)
7. Farmers plant clover, they raise vegetables. (or)
8. The Nile flooded the valley, most farms and crops were ruined. (and)
9. The Egyptians built a dam it helps the farmers. (and)
10. The dam holds back the water farmers need it. (but)

C. **Rewrite each run-on sentence as two separate sentences.**

Example: The Nile flows near the equator it flows through desert and farmland.

The Nile flows near the equator. It flows through desert and farmland.

11. The Nile Valley has rich soil Egyptians use it well.
12. Today, the valley is crowded, farmers grow food.
13. Crops are grown all year rice is grown in summer.
14. Millet is a summer crop corn is also a summer crop.
15. Cotton is important it is Egypt's biggest crop.

Writing Connection

Social Studies Use encyclopedias, atlases, and other resources to answer your questions about rivers. Work in pairs to record the answers. Then write a paragraph from your notes. Make sure there are no run-on sentences.

Remember

to avoid **run-on sentences** when you write. Change a run-on sentence to a compound sentence with a comma and a connecting word, or write it as two separate sentences.

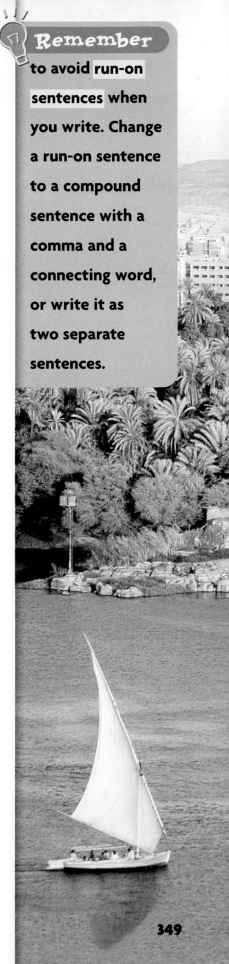

Complete Sentence

- a subject
- a predicate
- a complete thought

Connecting Words (Conjunctions)

- and
- or
- but

GRAMMAR — WRITING CONNECTION

Correcting Sentence Errors

Correct a sentence fragment by making it into a complete sentence. Correct a run-on sentence by using a comma and a connecting word or by writing separate sentences.

Examples:

Incorrect: Sailed down the Mississippi River.

Correct: The boys sailed down the Mississippi River.

Incorrect: They watched the river, Bob saw a fish.

Correct: They watched the river, and Bob saw a fish.

Guided Practice

A. The first group of words in each pair is not a sentence. Tell if the second group of words is a correct sentence. If not, explain what is wrong.

Example: Delicious fish in the Mississippi River.

Delicious fish, in the Mississippi River.
not correct; sentence fragment—no predicate

1. Is home to many animals.
   The Mississippi River is home to many animals.
2. The heron is a bird, it makes a nest in a tree.
   The heron is a bird. It makes a nest in a tree.
3. The egret looks like the heron the egret is white.
   The egret looks like the heron, the egret is white.
4. Is lined with sweet gum and tupelo trees.
   The Mississippi is lined with sweet gum and tupelo trees.
5. Steamboats and other ships.
   Steamboats and other ships on the river.

Independent Practice

B. Add a subject or a predicate to correct each sentence fragment.

Example: The Volga River. *The Volga River is busy.*

6. Work in the mines.
7. Miners are.
8. Russian storytellers.
9. Is long, cold, and dark.
10. Supply water for farms.

C. Write each run-on sentence correctly. Add a comma and the connecting word in parentheses.

Example: The river is long we sailed its entire length. (but)
The river is long, but we sailed its entire length.

11. The Volga is long, the people love the river. (and)
12. Some Russians grow wheat some work in mines. (and)
13. Other workers mine salt they may labor in the gas fields. (or)
14. Huge dams are costly they also are helpful. (but)
15. The Volga River is long, it is very deep. (and)

Remember to avoid sentence fragments and run-on sentences. Make sure that each sentence expresses at least one complete thought. In a compound sentence, place a comma and a connecting word between the complete thoughts.

Writing Connection

Technology With your group, use the answers to your research questions to make a graph or chart. You might make a bar graph that shows the lengths of rivers in your state. Include colors and pictures. If you wish, use a computer. Correct errors in any sentences you might write.

Extra Practice

A. Read each sentence fragment. Tell what is missing or what is wrong in each one. *pages 346–347*

Example: Depends on rivers for many things.
no subject

1. The slow-moving sloth.
2. Is a very wide river.
3. One important American river.
4. Are some of the important rivers in the world.
5. Can give us water, fish, and transportation.
6. A skunk or an opossum near the river.
7. Freezes only in the coldest months.
8. The Amazon River is very.
9. The Nile River.
10. Early settlers along the Mississippi River.

B. Write each run-on sentence correctly. Add a comma and the connecting word given in parentheses. *pages 348–349*

Example: You can read about rivers you might visit some. (or)
You can read about rivers, or you might visit some.

11. The river was wide it moved swiftly. (and)
12. The river delta is wide the mountain canyon is narrow. (but)
13. A dam stops floods it also traps good soil. (but)
14. Otters like to eat fish they play in the river. (and)
15. You can read stories about the Mississippi you can listen to songs about it. (or)

Remember

that a **sentence fragment** is not a complete sentence. Each sentence must have a subject and a predicate and express a complete thought. Remember also that a **run-on sentence** is not a proper sentence.

For more activities with sentence fragments and run-on sentences, visit *The Learning Site:*

www.harcourtschool.com

C. Add a subject or a predicate to correct each sentence fragment. *pages 350–351*

Example: Can be like a highway of water.
A great river can be like a highway of water.

16. Smaller rivers.
17. Tugboats and barges.
18. Are helped by dams.
19. Are found on the banks of the Nile River.
20. Is in South America.

D. If a sentence is correct, write *correct*. If it is a sentence fragment or a run-on sentence, identify the error and write it correctly. *pages 350–351*

Examples: Carry building materials.
fragment, no subject; Some riverboats carry building materials.

Some rivers have strong currents. *correct*

21. The Danube is the second-longest river in Europe it carries the most water.
22. The Danube begins in Germany, and it flows to eastern Europe.
23. Curves south at Budapest, Hungary.
24. The Danube is a subject in stories it is also a topic in songs.
25. It flows through the Black Forest and through eight countries.

Writing Connection

Writer's Craft: Elaboration Write a paragraph that explains the information in the graph or chart that your group made on page 351. Use complete sentences as you describe the information given in the visual aid. Tell why this information is important to know.

Chapter Review

Read the passage. Choose the best way to correct each sentence, and mark the letter for your answer. If the sentence is correct, mark the choice *No mistake.*

(1) Early traders traveled the Mississippi River. (2) They used flatboats they used rafts. (3) Settlers moved west. (4) Traveled on the river in canoes. (5) Trading posts. Soon became towns. (6) Small towns grew, and they became major cities.

TIP Remember that all sentences must have a subject and predicate and must express a complete thought. Remember to eliminate choices as you work each problem.

1 A Traveled the Mississippi River.

 B Early traders traveled.

 C Early traders used the Mississippi.

 D No mistake

2 F They used flatboats, they used rafts.

 G They used flatboats but used rafts.

 H They used flatboats, or they used rafts.

 J No mistake

3 A Settlers. Moved west.

 B Settlers, moved west.

 C Settlers moved, west.

 D No mistake

4 F They traveled on the river in canoes.

 G They traveled. On the river in canoes.

 H They traveled on the river, in canoes.

 J No mistake

5 A Trading posts, soon became towns

 B Trading posts soon became towns.

 C Trading posts soon, became towns.

 D No mistake

6 F Small towns grew, became major cities.

 G Small towns grew but they became major cities.

 H Small towns grew. Became major cities.

 J No mistake

For additional test preparation, visit *The Learning Site:*

www.harcourtschool.com

Using Visuals to Communicate Information

You have seen different kinds of illustrations in encyclopedias and other reference books. These illustrations, or **visuals**, probably helped you learn more about your research topic.

When you write a paragraph or essay that includes facts, you can add information by including visuals. Before you create a visual, think about who your audience will be. What information will they need? What **caption**, or words beneath the visual, will be most helpful?

These are some visuals and the information they communicate:

- **Maps** can show the location of a place, the distance between places, the path of a river, or the size of a country.

- **Tables and charts** can list information about amounts. You can organize information in a chart to compare facts.

- **Graphs** can be used to show how things change over time, such as the number of people in a city or the cost of an item.

- **Drawings and photographs** can give readers information that is not in the text. A photograph of a person, for example, may show something about his or her personality. Captions help readers understand exactly what the pictures show.

YOUR TURN

MAKE A GRAPH Look up the lengths of four different rivers in an encyclopedia. Using a ruler, chart the lengths on a bar graph. On the vertical side of the graph, mark the different lengths. On the horizontal line of the graph, write the names of the rivers. Then draw a bar showing how long each river is. Share it with your class. As a class, combine your graphs into one large bar graph. Which river is the longest? Which river is the shortest?

TIP Remember that maps, charts, graphs, pictures, and captions can be used to communicate important information.

Research
Report

Victoria water lilies
in the Amazon. ▼

Clouds hang over the
Manu River in Peru. ▼

A writer of a research report gathers facts about a topic from several sources. In his book, Saviour Pirotta gives facts about the rain forest. As you read, notice the subtopics he discusses.

Outstanding Science Trade Book Award

RIVERS in the RAIN FOREST

by Saviour Pirotta

Rivers are essential to rain forests. They provide the forest with water all year round. Rivers also provide a home to many different plants and animals. People rely on the rivers, too.

River Plants

Mangrove trees grow in swamps, at the mouths of rain forest rivers. Mangroves have special long roots, which help anchor them in the mud. Mangrove seeds sprout on the branches of their mother tree, instead of in the ground. This protects them from being washed away by the tide before they can grow into saplings.

Giant water lilies grow in rain forest rivers. Some grow big enough for a small child to sit on. Victoria water lilies grow in shallow water. Some can grow up to 6 feet (2 m) wide.

Research Report

▲ A basilisk runs across a stream.

Animals in Rivers

The rivers of the rain forest are home to many different fish, amphibians, reptiles, and mammals. The mudskipper lives in the mangroves. It is a fish, but it can also breathe out of water. Mudskippers use their fins to walk as well as swim.

Basilisks are amphibians. They can walk on water! Basilisks have long webbed toes on their back feet, which act as paddles. They can run across small streams on their back legs.

There are over 2,400 kinds of fish in the Amazon. Catfish are among the largest. They can grow over 6 feet (2 m) long. Catfish are a very important food for people.

The manatee is the biggest animal in the Amazon River. Manatees move very slowly, feeding on grasses on the riverbed.

▲ Manatees hold their breath for up to 15 minutes when they swim underwater.

◄ Two male mudskippers look at each other angrily, with their fins raised.

359

This man is using an ax
to hollow out a canoe. ▼

People and Rivers

Many rain forest people use the
rivers to get around. It is easier to
travel on the rivers than to fight
through thick forest.

The smallest boats on the rivers are
canoes. They are made by hollowing
out tree trunks. Some people have
motors attached to their canoes.
Canoes are used to get to school, to go
to riverside markets, and to go fishing.

Huge logs are towed down a river
on a raft in the Amazon, Brazil. ▼

On giant rain forest rivers, big freighters carry rubber, beef, and mineral ore to busy ports. Smaller boats are used to carry animals, coffee beans, and bananas to riverside markets. Big logs are tied together to make huge rafts.

People have made their fortunes by finding gold or diamonds in their rain forest rivers. Mining causes a lot of damage to rivers. It disturbs the water at riverbanks, where fish and other animals come to drink.

Rivers are being polluted by mining. We need to save the rivers, so that people can enjoy them in the future.

Canoes carry goods to a riverside market in Colombia. ▼

Vocabulary Power

am·phib·i·an
[am·fib′ē·ən] *n.* An animal that can live both on land and in water.

Analyze THE Model

1. What is the author's purpose?
2. Where does the author tell what his main topic is?
3. Into what subtopics has Pirotta organized his writing?
4. Identify at least one detail that he adds for each subtopic.

main topic

subtopic

facts and details

subtopic

facts and details

subtopic

READING — WRITING CONNECTION

Parts of a Research Report

Saviour Pirotta used facts to tell about the rain forest. As you read this research report, written by a student named James, note the facts and details he included.

MODEL

The Pyramids of Egypt

The huge pyramids of Egypt are amazing, especially since they were built completely by hand without any modern tools or machines.

The Structures

Pyramids were built in Egypt more than 4,500 years ago as tombs for the kings. In most pyramids, there was a secret room in which the king was buried. A king's collection of gold and other riches was buried with him.

The Workers

Egyptian peasants built the pyramids. They had a hard job. First, they had to cut the stones with saws. Then, they had to drag the heavy blocks to the pyramid and shove them in place. Each block weighed more than 2 tons! They also had to push the blocks up brick ramps to get them to the top of the pyramid. As they worked higher and higher, they had to build longer ramps.

The Great Pyramid

The pyramid built for King Khufu is the

largest Egyptian pyramid. It was built with more than two million blocks! The base of this pyramid is about the size of ten football fields. When the pyramid was built, it stood 481 feet high. The Great Pyramid is one of the Seven Wonders of the Ancient World.

Many people travel to Egypt to see the pyramids. People are always amazed at the size of the pyramids and the work that went into building them.

facts and details

conclusion

Analyze THE Model

1. Who is James's audience? What is his purpose?

2. Where does James state his main topic?

3. What subtopics does James write about?

Summarize THE Model

Use a chart like the one shown to list important information James covered in his research report. Then write a summary of his report.

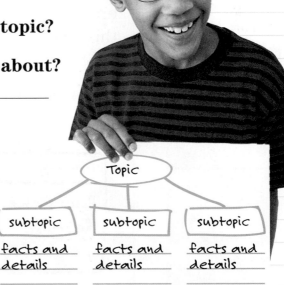

Writer's Craft

Paragraphing Each of James's paragraphs has a topic sentence, followed by details. Write each of James's topic sentences. Then add one detail which supports each topic sentence.

363

Prewriting

- Remember your audience and purpose.
- On a card, write the title, the author, and the page numbers of each source that you use.
- Support each subtopic with interesting facts and details.

Purpose and Audience

In this chapter, you will write a research report to learn more about the people and the geographical features of a state in the United States or of another country.

WRITING PROMPT Write a research report that tells how particular geographical features of a state or country affect the everyday lives of people there. Think about the kinds of information that would interest your classmates.

Before you begin researching your topic, think about the structure of your report. How many paragraphs will you have? How many subtopics do you need to support your first paragraph?

MODEL

After James chose his topic, he looked through several sources. He decided on three subtopics. He made this web to organize the notes from his research.

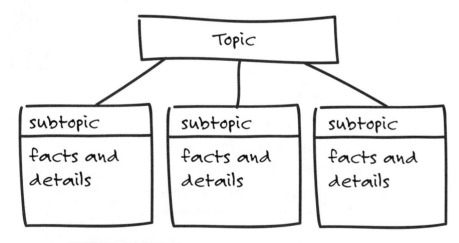

YOUR TURN

Choose a state or country to research for your report. Organize the subtopics, facts, and details from your research in a chart.

Organization and Elaboration

Follow these steps to help you organize your report:

STEP 1 **Introduce the Topic**

Use your first paragraph to introduce your main topic.

STEP 2 **Organize the Subtopics**

Determine your subtopics. Create a heading for each one.

STEP 3 **Add Supporting Facts and Details**

Add facts and details which support your subtopics.

STEP 4 **Conclude with a Summary**

Summarize your main topic and subtopics in your last paragraph.

MODEL

Here is the beginning of James's draft. How does James let the readers know what he will discuss first? What interesting facts does he include?

> The huge pyramids of Egypt are amazing, especially since they were built completely by hand, without any modern tools or machines.
>
> The Structures
>
> Pyramids were built in Egypt more than 4,500 years ago as tombs for the kings. In most pyramids, there was a secret room in which the king was buried.

YOUR TURN

Now draft your research report, using the steps above and your prewriting web.

Revising

Organization and Elaboration

Consider these questions as you read your draft:

- Does the order of my subtopics make sense?
- Do I need to add more facts and details?
- Which facts or details should I take out because they do not relate to my subtopics?
- Which sentences could I combine to make my report easier to read?

MODEL

Here is another part of James's research report. Notice that he added details to make some information clearer. He also combined two sentences.

> Egyptian ^ The Workers
>
> ^Peasants built the pyramids. They had a hard job. First, they had to cut the
> stones. _with saws_ Then, they had to drag the _heavy_ blocks to the pyramid. _and_ ~~They had to~~ shove them in place. Each block weighed _more than_ 2½ tons!
> They _also_ ^had to push the blocks up^ _brick_ ramps to get ^_them_ to the top of the pyramid. As they worked higher and higher, they had to build longer ramps ~~and pull them up.~~
> ~~Robbers broke into most pyramids to steal the treasures.~~

YOUR TURN

Revise your draft to make your research report as interesting as you can. Think about facts and details you might add to help your readers learn.

Strategies Good Writers Use

- Add facts and details that make the information clearer.
- Take out facts and details that are not about the topic.
- Revise sentences by using compound and complex constructions.

Set the titles for your subtopics in boldfaced type so that they are clear to the reader.

Checking Your Language

It is important to proofread your writing for mistakes in grammar, spelling, punctuation, and capitalization. By correcting mistakes, you will make it easier for your readers to understand the information in your report.

MODEL

Here is another part of James's report. James proofread it and corrected the mistakes he found. Notice the capitalization and punctuation corrections he made. What other errors did he fix?

> The Great Pyramid
>
> The pyramid built for ~~king~~ King Khufu is the ~~large~~ largest Egyptian pyramid. It was ~~builded~~ built with more than ② two ~~million~~ million blocks!
>
> The base of this pyramid is about the size of ⑩ ten football ~~feilds~~ fields. When the pyramid was built, it ~~standed~~ stood 481 feet high. The Great ~~pyramid~~ Pyramid is one of the seven Wonders of the ~~Ancient~~ Ancient world.

YOUR TURN

Proofread your revised research report three times. Each time, check for one of the following:
- **grammar mistakes**
- **spelling mistakes**
- **capitalization and punctuation mistakes**

Publishing

Sharing Your Work

Now you will share your research report with your audience. Use the following questions to help you decide how to publish your work:

1. Who is your audience? How can you present your report so that your audience will learn from it?

2. What would be the best way to give your audience a written report? Should you print in manuscript, write in cursive, or make a computer printout?

3. Should you read your report aloud?

4. Would a multimedia presentation be an interesting and useful way to present your report? To give a multimedia presentation, follow the steps on page 369.

USING YOUR

Handbook

• Use the rubric on page 510 to evaluate your report.

Reflecting on Your Writing

 Using Your Portfolio What did you learn about your writing in this chapter? Write your answer to each question below.

1. Did you find using a graphic organizer helpful during prewriting? Why or why not?

2. How did revising help you write a better research report?

Place these answers and your research report in your portfolio. Look over the examples of your writing in the portfolio. Think about the goals that you set earlier for improving your writing. Write one sentence about one way in which you have become a better writer. Write one sentence about what you would like to do better.

Giving a Multimedia Presentation

James decided to create a multimedia presentation to share his report with his classmates. You can design and give a multimedia presentation by following these steps:

STEP 1 Choose the kind of multimedia aids that would best suit your audience and purpose. Would drawings, diagrams, video segments, or music help your audience understand your information better?

STEP 2 Select or design visual media that will represent your message, meaning, and main idea. Plan when you will use multimedia aids in your presentation.

STEP 3 Arrange for any equipment you need, such as an audiotape player or a videocassette player.

STEP 4 Use natural gestures and body language during your presentation. Speak slowly and loudly enough for all to hear. Vary your tone of voice and pitch.

Strategies for Listeners

As you listen to your classmates' presentations, use these strategies to help you learn from their reports:

- Give the speaker your full attention.
- Identify the speaker's subtopics.
- Listen and look for facts and details in the multimedia aids.

Unit 5
Grammar
Review

CHAPTER 25

Prepositions
pages 308–317

Prepositions *pages 308–309*

Write the sentence. Underline each preposition.

1. Millie and Joseph live in a big city.
2. They like going to movies and to the theater.
3. They often go on weekends with their friends.
4. On Saturday they saw a play about jungle animals.
5. The theater is in their neighborhood, near the park.
6. The next day Millie and Joseph walked through the park.
7. They walked across the bridge that goes over the pond.
8. Then they walked by the aquarium and under the tunnel.
9. They went around the corner and into the zoo.
10. There are many activities in a big city!

Object of the Preposition *pages 310–311*

Write the prepositional phrase or phrases in each sentence. Underline the object of each preposition.

11. New York City has subways that run under the ground.
12. The subway trains take people from one part of the city to other parts.
13. Some tunnels in New York City go under the rivers.
14. You can travel on beautiful bridges.
15. The bridges go over the same rivers.

Using Prepositional Phrases

pages 312–313

Add a prepositional phrase, and write the new sentence. Your prepositional phrase can tell *when*, *where*, or *how*. Use the word in parentheses as a guide.

16. Lois and her mother are traveling. (where)
17. They flew. (how)
18. They arrived at the airport. (when)
19. They took a taxi. (where)
20. They got to the hotel. (when)

Independent Clauses
pages 318–319

Read each group of words. Label it *independent clause* or *phrase*. If it is an independent clause, write it correctly as a sentence. Underline the subject once and the predicate twice.

1. some foods were first eaten in particular places

2. chowder is a thick soup from New England

3. New England corn chowder and clam chowder

4. Native Americans introduced the colonists to corn

5. food dishes from the Southwest

Dependent Clauses
pages 320–321

Write the dependent clause in each sentence. Then circle the connecting word that begins the clause.

6. Since modern travel is quick and affordable, more people can try foods in different areas of the country.
7. Baked beans were not popular outside of New England before so many people began traveling more.
8. Because some foods from a region are so popular, visitors from other areas try these foods.
9. When Midwesterners traveled to New England, they discovered baked beans.
10. I eat hushpuppies whenever I travel to a southern state.

Distinguishing Independent and Dependent Clauses
pages 322–323

Write the sentence. Underline the independent clause once and the dependent clause twice.

11. When I cook fried rice, I follow a recipe.
12. I eat stuffed grape leaves when my family goes to a Greek restaurant.
13. Although I have never been to Maine, I have tasted Maine lobster.
14. While I was in Baltimore, I tried Maryland crab cakes.
15. I learned a little about French cooking because I watched a cooking show on television.

Unit 5
Grammar Review

CHAPTER 28

Complex
Sentences

pages 336–345

Complex Sentences   *pages 336–337*

Write whether each sentence is *complex* or *not complex*.

1. At the town meeting, everybody talked about the land.
2. The land had rich soil and would make good farmland.
3. The people wanted to save the forest, but they couldn't.
4. After the area was settled, more forests were cut down.
5. We plan to make a park for the city if we can.

More About Complex Sentences

pages 338–339

Combine each pair of sentences to make a complex sentence, using the word in the parentheses. Add a comma if necessary.

6. Eli's family bought land in the country. They planned to leave most of it as forest. (when)
7. They bought the land. They wanted trees. (because)
8. They built their house. Most of the land was still covered with forest. (after)
9. Another family built a house next door. Eli could see the house through the trees. (after)
10. Nobody else builds a house. We will have plenty of forest left. (if)

Commas in Complex Sentences

pages 340–341

Write the sentence. Add a comma if it is needed. If no comma is needed, write *no comma*.

11. When we bought the farm we planted crops.
12. Although we wanted to plant rice we didn't.
13. We changed our minds because of the climate.
14. Many crops need more rainfall than our area gets.
15. After we thought about it we planted another crop.

Sentence Fragments   *pages 346–347*

Write whether each group of words is a sentence or a sentence fragment. If the group of words is a sentence fragment, name the missing sentence part(s).

1. North America's Missouri River.
2. Joins the Mississippi River.
3. The junction is north of St. Louis.
4. Is over two thousand miles long.
5. The Missouri River begins in Montana.

Run-On Sentences   *pages 348–349*

Write each run-on sentence correctly. Use a comma and a connecting word *(and, or,* or *but).*

6. The Missouri was calm in summer it flooded in winter.
7. The flood ran through communities it damaged homes.
8. People built locks they constructed dams.
9. Dams hold back water, canals irrigate fields.
10. The Ohio River joins the Mississippi it flows south.
11. The Ohio River begins in Pittsburgh then it turns southwest.
12. The Ohio transports freight this waterway carries huge ships.
13. Cargo ships may haul coal they may ferry oil.
14. Freighters carry iron ore they may move other metals.
15. Cincinnati is a major city it is on the Ohio River.

Correcting Sentence Errors

pages 350–351

Rewrite each sentence fragment or run-on sentence correctly. Add missing parts where needed.

16. Flooded the entire plateau.
17. The Allegheny joins the Monongahela, the new river is called the Ohio.
18. Is a great shipping lane.
19. Mining and coal companies from West Virginia.
20. Mine gravel and ship it along the Ohio.

Tour Guide

Imagine that you have guests visiting from out of town. Where will you take them? Make a brochure describing things to see and do in your community.

Brainstorm and Research

- With a group, brainstorm a list of interesting places in your community.

- Research ideas using the Internet, a tourist information office, or a history museum.

- Make a list of four places to visit.

- Write a paragraph about each place. Include important facts visitors would want to know.

- Find or take pictures of the places you described.

Make a Tour Brochure

- Put together a brochure to let visitors know where you will be taking them. Use a computer if you like.

- Arrange your paragraphs, pictures, and photographs in a way that makes sense.

- Include a map and travel directions for each place.

Share Your Brochure

- Read your brochure to a classmate. Have you included the most important facts? Are your map and travel directions clear?

- Display your brochure on the classroom bulletin board.

- When you have visitors, use your brochure to show them around your community.

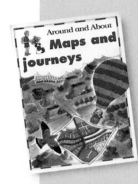

Maps and Journeys
by Kate Petty
NONFICTION
Harry and his dog Ralph study their city
and learn how to make maps by using
important landmarks.
Award-Winning Author

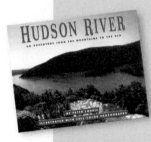

*Hudson River: An Adventure
from the Mountains to the Sea*
by Peter Lourie
NONFICTION
The author takes a canoe trip down the
Hudson River, from the mountains to
Manhattan, and points out many interesting
sites along the way.
Award-Winning Author

Unit 6

Grammar Usage and Mechanics

Writing Expressive Writing